ALED

ALED
The Autobiography

Aled Jones
with Darren Henley

First published in Great Britain in 2005 by
Virgin Books Ltd
Thames Wharf Studios
Rainville Road
London
W6 9HA

A catalogue record for this book is available from the
British Library.

ISBN 1 85227 2503

Typeset by TW Typesetting, Plymouth, Devon
Printed and bound in Great Britain by CPD Wales

CONTENTS

ACKNOWLEDGEMENTS

This book tells the story of the two distinct parts of my career. As a boy soprano, so many amazing things happened to me in such an incredibly short period of time that I have had to rely on many people to help me fill in the gaps in my own memories. My Mam and Dad were with me on every step of that exciting journey, something for which I will always be in their debt. I also owe so much to a wonderful lady called Hefina Orwig Evans, without whom the journey would never have even begun. When she died, I discovered that she had kept scrapbooks of all the newspaper cuttings about me as a boy. These have proved invaluable in helping to jog my memory.

My wife Claire has been at my side throughout the second part of my career. She has read and re-read every single word in this book and without her love, support and eminently sensible suggestions, I would never have had the strength to get it finished.

Thank you also to my manager Peter Price and my lawyer Paul Russell, who have helped me so much. All of the team at Virgin Books have been nothing short of brilliant, with special thanks to KT Forster, Stuart Slater, Gareth Fletcher and Ian Allen.

Finally, I would like to express my sincere gratitude to Darren Henley, whose tireless work and boundless enthusiasm has made this process such a pleasure. Through writing this book together with him, I have gained a true friend.

1. BY ROYAL COMMAND

The first time I heard about being summoned before the Prince of Wales was when I came home from school on a Monday afternoon. As usual, I had spent the day at David Hughes Comprehensive in Menai Bridge and had returned home on the school bus, with more pupils crammed on board than there were seats. I always stood up at the front with my mates. We were typical fourteen-year-olds with scuffed shoes and ties that had been ripped off and stuffed in our sports bags the moment we left the school buildings.

It was 1985, I was at the height of my career as a boy soprano and there was a great offer of some sort waiting for me nearly every day when I arrived home. All important decisions in our house would be made around the kitchen table. Mam was the teacher of the reception class at the local primary school, so she got home first and cooked the evening meal. Dad would come home from his job as an engineer. We would all sit around the table and invariably there would be a letter inviting me to sing in one concert or another.

On this particular day, though, my parents were both white-faced. Mam asked, 'How do you feel about singing for Prince Charles and Princess Diana?'

When the call came through to my parents from Prince Charles's private secretary earlier that day, they could not believe it, presuming it to be a practical joke. The official said to them, 'Prince Charles has loved your son's voice for a long time. He knows that he's thirteen and would like to hear him sing for himself before his voice breaks. So would he be kind enough to come down to Kensington Palace and perform for the Prince and Princess of Wales?'

'Oh, yeah!' was my immediate reply, because secretly I loved Princess Diana, I really did. I thought that she was the best thing in the world. Then, when Mam and Dad told me where I would be singing, in the Prince and Princess's private living room at Kensington Palace, I just didn't know what to make of it. It was all going to happen just three days later.

The first thing that went through my mind was that it probably wouldn't get any bigger than singing for royalty. People who live in North Wales don't often get the opportunity to see the royal family. It was to be the biggest thing that I could have done at that time. What made me even more nervous was that the Prince and Princess were inviting me into their house. All sorts of silly questions flashed through my mind. What would I wear? What would I have to eat? What would happen if I made a mistake? Lying in bed that night, I felt a mixture of nervousness and real excitement. The next morning the big question was: what was I going to sing?

I was asked to bring a pianist with me and I chose one of the best I have ever worked with – a lady called Annette Bryn Parri. When she found out that she was going to be playing at Kensington Palace, she was as amazed as I was.

What happened to me as a child was easy for me because I didn't fully appreciate what was going on, but for my parents it must have been the biggest shock of their lives. They both continued with their normal jobs – Dad worked really hard and was unable to get time off to come down to London for my royal command performance. So it was myself, Mam and Annette who stood on the platform of Bangor station waiting for the train to London. As I shivered in the wind, I became convinced that it was one of the coldest places anywhere in the world.

We stayed at the Royal Garden Hotel, right next to Kensington Palace. That evening, one of the Prince's equerries came to the hotel to explain what would happen. That's when the precision of it all hit me – everything was planned down to an exact time. Before I went to bed, I looked out of the window of my room. I could see policemen walking along the private path to the Palace, which was lit by the glow of these very old-fashioned lanterns. That was the path I would be taking the following evening.

The day of my special performance came and went quickly. Soon it was time to get dressed for the evening. I wore a pair of grey trousers, a white shirt and a red bow tie, much to my embarrassment as I look back on it now. Bow ties were something of a trademark of mine at the time, because the lady who looked after the wardrobe for a BBC Wales television series I had made had decided that I would wear a different-coloured one for each programme. I ended up with more than twenty of them in every embarrassing colour imaginable. Needless to say, they are no longer part of my stage wardrobe these days.

A Welsh businessman who lived in London, Simon Davies, offered to drive us to the Palace in his Rolls-Royce. By this stage, I was so nervous that I couldn't manage to open the car door. I sat in the front and sank deep into the massive leather seats. As we drew up to the first guard post outside Kensington Palace, a policeman came out. He was expecting us and said, 'On you go, Mr Jones.' We continued along the drive. The lanterns seemed to be a different colour from normal streetlamps, more like those old sulphur ones with an orange glow. It was all very Dickensian, very old London. We stopped at a second guard post and another policeman checked who we were, before waving us through. Eventually, we arrived at the back door of Kensington Palace. I was aware that we were going to a pretty awesome house.

The equerry whom we had met the night before greeted us at the door, along with the butler. He said, 'They're very excited about you coming. They've been talking about it all day.' I couldn't quite believe it – I was thirteen and this was the future king. Why would he be excited about meeting me? Surely it should have been the other way around?

Mam, Annette and I were whisked into the Prince and Princess's private living room. We sat there on our own waiting for them and I suppose that at that moment I was more nervous than at any other time in my career. Even Annette, who was always very level-headed, said, 'I can't believe we're really in their house.' It definitely was a home and nothing like the sort of stateroom that you might imagine; you could tell that it was a room that they actually used. There were sofas everywhere, photos of Prince William and Prince Harry as babies and pictures of the Prince and Princess wearing normal clothes. These were all shots that you would never see in the papers.

Moments after we had sat down, the door opened and Prince Charles walked in. He was so gracious and such a lovely man, particularly with Mam and Annette. The first thing he said was, 'You must have a drink.' Mam and Annette didn't know if he meant a cup of tea, a cup of coffee or wine. He must have sensed their confusion and I will never forget how he leaned forward, touched Mam's knee and said, 'You'd fancy a gin and tonic, wouldn't you?'

It broke the ice completely and everyone just relaxed. I was amazed that moments later a footman appeared with one of the largest gin and tonics I had ever seen and placed it in Mam's hand. Everything going on inside the room was obviously being noted and watched by someone outside and I was fascinated about how that worked.

Prince Charles explained that Princess Diana would be a little late because she had been swimming. At that time, she swam every night. When the Princess arrived, she still had wet hair from the pool. She gave me a kiss and curled up in a chair next to her husband. It was time for my performance.

I started with Handel's 'Where E'er You Walk'. After I had finished singing, they clapped; it seemed a little uncomfortable because it wasn't a proper concert and there were just the two of them sitting there in front of me. Prince Charles said, 'This doesn't seem right. I don't think we're going to clap any more, but just to let you know that it's brilliant. I love it.' I bowed for what must have been the tenth time because I felt that I had to – I was with royalty after all – and both the Prince and Princess told me that there was no need to keep on doing it. They reassured me that I could just relax and be myself, which was a real relief.

I sang for more than an hour, with nobody else in the room except my Mam, Annette and the Prince and Princess of Wales. My performance included Rod Stewart's 'Sailing' and the Beatles songs 'Hey Jude' and 'Yesterday', as well as Handel's 'Ombra Mai Fu'.

Finally the Prince said, 'You've done enough work. Come and sit down with us.' He told me that he preferred the Handel, while the Princess said that she liked the pop songs the best. The Prince seemed particularly interested in music, asking how the voice was going and whether I felt it was about to break.

As we were chatting, I knocked a glass of water off the table. I thought to myself that this was just the most dreadful thing I had ever done. My Mam panicked like mad, leaped up, went bright red and spluttered, 'Sorry! Sorry!' Diana jumped up, rubbed the wet carpet with her foot and said, 'Oh, don't worry. The boys do it in this room all the time.' It was a lovely thing to say to put us all at ease. I was just relieved not to have been thrown in the Tower.

I had met Diana before because we had both done some charity work for Barnardo's. Believe it or not, the TV presenter Anne Diamond, the Princess and I were the only clients of the same hairdresser – a Scotsman named Richard Dalton. The Princess and I would send short notes to each other, using Richard as a courier. They were just silly little notes – mine to her might say, 'Hi, how are you?' and she would then send one back saying, 'I heard you singing on the television, and it was great.'

Each time that I saw Diana, I always got a sense of her playful character. That evening in Kensington Palace, she told me that she and the Prince had a present for me. Being my age, I couldn't wait to see what it was. But I think that she was even more excited than I was. She insisted that I opened it there and then. It was a framed photograph of both of them together, signed personally for me by them both.

After more than an hour and a half of chatting, we said our goodbyes and the Prince and Princess thanked me for coming. Simon Davies was sitting on the stairs outside with the equerry and the butler. He took us to his Rolls-Royce and said, 'You can't have an evening like this and just go back to the hotel, so I'm going to take you all for dinner at the Dorchester.'

I hadn't really taken in what I had just done. Mam was exhausted, but Annette felt the same as me, just in awe of what had happened to us. Lots of people met the Prince and Princess of Wales and lots of people had time with them, but to spend almost three hours in their living room was something I had never expected to do.

I had never been to the Dorchester before either. I didn't know which knife and fork to use because there were seven sets in front of us. The plates were huge and had tiny bits of food in the middle of them. The chef himself, Anton Mossimon, came up to the table to shake my hand.

It was all such an experience for me, but my life at the time was filled with huge contrasts. The next day I would be back at school and I was already looking forward to seeing my girlfriend again. I would never tell my school friends what I had been doing the day before. In many ways, I was leading two separate lives: my school life, which I really enjoyed with my friends and my girlfriend, and then this very special other life which gave me the added bonus of doing amazing things that were beyond the dreams of most teenagers. I always kept the two lives separate. It wasn't something Mam and Dad told me to do, I just worked it out for myself because it seemed the most natural thing to do.

After dinner at the Dorchester, we went back to the hotel and in true Welsh fashion, Mam and Annette had a nightcap while we relived what had happened. The next morning saw reality dawn as we went back home on the train to Bangor.

2. ANGLESEY LIFE

I was born on 29 December 1970 at St David's Hospital in Bangor. It was a cold Christmas that year and the snow had started falling heavily on Boxing Day. The district nurse was concerned that Mam would be prevented from reaching the hospital by the bad weather so she was admitted early to the maternity ward. I came into the world by Caesarean section two days later. Mam wanted a boy and had even chosen my name. So the very first words that she heard when she came round from the anaesthetic were 'Aled's here'. As predicted, I was very heavy, weighing in at a whopping 9 lb 14 oz.

My Mam, Nêst, and my Dad, Derek, had moved to Anglesey, an island off the North Wales coast, a few years before I was born. We lived in a tiny village on the south side of the island called Llandegfan. It's the sort of place where everyone knows everyone else, with a post office, a convenience store and a tiny hairdresser. Menai Bridge is the village just along the road where, as you might guess from the name, you will find the two bridges which link Anglesey to the rest of Wales. Menai Bridge is not a big place either, but it does have quite a few shops. Now, more than thirty years later, when I drive through on my way home, it still makes me smile that many of these shops are just the same as when I was a boy. There are a couple of Chinese takeaways and the first curry house arrived when I was sixteen – a big event for me.

The most cosmopolitan part of the island is known as Million-aire's Row. It runs in a strip from Menai Bridge to another town called Beaumaris. It's here that big stars such as Roger Moore have owned houses over the years. The view out to sea is beautiful, absolutely stunning. When I was eighteen, I couldn't wait to leave the island, but now that I am a lot older and a little bit wiser, I realise just what a wonderful haven it is.

Anglesey is a very quiet place and life definitely moves at a much slower pace than in some other parts of the country. The people of Anglesey are very proud to be both Welsh and Welsh-speaking. Welsh was the only language I spoke until I was around five years old. We were taught totally in Welsh for the first few years at school, with English being taught as a second language.

The Jones family home was always a very happy house, with Dad and Mam both working only a short distance away. Both sets of grandparents lived close by and this group of people made my world a very secure and loving place.

Mam went back to work at the local primary school when I was just seven weeks old. My father's mother looked after me while Mam was working and would turn up every morning just before she went off to school. I called my grandparents Nain and Taid– the Welsh words for grandma and grandad. My maternal grandparents were known as Nain and Taid Caernarfon and I called my paternal grandparents Nain and Taid Llanwnda – with both sets being named after the places where they lived.

Once Mam had gone, Nain Llanwnda would then spend the rest of the day really spoiling me, while we constantly played all sorts of games. A particular favourite involved me placing a huge blackboard on Nain's knees, which I would then sit on top of with all of my teddies. Even though she was quite a big woman, she would end up being crushed under a mountain of soft toys. Nain was an incredibly kind person and a brilliant cook who loved her food. She filled my early years with laughter wherever we were together, whether it was at home, on the beach or out walking. I was very active as a small child and never managed to sleep fully through the night until I was three years old, although I did nap during the day with Nain Llanwnda, which probably explains it.

I have two particular memories of those early years, both of which involve food. Every afternoon, we would wait for Joe, the Polish bread man, to drive by in his white van. Without fail, Nain would buy me a currant bun. One time, I was on my tricycle waiting for the man when I did a wheelie and cut my head open on the wall. Nain was in a terrible state of panic and called Mam home from school. I was rushed off to the hospital to be stitched up. The scar on the back of my head is still with me today, and at the time I wore it proudly as a badge of courage. My second food-related memory concerns the very sweet tooth that I had developed. The absolute highlight of my day came at lunchtime when, as a special treat, Nain would give me a cube of raw jelly to chew on. I am sure that I can trace my love of sweet food back to this time, as one cube inevitably led to the whole pack disappearing into my stomach during the rest of the afternoon.

By the time I was two years old, my parents discovered that I had an uncanny knack of reproducing everyday sounds. I could harmonise with a sound and sing tunes with it in the same key. So if Mam was using a hairdryer, or the bath was running, I would make up a new melody around the sounds and rhythms. My parents tell me that this constant mimicking of noises was the first sign they saw that I was actively showing an interest in music. At around this time, my favourite television show was an Asian magazine programme broadcast on Sunday mornings. I would sit naked on a cushion in front of the television each week watching the programme and singing along to the music. The words meant absolutely nothing to me at all, but I was captivated by the tunes and would join in with the sitar melodies.

The other programme that I never missed was *Doctor Who*. True to tradition, the moment the music started, I would dive behind our leather sofa, from where I would watch the whole episode. I was particularly frightened of the Daleks and would hide every time they came on screen. But despite my fear, I still desperately wanted to watch it each week. One day when she was cleaning, Mam discovered that I had been nervously gnawing away at the back of the sofa and that her pride and joy now had teeth marks all the way along the top from one end to the other. I got an almighty telling off and Mam got a new sofa, because the existing one was completely ruined.

My grandfather on my mother's side, Taid Caernarfon, had a great sense of humour and I always felt so close to him, probably because of his cheeky nature. He and my grandmother would keep a big glass jar of sweets underneath the television in their house, always filled with the lemon or strawberry bonbons which I absolutely loved. I would often sit on his knee eating sweets while he would make incredibly detailed Plasticine men and teach me naughty words in Welsh. I'm not sure if that's what all grandfathers did then – but I loved him for it. He taught me at a very early age that if Mam was a long time in a shop and I shouted '*cachu babŵn*', the Welsh for 'baboon poo', I could instantly persuade her to stop whatever she was doing in the shop and rush me outside in a state of extreme embarrassment.

My other grandfather was far more serious. He was a quieter man, with big vein-covered hands that I seem to have inherited, but he was also very musical. Songs were already a very big part of my life, even though I was just a toddler. I would sit in Taid Llanwnda's rocking chair and he would serenade me with his beautiful deep bass voice. Music was particularly strong in Dad's family going back many years. Many of my uncles had excellent voices that they put to good use competing in Eisteddfodau and singing in choirs. Music also played a large part in Mam's side of the family. My great-grandmother sang with the Moody Manners opera company in Ireland and also played the organ in church. Nain Caernarfon played the piano and accompanied many singers and my Uncle Arthur (actually my great-uncle) worked for Riccordi Music in London for many years.

Nain and Taid Caernarfon had big leather sofas and I was often to be found standing on a small table next to them in the front window of their house singing hymns.

I think that Mam's kindness and gregariousness came from her mother, who was always the life and soul of the party. Having said that, Nain suffered terribly from diabetes and I saw my first injection with her. I was far too young to understand that the insulin she was injecting from this big metal syringe was helping her to lead a normal life and I found the experience very frightening every time I saw her do it.

Nain and Taid Caernarfon had a dog called Spot, a scruffy little Jack Russell, with which I was totally in love. He was there every week when I visited Nain and Taid's house. I would use a belt as a lead and take him for walks down to Meira's Shop, a traditional general store that sold everything from cat food to chocolate. The big lure for me at the shop was one of Meira's *teisan gwstad*, which were custard cakes. I would be so excited about scoffing one of these treats that I would invariably zoom off back to Nain and Taid's house on a custard-induced high leaving poor old Spot tied up to the lamppost outside the shop. When I got back to him, the poor thing always had a rather lost, forgotten look on his face.

A little strangely, Nain used to keep crisps in the oven to keep them fresh – these were not home-made crisps, but crisps bought in paper bags from the shop. I got a nasty surprise on one particular occasion when I stuck my head in the oven to find the crisps and instead there was a roast chicken cooking at full blast. I thought that my head was going to explode from the heat. I still don't really understand why Nain thought that crisps would be fresher if they were kept in the oven, though. I have found over the years that it is best not to delve too deeply into these Welsh customs.

My early childhood was a very happy time, but also very peaceful. I would spend at least one afternoon each weekend either in Caernarfon or in Llanwnda. It was one of the most special times of my life because of the relationships that I built up with my grandparents. It always seemed to be summertime and I would spend hours watering cucumbers in Taid Caernarfon's garden, or playing football in Taid Llanwnda's yard, being careful not to hit the windows of his car.

Our first family home was a bungalow on a housing estate called Frondeg. I had great friends there, the best of whom was Lee Dunphy. We had a unique relationship, where we would play every morning and afternoon up until it was time for us to go inside for lunch or dinner. Just before our Mams called us, we would have play fights. Then we would say, 'See you later!' or 'See you tomorrow!' That was the daily routine, with us both making our way home bruised and battered, but still the best of friends.

Our favourite game was called 'Block-One-Two-Three'. One person would be 'on', standing by a lamppost, and the rest of us would have to run up to them and shout 'Block-One-Two-Three' without being spotted. If they saw you first, then you were 'out'. We would play this for hours every day from teatime until it got dark in the evening. We all enjoyed such pleasant childhoods, without having a care in the world. In our small corner of North Wales, life seemed very secure.

Dad is a great nature man and he taught me to climb trees at a very early age. There was only one tree on Frondeg and it seemed to me to be particularly tall. Usually, only the older kids were physically able to climb the tree, but I found that with a bit of effort

I could manage to clamber up to the very top branches. Climbing that tree was such an achievement for me.

In those days, parents had no fears about letting their children play outside unsupervised. Anglesey felt like a safe place. However, later on, when I was thirteen, our bright yellow Vauxhall Cavalier (with leopard-skin seat covers!), was stolen from outside our house and Mam and Dad were forced to acknowledge that maybe the island was not as crime-free as it had once been. When the car was recovered, we found out that the thieves had used it in a robbery and had left some of their haul behind – three pieces of frozen chicken that had defrosted under the passenger seat.

When I was five years old, it was time to go to school. As Mam taught the reception class at the local primary, she decided that it would be better for me if I went to the next nearest school at Menai Bridge. I simply did not want to go, so in the end I was bribed. Dad promised me that if I went to this different school down the road, he would buy me a brand new bike. Even so, I still only lasted the morning. I dissolved into tears the moment I was left in the classroom and then sobbed hysterically for the rest of the time I was there. I was devastated, because all of my friends from home were back at Llandegfan Primary and I knew absolutely nobody at Menai Bridge. Even worse, because everyone there came from a tight-knit community just like my own, all of my new classmates already knew each other. Although I was only there for the morning, I was frantically upset. By lunchtime, the teachers were seriously concerned about me and my parents were called to take me home.

That evening, I sat on Mam's lap while she phoned Mr McLean, the headmaster of Llandegfan Primary, a kind man with a ginger and white beard – and her boss. She asked him if I could join her class. He said 'yes' and that was that. The next day I was there with all my friends and I never looked back.

Being the son or daughter of a class teacher is tough in the extreme – and don't let anyone try to convince you any different. Mam was keen to show no favours towards me because I was her son. In reality, this meant that everyone else would get away with murder and I would get away with absolutely nothing. On a couple of occasions, I got into huge trouble because I would find out at home what the teachers were doing or thinking and would tell my friends. I got the worst telling off of all when I discovered that the school was about to be given a new, very cool, bright-yellow football kit. I went and blabbed this incredibly exciting headline news before the teacher had told the team. I got into terrible trouble, although I had not meant any harm. I was just on the verge of getting into the team myself and when I found out about the new kit I thought, 'Wow! This is so rock'n'roll. I've got to tell everyone else.'

My passion for football developed at primary school and I did eventually get to play for the team. When people learn that I am still a much keener follower of football than rugby, I am sometimes accused of being un-Welsh, but in fact, in North Wales, rugby comes a very firm second to football. Geographically, you are much closer to cities in the northwest of England such as Liverpool, than you are to the Welsh capital, Cardiff. Although I support Arsenal these days, my second-favourite team has always been Bangor City, and I even went to a couple of their matches while I was a kid.

Llandegfan was only a small village and with just thirty people in my class, my friends in school became my friends out of school. They were really good pals too and the minute that school finished, we would be in and out of one another's gardens playing football, climbing trees, or just generally hanging around. One thing that does occur to me now, as I think back on this early period of my life, is how I always seemed to push myself forwards as the boss of our gangs. I was never aware of it at the time, but my group of friends would always end up doing whatever I wanted to do, which seems really awful now. I am not sure that I am a very good leader, but despite that, it was always me deciding which game we would play at break time and the others seemed to follow without any argument. I suppose I have always been quite a competitive person, although I am not sure from where this drive originally came.

When I was nine, the whole of our class went to Butlin's in Pwllheli for a week to rehearse for a joint production with some other schools in the area. We all fancied the girls from the village called Llanfairpwllgwyngyllgogerychwyrndrobwllllantysiliogogo-goch (which translates as 'The church of St Mary in a hollow of white hazel near a rapid whirlpool and near St Tysilio's church by the red cave') although to local people it's always known as Llanfair PG. A group of us discovered that they were in chalets just down the pathway from ours, so in the dead of night we crept out and knocked on their door, before running back to our chalet. It was all so naïve and I think we would have died of fright if the girls had actually opened the door. We decided to give it another go to see if they would let us into their chalet but, just as we were about to knock, the door of the next-door chalet burst open and their teacher stood in front of us. He shouted angrily, before telling us that we would all be sent home in the morning. We trudged back to our chalet and stayed up talking for half the night, terrified of the telling-off we would receive when we arrived home early. In the end, the teachers relented and we were punished with a morning's worth of litter-picking around Butlin's.

If you ask someone from outside of Wales to describe my homeland, singing is usually mentioned alongside rugby pretty early in the description. It's true – singing is a way of life in Wales and has been from the year dot. I know that people sing in schools and nurseries in other parts of the UK, but on Anglesey there really would not be an hour at school when music was not involved in some way. It was always there and was always made into the highlight of the day. Singing happened everywhere in Wales, though: in pubs, at sporting occasions and as part of religious worship. Everybody I knew went to church or chapel on Sundays. There was never any choice or debate – it was just something everyone did.

My very first concert was in the local parish hall. Up until then, I hated singing in public, even though my grandparents were always persuading me to stand up and perform. I used to be so embarrassed, but on this occasion a man came up to me after I had performed and said, 'Oh, that was lovely. Here's fifty pence. Go and buy yourself an ice cream.' I thought, 'Wow! This is fantastic!' And from then onwards, it was virtually impossible to stop me singing. I suppose I enjoyed hearing applause for what I was doing, although I am certain that the possibility of earning 50p each time I opened my mouth was a much more appealing prospect. For the very first time, I realised that singing was cool and something that was natural to me.

Once I was seven years old, I began regularly to take part in Eisteddfodau. These competitions are a way of life in North Wales with children performing every weekend in towns and villages across the country. I entered a few times and got nowhere, but in 1979 I won first prize at the Eisteddfod at Bontnewydd near Caernarfon, which was the village where my grandparents lived and where my Dad was born. It was horrendous because there were so many children competing and I was up last, which meant I would get to do my party piece very late in the evening. Nowadays, they only allow as few as six youngsters to go on stage, but back then, whoever turned up was allowed to perform. Even though it took such a long time, I think the old way was probably better because at least everyone was given the chance to have a go. I sang 'Morning Has Broken' in Welsh and Taid Llanwnda was so proud when I won first prize. Once the competition was over, I took great delight in wearing the first-prize rosette around the house for a long time afterwards.

The highlight of my competitive career was two firsts at the National Urdd Eisteddfod – with top prizes in the solo under-twelve-year-old category and also in the *cerdd dant*, which is a type of performance unique to Wales. A harp, which is playing a completely different tune to the one that they are singing, accompanies the vocalist, making it incredibly difficult to get the hang of. The Urdd is a youth fellowship that is part of many Welsh youngsters' growing-up process, and the national final celebrates the best of Welsh youth from every corner of the country. Every schoolchild from primary age upwards can compete in categories ranging from solo voice to playing the harp. Dad was listening to the competition being broadcast live on Radio Cymru, but was infuriated because every time I was about to sing, the station cut away from the Eisteddfod for coverage of the Pope's visit to Britain.

Everyone would have lessons ahead of the Eisteddfodau so that they could learn their performance piece to perfection. A lovely lady called Nia Jones, who was a very skilled and gentle teacher, taught me. Some of the children were quite obviously super-coached and faced intense pressure to perform well on the day. I wonder if for some of them it killed off their love of music. Like it or loathe it, though, it was just one of those things that we were expected to do as children – and if you could not sing a note, then you would recite Welsh poetry or prose. If you were unable even to manage that, then you would have to put on a pair of clogs and dance.

Singing was still a very important part of my life at school, with a service every day. I was also in the cubs and we all sang in a big end-of-year show. The highlight of the cubs' year was the annual camp in a field about five miles away from home. It was great fun, with six of us sleeping in each tent. We learned to cook food on the campfire and spent the days earning our badges.

In 1980, at the age of nine, I made my first-ever television recording for BBC Wales. It was a lovely Welsh carol called 'Hwiangerdd Mair', which means 'Mary's Lullaby'. By then, we had moved into a new house, which Mam and Dad were still in the process of renovating. We didn't yet have a proper floor in the living room and I watched the BBC Wales programme on a battered old TV. I thought to myself, 'I can't believe it, I'm on television.' It all seemed very surreal. I remember being very proud, although it was really no big thing because the BBC went around all of the little schools that year, as they did every Christmas.

Before that moment, television had been something that had failed to grab my imagination. I didn't watch it much as a tiny kid, although Mam would always tune into *Coronation Street* without fail. All of a sudden, there I was actually on television myself, although I was too young to understand much about how it all worked. It was a few years later, when I performed in a BBC programme from Israel, that I first understood how powerful a single television show could be.

A year after the BBC Wales broadcast, I played the lead role in the Llandegfan Primary School production of Andrew Lloyd Webber and Tim Rice's *Joseph and the Amazing Technicolor Dreamcoat*. I was standing in the playground when I was told that I was going to play Joseph himself. I did not have to audition because the headmaster, Edward Morris Jones, had simply chosen who would play each role. He took over from Mr Mclean as Mam's boss and was one of the people who cultivated my love of music as a youngster. All the children saw him as something of a celebrity on Anglesey because he could often be heard performing songs while accompanying himself on the guitar. Back then, *Joseph* was only about 35 minutes long – the composer and lyricist lengthened it considerably before it became the show that we know and love today. My school was one of the first to do it and there was a big wave of anticipation because the headmaster had written to Andrew Lloyd Webber to ask permission to stage the performance. We were all very excited when the agreement came through. My coat was made from a pair of Mam's old curtains and I loved being Joseph, just as I did some fifteen years later, when I played the same role in a UK tour of the West End production.

But when I was eleven years old and standing on the stage in the hall at Llandegfan Primary School, taking my bow at the end of the show, I could not possibly have predicted that before I would perform *Joseph* again, I would already have had an entire career as an international singer that had a beginning, a middle and an end.

3. CASSOCKS, CONKERS AND FLORAL GUMS

I only ever became a choirboy because of a burning ambition to learn how to play Beatles songs on an old black piano that Mam had been left in a will. Elsie Francis, a teacher at Llandegfan School with Mam, suggested that we go to Bangor Cathedral to see the choirmaster, because he gave piano lessons.

I had never been inside a cathedral before and as soon as I walked through the door I was instantly struck by both the size and the smell of the place. I have since discovered that Bangor is a particularly small cathedral, but that every single one of them shares the same smell – a unique mustiness, which is very hard to describe. I suppose the best way of summing it up is to say that they smell 'old'. All I know is that I instantly feel at home in cathedrals as soon as I enter one. For a small nine-year-old boy from Llandegfan, Bangor Cathedral was an awesome building. I walked down the aisle and was blown away because I had never seen anything like it in my life. I turned to Mam and said, 'Wow! This is massive!' I could tell that the building had an immense history and I felt privileged to be there. I stepped gingerly between the choir stalls, overcome by the need to be careful not to damage the ancient tiles on the floor. I had been used to Llandegfan parish church with its tiny organ. Here in front of me was a mighty instrument with pipes as wide as my body that towered upwards towards the ceiling.

I had also never met anyone quite like the choirmaster, Andrew Goodwin. He agreed to teach me piano and asked me to sing a few scales to see what my musicality was like. He then turned to me and said, 'Please could you leave the room for a couple of minutes, because I'd like to talk to your mother?' At the time, this struck me as being rather odd, but I did as I was told and waited outside. I presumed that he was telling Mam that my singing was no good and that she should take me away.

In fact, he told Mam that he thought I had potential as a chorister and that, in his opinion, I could even make it in one of the big cathedral choirs. He wrote Mam a letter shortly afterwards:

Dear Mrs Jones,

I enclose, as arranged, details of the Cathedral choir together with a copy of the current service list.

I did not want to say in front of Aled on Saturday but I think, from what I heard of his voice, that he would be good enough to apply for entry to a choir school at one of the large Cathedrals. This idea may not appeal to you at all, but if you would like to pursue it, I could advise you accordingly. In fact, many Cathedrals will be holding auditions during the coming month or so.

In any case, I shall expect Aled for his first lesson on Friday 1st February, at 7.10 p.m.

Yours sincerely,

Andrew Goodwin

Organist and Master of the Choristers of Bangor Cathedral

Although the prospect of me attending any other cathedral choir apart from Bangor was promptly ruled out, the letter still sparked a debate in the Jones household. As with all of our big discussions, it took place in the kitchen. I sat with my feet dangling over the edge of the work surface while I listened to the arguments for and against. In the end, it was my decision and I felt that yes, I did want to become a choirboy. It was the first time that my parents had allowed me to make a decision about my singing career – something that they would continue to do time and time again over the next few years. Bearing in mind I was only nine, they treated me as though I were more mature.

Joining the cathedral was a massive commitment and the odd thing is that I kept on going, even though sometimes I didn't like it. Before the Friday evening rehearsals, I would have butterflies in my stomach as I walked all the way along the pathway and right up to the moment that I struggled to turn the big stiff handle on the back door of the cathedral. After giving the heavy door a final shove, I would compose myself as I ran up the staircase inside. Nobody knew how scared I really felt. The rehearsals ran from twenty past four until six o'clock and, believe me, this was the longest hour and forty minutes in the world. But I suppose I secretly also really enjoyed it, because there is nothing quite so rewarding as learning to read music and singing a note so pure that it reverberates around God's house. It makes you feel very powerful to be able to do that as a young boy.

We would go through all of the music for the next week. There would be more rehearsals on two Saturday mornings in the month from ten o'clock until midday, afternoon services on Tuesdays and Thursdays and then two services each week on Sundays – one at eleven o'clock in the morning and one at quarter past three in the afternoon. The only time off was for six weeks in the summer during the school holidays. Not only did the cathedral have a distinctive smell, but so did the choir room. It's something I always associate with a mixture of fear and excitement and it was only when I visited the cathedral again many years later that I finally realised that the unique odour came from the Calor Gas heaters.

When you first join the choir, you are still very much on trial and I hated my time as a probationer, yearning for the day when I would be a proper choirboy. To make the move up, you had to learn the service, to know the Creed off by heart and to be able to read music, so I had a lot of hard work to do. I felt so, so young as a probationer and really looked up to the other choirboys. Despite my apprehension on the way to the Friday night rehearsals, I grew to love the cathedral enormously.

At the time, Bangor Cathedral did not have a huge choir like Canterbury or Westminster. On a snowy, windy day in North Wales, there might only be six boys in total – three on either side of the cathedral. If you were to visit on a Sunday these days, the choir is far better populated.

All of the choristers lived in fear of hearing the words from Mr Goodwin: 'See me afterwards, boy.' I found him a slightly scary figure, but he taught me deportment and breathing and he was a hard taskmaster. I do believe that people who become good at things in the entertainment world, or in sport or the arts all have to work exceptionally hard. When they are questioned about their success, you often hear them say that 'it just comes naturally' to them, but when you scratch away at the surface, you usually find that there has been a period of intense effort early in their careers. Without a doubt, this was my time for hard graft.

Andrew Goodwin was a good coach and a very disciplined teacher, but we never had an easy relationship while I was a choirboy. Some of the children in the choir during the time I was there came from the very toughest parts of Bangor. One minute, we would all be normal schoolboys with battered shoes and holes in our trousers. The next, we would be angelic-looking choristers wearing cassocks and singing Stanford in G or Dyson in F. The fact that we were able to make this switch was all down to Mr Goodwin and the training he gave us. I really respect him for all that he taught me. In fact, he is still Master of the Choristers in Bangor Cathedral and it is a testament to his skill that so many boys have been given the opportunity to learn about a cathedral choir.

After the Friday night rehearsal, we would tear down the stairs from the choir room to the youth club, because that was when we got to meet girls, which was definitely one of the big pluses about being in the choir. The social life surrounding the choir was very varied and each Friday we would play football, go to the cinema, eat hotdogs and generally have a great time. Although we occasionally got some stick from our mates for wearing 'dresses' on Sundays, the girls seemed to love it that the boys were choristers. And to us, that was the important thing.

When choirboys get together, mischief tends to be high on the agenda. We would always mess around during services and I have to confess that I often didn't listen to a sermon all the way through. I would like to apologise now to the dean, Ivor Rees, whom all of the choirboys loved because he was such great fun. I consider him to be a friend now, so I hope he won't mind too much if we were not listening as hard as we should have been.

Before the Sunday service, we would all visit the sweetshop just up the road from the cathedral, to stock up on goodies to sustain us through the service. The pockets in choirboys' cassocks are notoriously massive, so we would manage to cram in at least three 'quarters' of sweets. Floral gums were our particular favourites, for wholly practical reasons. They were small versions of midget gems, which tasted like perfume. We would eat so many of them because they were tiny enough for us to be able to get rid of them quickly when we were about to sing. A company called Squirrel made them and I remember being horrified when I heard that their factory had burned down. These days, you can still buy floral gums, but somehow they don't quite taste the same to me as the ones that were made in the original factory.

Floral gums were also great for use as ammunition. Our favourite game during the service was to flick a floral gum from the choir stalls on one side of the cathedral to those on the other side, with the aim of getting them to land on the slanted music shelf.

Other schoolboy pranks would involve the list of music for the whole month, which would be in the choir stalls on a piece of white paper. We never tired of changing composers' names or the titles of pieces of music into funny or risqué words. In one three-week period, I also learned to draw perfectly the logo used on the front of Motörhead albums. An older choirboy who sat next to me taught me and I can still reproduce it to this day, although it's not something I'm often asked to do.

Whenever we were caught misbehaving, Mr Goodwin would become apoplectic. One time, we put Blu-tack under the keys of his piano so that when he sat down to play, no sound came out. As you can imagine, it went down like a lead balloon. On another occasion, he gave a group of us a severe dressing down because we had dared to write in the cathedral visitors' book during a break between services. Bless our hearts; all we had actually written was 'We think this place is ace'. The choirmaster went absolutely spare and, as a punishment, he sent us to the dean to apologise in person. Now the dean, Ivor Rees, was a very different sort of character. When we turned up in his office he said, 'Oh, don't worry boys. I love it that you think the cathedral is ace. Come in and have a cup of tea and a slice of cake.'

One of the best moments of my childhood happened on the way into the cathedral one Sunday morning. As I walked up to the door, there was a sudden gust of wind and dozens of conkers fell out of the tree by the pathway. I was thrilled because there were very few horse chestnut trees near our house on Anglesey, so I set about gathering up as many as I could, even though I was already ten minutes late for the service. Along with all my friends, I was obsessed with conkers and if any of us did find a tree we would think nothing of sneaking into someone's garden to steal its fruit. We went about our mission with a real zeal, feeling it was truly what we had been put on the earth to do. So the cathedral conker tree shedding its load right in front of me was just unbelievable and it kept me happy for months. To harden to full effect, I put some in the oven, some in vinegar and some in cow pats – I took the world of conkers very seriously.

One Friday evening I went along to the rehearsal as usual and was told that I was to sing my very first solo two days later, news which struck fear into my heart. I took the part home and rehearsed it with the piano all day on the Saturday. On the Sunday morning, I rehearsed constantly and my nerves were such that I could not manage to eat a scrap of food for either breakfast or lunch. It was a pattern that would continue right through my time in the choir. I took it really seriously and worked as hard as I could on each piece. If my solo came in the 3.15 p.m. service on the Sunday, I would rush home after the morning service and would carry on rehearsing right up until the time we had to turn around and go back to Bangor for the afternoon service. There was a time towards the end of my period in the choir when I was the only one doing solos, but I still managed to cope with the pressure.

Despite the amount of solo singing that I was doing, I never became head chorister. It was a job that I did not want to do – I could never have stood the pressure of being the main man. I always stood at the end of the row of choirboys, where I was much happier because it meant that I would not have to conduct the choir when the choirmaster was playing the organ. This was a truly terrifying experience, where you would have to start both the rest of the choir and the organ. I only did it twice and I was awful on both occasions.

Christmas was a very special time in the cathedral. In the week before, we would sing at the Service of Nine Lessons and Carols, which was one of our most testing times of the year. We had to jump between three hymn books during the service very quickly without dropping one, so the pressure was always on. Midnight mass was every choirboy's favourite service in the calendar. First, because we were all allowed to stay up late, but mainly because it meant that Christmas presents were just around the corner. We would whisper to each other at the start of the service, 'What presents are you hoping to get tomorrow?' Then, during the service the cathedral clock would strike twelve and the question would change: 'What do you want to get today?'

I always enjoyed going into the cathedral on Christmas Day. During the Christmas morning service in 1981, I received the Mary

Robinson Prize for the chorister who had made most progress during the year and who had achieved a high musical standard. The prize was a twenty-pound book token. That ranked as my best ever Christmas at the Cathedral. The worst was the year when I had an abscess in my mouth and was in agony – I carried on singing throughout, but was thoroughly miserable. There were no dentists open around Christmas and I was treated as an emergency on Christmas morning. That year, we decided to move Christmas Day to my birthday four days later, so that we could still celebrate in style.

In March 1983, when I was twelve, I was asked by Wyn Thomas, the Professor of Music at the University of Wales in Bangor, to sing in a performance of Mendelssohn's oratorio *Elijah* in the Pritchard Jones Hall of the university. I would be performing alongside the university's choir and orchestra with professional soloists including Janet Price, Margaret Cable, Neil Jenkins and Ian Caddy. It was to be my first professional engagement, for which I was actually paid hard cash. I loved working with Margaret Cable – what a voice! I also got my first glimpse of how professional singers actually operate. I was surprised how relaxed Ian Caddy was during the rehearsals. He would sit quietly reading a book while the others rehearsed and then when it was his turn to perform, he would stand up and sing his part effortlessly and brilliantly, before sitting back down and getting on with his book again. It gave me a taste of how singing operated as a real job and I loved it. I was full of admiration not only for the soloists, but also for the orchestra, because believe it or not, this was the first time that I had ever heard a full orchestra playing live. I was blown away by the magnitude of the sound a group of musicians could create. I have always had a soft spot for the Pritchard Jones Hall and was very proud to be awarded an honorary degree by the University of North Wales in the very same hall more than two decades after making my debut there.

That summer, the Bangor Cathedral Choir hit the road, going on tour to what was then West Germany. To help cover the costs of our trip, we staged another concert in the Pritchard Jones Hall. I was one of the more senior choristers by then and ended up singing many of the solos because most of the rest of the choir hardly knew any of the pieces. So I had to push things along as best I could. The piece that got us all stumped completely was *Zadok the Priest*, which is not known as being a solo work, although I was told afterwards that at one point the congregation could only hear my voice still going.

When the day came for us to leave Anglesey for Germany, we piled into the coach in a state of high excitement. The dean and his wife led the trip, which for virtually all of us was the first time we had been away from home. Before we went, we had been told to choose roommates for the trip. My parents sensibly made me pick boys who were quiet, whereas really I should have shared a room with my mates. The journey to Germany seemed to last for ever. We were on a boat for hours and hours, travelling in Z-Class – the cheapest of the cheap – with six of us sharing a berth right next to the engines. We were woken up throughout the night by drunks singing in the corridor outside. Once we docked, it was back on the bus for hours more of uncomfortably squashed travel. Despite our mode of transport, I loved every minute of the trip.

The tour proved to be a success, with performances in Soest, Mannheim, Speyer and Worms. As well as the singing, we had a great laugh. We were at that age when souvenir shops have a magnetic draw. One of the choirboys bought a pair of white clogs and we all decided to copy. The sight of a group of choirboys clomping around Germany wearing this strange footwear with their jeans must have looked bizarre in the extreme.

A year after the trip to Germany, I made my first tentative steps into the media world with a performance for television on a Welsh version of *Songs of Praise*, called *Dechrau Canu, Dechrau Canmol*, which translates as 'Start Singing, Start Praising'. The programme has been going for decades and comes from a different village in Wales every week. I was chosen to sing because it was coming from Beaumaris church on Anglesey and I was a local lad. Once we knew that I was doing the TV show, Andrew Goodwin suggested that I have extra singing lessons and he recommended that I go to see Julie Wynne and Robert Wyn Roberts. They were boyfriend and girlfriend, and had just finished studying at the Royal Northern College of Music in Manchester. They were both great fun to work with, as they were much closer to my age than any other music teachers I had encountered before. With a lot of hard work and plenty of laughs along the way, they coached me brilliantly to bring my two pieces for the programme up to scratch.

On the day of recording, I sang Franck's 'Panis Angelicus' and a Welsh version of the 'Pie Jesu' from Faure's *Requiem*. Although I had appeared on BBC Wales when I was much smaller, this was the first time I had properly recorded anything. Up until then, I had only needed to be aware of singing, but with cameras, lighting and sound people involved, I quickly had to learn a whole new way of working. I was surprised that everything had to be sung over and over again so that the technical people could get the right shots. Even though it was totally alien to me, I took everything in my stride – probably because when you boil it down to its simplest level, I was still only singing in church. This time, there just happened to be cameras there as well.

Now when I say that this was my first recording, I suppose I am not entirely telling the truth because all the way through my time in the cathedral choir, Mam used to bring a tape recorder to the services to record my singing. But not a small unobtrusive Dictaphone, oh no. Instead she used to cart around a huge cassette recorder. She would walk into the cathedral with this machine each week, completely ignoring the questioning stares from the rest of the congregation. In the evensong service, there would only be around ten people there, all of whom would sit near the choristers in the top part of the cathedral. Just as I would be about to launch into 'O for the wings of a dove', the building would echo with a deafening 'Clunk! Clunk!' as Mam pressed the play and record buttons on the tape recorder. It still makes me blush when I think of it now.

A lady called Hefina Orwig Evans, who was another regular attendee at the cathedral, decided that Mam should not have to make do with her own home-made recordings. So she took it upon herself to write to a local company, Sain Records, to recommend that they make a record of one of my performances:

Dear Friends,

A twelve-year-old boy from David Hughes Comprehensive, Menai Bridge, called Aled Jones, has a special voice. He won First Prize in the Urdd National Eisteddfod last year and First Prize for the Cerdd Dant solo.

He is the chief soloist with Bangor Cathedral Choir and the Choir will be singing on the 500th Anniversary of Martin Luther's birth in Worms in July, with Aled as soloist.

On Sunday night, there was a 'Festival of Song' in the Cathedral and Aled, with the Choir, sang 'Hear My Prayer' quite outstandingly. I thought that night what a tragedy it would be for his voice to break and there be no record of him. Before he went to David Hughes Comprehensive, Aled was a pupil at Llandegfan, where Edward Morris Jones is head-master, and he could confirm he has a special voice.

I wonder if you are interested? I am not a relative of his and there is no connection other than that I have this great desire to have a record of his voice.

Yours truly

Hefina Orwig Evans (Mrs)

The first we knew of this was when a letter from Sain landed on the doormat inviting me to make a record for them. They wanted me to sing half an album's worth of songs, with the rest of the disc coming from another boy soprano. For some reason, things didn't come together with the other choirboy, so they took a gamble and asked me to do the entire album.

Making a record was a whole new experience for me and the process took some getting used to. Andrew Goodwin accompanied me on the organ and I sang from the cathedral pulpit. Because we were so far apart and unable to see each other, my singing teacher Robert Wyn Roberts stood underneath the pulpit relaying the beat to me. I rehearsed hard for weeks beforehand and learned songs in Welsh, English, Latin and Italian.

We made the whole album in around four hours, which by most music-industry standards is ludicrously quick, although it is a discipline which I have kept with me ever since. I don't believe that you make a better album by going to four different studios and using a barrage of computer experts to patch together each song from dozens of different takes. When I recorded with Sain Records, an engineer and a producer would park their van outside Bangor Cathedral. A couple of thick wires would then be fed through the door and attached to two microphones – one in the pulpit and one by the organ. Then I would sing. And it was as simple as that.

It didn't seem odd to me that I was the focus of attention during the recording process and after the album was released: being an only child, it was something that had always happened to me. My grandparents had always fussed around me and the experience I went through at this time wasn't much different. The fact that my first album didn't cause an explosion of popularity for me, but rather a gradual build-up of awareness of my work, meant that I had time to get my head around what was going on at each stage. As a child, I am not sure that you always appreciate the magnitude of some of the things that you do, so I always just 'got up there and did it', whether it was a record, a television performance or a live concert.

A proud Mr Goodwin showed the finished album to all of the choirboys after a Christmas concert performance at Penrhyn Castle. It seemed odd to see my photograph on the cover of an album that was actually going to be on sale in the shops. I remember holding it and thinking, 'Well you can never take this away from me. I've actually recorded an album.'

I sat down with Mam at home to listen to it. I remember thinking to myself how bizarre it was to hear my own voice coming out of the speakers attached to our record player. I was much more interested in the cover design and the sleeve notes than I was in the actual album. This fascination had been sparked the Christmas before when I was given my first-ever album. Each year, the choristers of Bangor Cathedral bought each other presents and mine was an album by the rock band Queen, which included my then-favourite song, 'Bohemian Rhapsody'. I was delighted and played it over and over again. I became so interested in how they packaged everything about the record that I even went out and bought a book about the group, which told the story of how they went about developing their own unique look, alongside their own sound.

Just after the release of my first album, I competed in the National Eisteddfod, which is regarded as being very prestigious, being the biggest event of its kind in Wales each year. The preliminary part of the competition was open to everyone. I was nervous as I went on stage to sing and cannot have put in a very good performance as I failed to move on any further. Here I was with an album out, but I couldn't even get past the first stage of a singing competition – what a leveller!

My parents had always been great fans of the broadcaster Richard Baker, so imagine their shock when, one evening at around eight o'clock, he phoned up our house to tell us that he would be playing a track from my album on his *Baker's Dozen* radio programme the following week. Just as I have Hefina Orwig Evans to thank for putting Sain Records in touch with me, I have another lady to thank for getting that record its first national radio airplay. Unbeknown to me, or to Mam and Dad, it was Pam Wilkinson, the mother of Thomas, my best friend at the cathedral, who had gone to the trouble of sending a copy of the album to Richard Baker. For him to play the piece on the radio was amazing enough, but to take the trouble of phoning up to tell us beforehand was especially caring. I am sure that giving this level of attention to his listeners is almost certainly one of the reasons why he has remained a truly great broadcaster for so many years. The airing that he gave the album on *Baker's Dozen* was the first radio airplay it had received outside of Wales. I interviewed Richard recently for my BBC Wales radio programme and he still remembers making that call.

My own knowledge of Richard Baker at the time was limited to a cassette of favourite pieces from his programme *These You Have Loved*. I would sing along to it on our sailing trips on Dad's small boat, which he kept moored in Beaumaris. I hated it when the sea became choppy and would disappear below deck to listen to the tape to take my mind off feeling seasick. These trips always ended up with Mam, Dad and me playing cards or dominoes onboard in the evening, after cooking and eating the fish we had caught that day – often with the *These You Have Loved* tape as the only accompaniment, apart from the sound of the waves slapping against the hull.

The recording of my second album on the Sain label followed shortly after the release of my first. It did not go on sale until the following year and, in fact, the record very nearly didn't happen at all because the original recording made in Bangor Cathedral failed to come out properly. We only found this out six months after completing the recording when a very sheepish sound engineer knocked on our door and confessed. We had to do the whole thing all over again in another four-hour session, this time in Beaumaris Church.

My first record happened to be on sale in the foyer of St David's Hall in Cardiff on the night a BBC producer was there to see a concert. He bought my album and gave it a listen because he was looking for a boy soprano to sing in Handel's oratorio *Jephtha*. Already confirmed for the performance were such great names as Emma Kirkby, Anthony Rolfe Johnson and Alfreda Hodgson. When the producer listened to my album, he said, 'He's the one,' and phoned the conductor Sir Neville Marriner.

I had never been to Cardiff before, let alone St David's Hall, but I was acutely aware that this was the major league – far bigger than anything else I had done previously. This was serious stuff. I have to confess that I had absolutely no idea who Neville Marriner was when I met him. He walked into the rehearsal room with a baton in his hand and tapped me on the head with it. I had been told to learn the part of the angel, which starts with a recit – the sung part that tells the story before the main song. An aria follows on immediately afterwards, which my singing teachers had said I might as well learn anyway. When I was booked, it was on the understanding that I would only do the recit. In fact, I had been told that there would be no chance at all of me singing the aria as well. The morning before the concert, I stood in front of Neville and sang my part, but then I carried on into the aria. He turned to the other people in the room and said, 'Right, he's got to do the aria as well.' Julie and Robert were so proud that I was performing this concert and they gave me a good-luck card with a picture of a frog on the front, which I loved. I suppose that it showed that I was still a little kid, far more interested in childish things than in what I was about to be doing.

So the next evening I stood at the top of St David's Hall wearing a ridiculously large home-made velvet bow tie, which Mam had created herself. From my vantage point, I looked down on Neville Marriner, the BBC Welsh Symphony Orchestra and the soloists on stage. I was in a world of my own with my eyes glued on the conductor. He was lovely to work with because he is such a mild-mannered man and a phenomenal musician. As we stood there, I could feel him willing me on all the way. It might as well have just been the two of us in the hall, because I was completely unaware of anything else that was going on around us. My performance went down well, although I am not convinced that my singing was that great. Alfreda Hodgson dragged me on to the stage for the curtain call at the end and there were huge cheers – mostly from my dad, I think. It was the biggest thing that had ever happened to me.

4. VOICES FROM THE HOLY LAND

The two gentlemen who ran the music department of BBC Wales when I was a boy were Hefin Owen and Mervyn Williams. Mervyn was the boss, but together they produced much of the BBC's networked classical-music output. They had recorded *Jephtha* with Neville Marriner at St David's Hall so when, just a month later, they were commissioned to work on three big-budget music specials with an executive producer from the BBC in London called Rodney Greenberg, I was still fresh in their minds. The programmes were to be a joint production with Israeli television.

They had been asked to make three programmes in Israel – one for Christmas 1984 and two for Easter 1985. Mervyn told his colleagues in London about the little lad from Anglesey who had performed in concert with the BBC Welsh Symphony Orchestra and Chorus. He persuaded them to use me as the soloist throughout the three programmes, as we recorded songs at all of the religiously significant places in the Holy Land.

I actually ended up going to the Middle East twice. The first trip was to promote the programme on daytime television in Israel – at the time, a visit by a hundred-strong choir and production team from the UK was big news. Mam and Dad were unable to get the time off work, so off I went with my singing teacher Julie Wynn on El Al. The flight passed off without incident and I was thrilled to find that we were staying in the luxurious surroundings of the Hilton Tel Aviv.

The evening we arrived, I was supposed to have a rehearsal with the pianist, a twelve-year-old Israeli boy called Shlomi. He was a great guy and an incredibly gifted pianist. When we met, he was suited and booted with big hair, very different from the kids I was used to mixing with at home. He was undoubtedly a musical genius, though, and just a couple of years later he gave a concert performance in London's Royal Festival Hall. Whereas singing for me was just fun, playing the piano was already a career for him.

After the rehearsal, Julie and I went back to the hotel. A few minutes later, she took a call telling us that the Israeli TV staff had gone on strike and we would therefore not be able to do the programme the next day. So Julie and I instead spent the whole time in the Hilton's jacuzzi – a brand-new experience for me – before jumping back on the plane and flying home. The fact that we didn't make any television programmes at all didn't stop it from being an incredibly exciting experience.

My second trip to Israel was very different with far more hard work than the first. I had already recorded all of the music for the three programmes with the BBC Welsh Chorus led by their conductor, John Hugh Thomas. We did it in one afternoon in a church in an area of Cardiff called Splot, which, it has to be said, was then not the most attractive part of the city. It was too complicated to try to record the sound when we were actually standing outside in Israel, so we would be miming instead. The week before we were to depart for the Holy Land, I was given an audiotape of our recordings so that I could practise my lip-synching in front of the mirror at home. It was at this moment that I realised how big the three programmes really were. Nothing like it had been attempted before and, after all, they were going to be on BBC1, the same side as *EastEnders*. To this day, I pride myself on my miming. I love doing it and take great pleasure in getting it just perfect.

Security is understandably tight when you fly El Al and even back then you had to arrive at the airport three hours before the flight, ready to face an interrogation about your reasons for visiting Israel. Mam, Dad and I checked in without the choir, who had already gone through en masse. This young security guy told us to go into the next room. I was so excited that I jabbered away about all sorts of inconsequential nonsense until Dad threw me a look that said, 'Please button it, or we're going to get arrested!'

'Why are you going to Israel?' asked the security official.

'I'm going to do some BBC programmes and I'm going on a few chat shows,' I replied.

'Which chat shows are you going on?' I mentioned the name of one particular chat-show host.

'Really, what are you doing on there?'

'I'm a singer.'

'Hold on,' said the guard, picking up the telephone. After a brief conversation in Hebrew, he turned back to me, his tone mellowing considerably, and said, 'Oh, yes, you are going on that programme. My uncle is the presenter.' From that moment on, we were treated royally.

When we arrived on Israeli soil at four o'clock in the morning, the television crew were waiting for us. With them was a very formidable senior executive from Israeli TV, by the name of David Goldstein. He was a powerful man who had previously been a senior officer in the Israeli army. I would soon find out that he viewed television production in much the same way as generals view a military campaign. We were taken by bus to the kibbutz where we staying. The whole country was incredibly busy, full of people bustling in all directions – just about as far from Anglesey as you could get.

Filming quickly got under way, and in those days it really was filming, with the action recorded on to big reels of tape rather than the videotapes or hard discs that we are used to now. That meant that every single scene started off with a shot of the clapperboard containing the title of the programme and details of what was being recorded, so that the film editor back home had some idea of what was going on when he came to put the programme together. I got to know the clapperboard man and started to mess around with him. One morning, David Goldstein caught him pretending to sing with me. He dived down, grabbed a rock and threw it at the clapperboard man, hitting him on the back. 'Don't mess around! It's money!' he barked.

It became clear to us very quickly that the ancient and modern Israeli worlds are forced to sit very closely together. Nowhere was this more so than at the Garden of Gethsemane, which on paper sounds stunning. However, when we arrived there we were surprised to find that they were filming from the other side of one of Israel's busiest roads. The sight must have been rather surprising for the drivers zooming past on the motorway, as a hundred-strong

Welsh choir and a blond-haired kid wearing a cassock and surplice stood singing right next to the road on the steps which led up to the garden.

The days of filming were long, very long. The fiery intensity of the sun did nothing to make them go by any quicker. I was so hot in my cassock, which had been designed for use back home in draughty Bangor Cathedral, that I would wear nothing underneath but a pair of shorts. We worked all day, only breaking for the delicious packed lunch provided for us by the kibbutz. Each day, our parcels were filled with completely new taste experiences for me including, most memorably, gherkins.

One evening, towards the end of a particularly hot session of filming, Mr Goldstein came along and said to me, 'Are you cold?'

'No, really, it's lovely and warm,' I replied.

'It's getting cold. You should wear your jumper,' he said firmly.

'No, really I'm fine, thanks.'

'Wear your jumper!' he boomed. Mam said afterwards it was the quickest I had ever put on an item of clothing or obeyed someone in my life.

The best day of the whole trip came when we were given a whole 24 hours with no work to do. Mam, Dad, Julie and I decided to fulfil our ambition to float in the Dead Sea. We were so un-starlike, without the entourages who surround singers now. It was just the four of us and we jumped on a local bus for the two-hour journey. Some of our fellow passengers were soldiers, presumably going home on leave, and we were rather perturbed to see them putting their rifles in the overhead locker.

Still, it was all a bit of an adventure, although the journey to the Dead Sea was very hot, very long and very dusty. I was amazed to be standing by a 'Sea Level' sign on the roadside with the Dead Sea appearing to be miles below in the distance. Anyone going there who thinks it is an idyllic area should think again, because it is the rockiest, most uncomfortable place to be. You cannot just swim in the sea; instead you have to run through the water to actually get anywhere. Julie had brought the local paper from Bangor with her, so that she could have her photo taken floating in the sea while pretending to read it. We were typical tourists.

Although the experience of floating was fantastic, it was impossible to relax completely because army helicopters would constantly buzz overhead. At the time, I was far more concerned about avoiding getting any of the salt water in my eyes or mouth. Even the smallest amount forces you to scurry out of the sea to douse yourself with fresh water because the saltiness stings so much.

I had bonded with quite a few people in the choir, some of whom still come to my concerts now, and they were really lovely people. One man called Don Smith, who sang the solo on 'My Lord, What a Morning', was a particular favourite of mine because he had one of the finest voices I had heard. To this day, I still think of Israel whenever I hear that song. I was very upset when just before we were due to film in the dark, he fell down a hole in a church and hurt himself quite badly.

My biggest disappointment on the trip was when I was recording 'O Holy Night' in a cave right at the end of the day. The entire choir had been let off early because their part had been filmed, so they all rushed off to a local swimming pool. I was desperate to go swimming with them, so I really concentrated hard on singing the song to the best of my ability, hoping that I would get back to the pool. I was so disappointed when the filming overran and I missed the swim.

Although it was a big-budget production in terms of the overall cost of making the programmes, the BBC's funds would not extend to Mam and Dad staying with me in Israel for the whole trip. They were due to go home the day after my only live concert during the trip, in the Tel Aviv auditorium, which had been built to host the Eurovision Song Contest a few years before. David Goldstein was sitting in the front row and came backstage during the interval. 'It is fantastic, your voice is excellent!' he shouted, proceeding to slap me across the face really hard. This was his way of telling me that I was doing a really good job, but I was really shocked as Mam and Dad were due to fly home the next day leaving me with Julie, my singing teacher, and Hefin, the BBC producer, as my guardians for the rest of the trip. I was already feeling a little apprehensive, but I put the worries to the back of my mind and went back on stage for the second half, singing my heart out.

The response from the audience was amazing and I did three encores. By this point the choir must have been itching to get to the bar and were probably thinking, 'Come on, little brat, get off stage.' As I took my final bow, the pianist who was accompanying me said, 'Let's do the same thing again.' I felt it was time to finish so there was this awful moment where I just froze on stage.

I walked into the wings, burst into tears and said to Mam and Dad, 'I don't want you to go home early.' I then had to compose myself and turn round and sing Schubert's 'Heidenröslein' again. The next morning, Mam and Dad left for Britain; although I was very upset when they flew out, I had to get over it and Julie looked after me very well.

The morning after Mam and Dad left, we were due to film in Jerusalem and, as usual, Julie and I travelled in the back of a jeep with four armed guards. Suddenly, as we got to the outskirts of the city, a soldier ordered the driver of the jeep to stop. A bomb had gone off an hour earlier just around the corner from where we were due to start filming. Although you could not tell in the programmes that were broadcast, I had a very uneasy feeling inside for much of the remainder of the trip.

The armed guards themselves unwittingly got me into trouble after I was photographed with them wearing one of their berets and holding a sub-machine-gun. The picture was published in a book written about my childhood career and as soon as it came out there was a huge row. People were really horrible about it and said some terrible things about me, but as a kid you really don't understand the political implications of international conflict. So in hindsight, I do regret having the picture taken, but at the time, none of us understood how offensive it might be to some people. I loved the guards and felt very safe with them and they wanted to spoil me the only way they knew how. By the time that the picture was taken, they had become my friends.

Hefin and I flew back into Heathrow together. After we landed we had to pick up the tapes from the luggage carousel at the airport. He thought that the tapes had been loaded on to the plane, but was not entirely sure because there had been a small disagreement with the Israeli TV producers just before we had left. After an hour of waiting, the conveyor belt was still empty. Two hours later, there was still nothing. By this point, Hefin was sweating profusely and was making increasingly panicked calls on the payphone in the baggage-collection hall. At the time, I didn't really understand the significance, but looking back, I can see that those tapes represented two weeks of work involving more than a hundred people.

Eventually, after what seemed like an eternity, the first metal case of tapes came through the rubber strips and on to the carousel.

Then came the second one. I have never seen anyone looking as relieved as Hefin did at that moment.

The best thing about the Israel trip happening when it did was that it meant I had developed a relationship with Mervyn and Hefin from BBC Wales. They went on to record virtually all of my albums as a boy. They also made two series of programmes called *Aled,* which were recorded in the Margam Orangery, a beautiful wooden-floored building just outside Cardiff. I presented two versions of the programme – one in English and one in Welsh. I was very lucky to be singing alongside the pianist Ingrid Surgenor, who is one of the most respected accompanists in the world. It is not automatic when you perform with another musician that you gel together perfectly, even after rehearsing hard. When it does happen, as it always does for me with Ingrid, the effect is effortlessly magical.

Hefin and Mervyn never exploited me as a 'child star' and the bond of trust that Mam, Dad and I had built up with them was very important. Working with them taught me the lesson of how important it is to have a team of people around you that you can count on – and it is something that has stayed with me ever since.

Mam and Dad were at the very centre of my team. Although I realise now that my childhood was very different from that of other kids, most of the time it was actually very simple and monotonous. Even school was incredibly normal, with no talk of the good things in life such as electronic gadgetry or the bad things in life such as drugs. We simply played football whenever we could – usually in teams made up of the English versus the Welsh.

I am incredibly close to my parents and even though my home is now in London, I still see them regularly. Everyone always asks me if my relationship with my parents was different because I was working as a child, but I really do not believe this to be true. Whether we were in Hollywood or back at home, life remained completely the same. Looking back, I think that keeping your feet on the ground is the single most important thing about being famous as a child. I had only been on holiday with them once before I had started singing – and that was only as far away as Minorca. Going away on an aeroplane was something completely out of the ordinary for us back then. Mam was terrified of flying and spilled coffee over the brand-new suit she had bought for the trip. How things had changed just a few years later when we thought nothing of hopping on a plane, although Mam has always remained a nervous flyer.

One of the biggest problems we had at that time was having to refuse most of the requests for performances or appearances that came in each day. With both of my parents working full time, we tried to arrange everything for weekends or school holidays. On the rare occasions when I did something during school time, it was always Dad who accompanied me, as his holiday arrangements were more flexible. It has to be said that if we had accepted all the engagements on offer at that time then I would have been singing every night of the week. However, it was still very difficult to refuse people as most of the requests came from charitable organisations and, of course, each thought their charity or event to be the most worthy.

On one occasion, I had agreed to sing at a charity concert in a small chapel in North Wales. It was a firm booking, which had been agreed six months earlier. Just a week before the concert, we received a phone call from Valerie Solti, the wife of the great conductor Sir Georg Solti. She was arranging a soiree at Clarence House for the Queen Mother. She asked if I would be available to sing at the event. Dad had to tell her that, with great regret, I would have to turn down her kind offer.

Another major problem we had was double-booking. One or other of my parents would forget to record concert dates in the diary. On one occasion, we had agreed that I would take part in an evening charity concert in North Wales. But the booking was not written down in the diary. Later I agreed to sing in a matinee concert in the Barbican Theatre in London on the same day. When we discovered the double-booking, the only way I could attend both venues was by chartering a light aircraft to fly to and return from London in time for the evening concert.

At that time there was no private airport close to my home, but fortunately we were allowed to use the runway at RAF Valley, which is about twenty miles away. On the morning of our flight we were actually queuing up behind Hawk trainer jet aircraft. This was an amazing experience, as on take-off they peeled one way, while we went the other. This was my first time in a small aircraft and I was very excited and also rather nervous. It did not help when Dad asked the pilot if he would fly around the summit of Snowdon so that he could take some photographs. I was secretly relieved when we descended through thick cloud to land at Denham airport outside London where a car was waiting to take us to the Barbican.

Mam and Dad have always provided me with an incredibly stable home life, something for which I owe them an enormous amount. They must have been fazed by what happened to me as a boy, but they seemed to take it all very matter-of-factly. No one at home made a big fuss about the amazing things that were happening to me.

Occasionally I am asked in interviews what my advice to a 'child star' would be. My answer is always the same and it is directed at the parents, rather than the youngster: just let it happen. The parents of a child who works in the entertainment world should never become pains in the neck to the people working with them. Mam and Dad never were; they just went with the flow and, with hindsight, it was the best thing that they ever did. They were never too pushy because we had a normal life that we went back to at the end of each day's recording or filming. Some people might say that was a mistake and that if we had moved to America, I might now be worth billions of dollars, but the fact is that we would always come back to Llandegfan because that was our base. Our universe had this little Welsh village rather than London or Los Angeles at its centre, with everywhere else orbiting around it. That has remained so important to me ever since.

5. *THE TREBLE*

For the first few months of 1985, I could not so much as sneeze without it being recorded for posterity by a television crew who were making a documentary about me for BBC1 called *The Treble*. The woman behind the programme was an absolute genius of a TV producer called Angela Pope.

She led the pack of nine people who followed me everywhere during that time. And when I say everywhere, I mean everywhere. They were at every concert, every television interview, every meeting about my career. They were there when I woke up in the morning and they were there when I went to sleep in the evening. They virtually moved into our house, with Mam providing endless cups of tea and plates of biscuits.

Angela wanted to tell the story of how my career had begun, so many of the major incidents in my childhood career were re-enacted for the cameras. They even hired a studio in London so that they could record me 'meeting' Neville Marriner for the first time.

The dramatic highlight of the documentary saw Mam greeting me on the doorstep to tell me that I had been invited to sing in one of the 'Pops '85' series of concerts at St David's Hall in Cardiff alongside the legendary Welsh tenor Stuart Burrows. Now, viewers of the documentary might have been forgiven for thinking that the only thing I did was listen to his albums, all day every day, which was not quite the case. However, I did listen to his music a lot and I admired him enormously. He is an amazing lyric tenor and, to my mind, nobody in the world has ever bettered him.

Angela seized on this concert as one of the central points for the documentary, so we were filmed leaving Llandegfan in our bright yellow Vauxhall Cavalier with the leopard-skin seat covers and heading through the snow to Cardiff. It was undoubtedly an important concert, with the other soloist being a Finnish soprano called Karita Mattila, who was the first-ever winner of the Cardiff Singer of the World competition and who is now a world-renowned performer. As well as performing for the audience in St David's Hall, we were also being recorded for a television and radio broadcast by the BBC.

Stuart himself had a very successful career as a boy soprano and, as part of the documentary, Angela arranged for me to interview him. It came across on the programme as being completely natural, because she never told me what I would be doing on film beforehand, preferring to ambush me with a request there and then. Stuart and I talked about my voice breaking and I told him that I had heard that a boy should not sing for two years afterwards.

'I wouldn't contemplate singing, not for two years but four years,' he replied. At this point the colour completely drained out of my face. He went on: 'It depends when the voice breaks. I know it's agony, because you want to sing, because you're musical. Mentally, you think you can do it, but your body tells you physically that you can't.'

'When will I know when I must stop singing?' I asked.

'This is a very good question – it's the million-dollar question – because you find that there are times when you are singing well.'

By now, I was well and truly crestfallen. The scene ended with me saying, 'I just can't think of myself not being able to sing – having to be quiet for four years – because when I'm at home I just sing every minute of the day.'

People talked to me about my voice breaking all the time, but it was never something that scared me. As it turned out, I still had almost two years of singing ahead of me after the interview with Stuart. In my late teens, people in Wales often stopped me and asked, 'Did you listen to Stuart Burrows?' and I always jokingly replied, 'He didn't want me to sing for four years because he was scared I would come back and take his record sales from him.' This was, of course, completely untrue and Stuart's advice was absolutely right.

Stuart presented the concert, as well as singing for much of it. He stood on stage and introduced me, saying, 'Now, Aled and I thought long and hard about what we could sing together and we have decided to perform "Panis Angelicus" ...' The audience all murmured approvingly before he added the words, '... in Welsh.' At this point the audience broke into wild applause. They gave me a very warm reception for my other numbers: Handel's 'Where E'er You Walk' and Simon and Garfunkel's 'Bridge Over Troubled Water'.

The concert was a great success, but the sad thing was that I was at my lowest point as a boy afterwards. The following morning, we drove back to North Wales through increasingly treacherous weather in our mightily embarrassing car. What had started out as snow flurries when we had left Llandegfan had now turned into blizzards. The snow was lying all around us and although the journey from South to North Wales is beautiful, it is not easy, taking at least five hours. All the way back, I was curled up in the back seat of the car. After a while, Mam and Dad realised that I was sobbing quietly to myself.

'What's the matter?' Mam asked, the concern very clear in her voice.

'It's the best thing I've ever done in my life,' I replied. 'What if I don't ever get another chance to do anything like that ever again?'

'Oh, you will. I'm sure you will,' she said gently. 'But even if you don't, then don't worry, because it's been a brilliant experience which we've all enjoyed.'

I was inconsolable – here I was doing a concert to a full house at St David's Hall in Cardiff, the national concert hall of Wales, with the BBC Welsh Symphony Orchestra. I had only done the Neville Marriner concert with an orchestra before. The documentary people had added to the excitement and glamour of the evening, with one hundred per cent of the attention focused on me. Then all of a sudden, I had been left sitting with Mam and Dad in the car and it was back to school and back to reality. At that moment, I found it really tough to deal with. I was frightened because I had enjoyed singing on stage more than ever. I think I had also had my first real glimpse of what I thought that life could be like as a grown-up at the party afterwards.

I did a lot of thinking over the next few days and very quickly snapped out of the low, as I realised that you can always strive for new highs and that you should never dwell too much on the past. Even though I was just fourteen, I decided that if you want something enough in your life and are prepared to really work at it, then it will happen again. I made a promise to myself never to worry about the future from that moment onwards and instead vowed to enjoy the present. It's a promise that, by and large, I have managed to keep over the years since.

The Stuart Burrows concert was produced for television by my old friends Hefin Owen and Mervyn Williams from BBC Wales, but I was shocked when it finally went out nationally on BBC2 the following year, because I looked terrible. The make-up lady had given me a very odd tanned skin tone, I was wearing a yellow bow tie and trousers that were too short, and to top it all, when I bowed it looked as though I was going to dive into the audience. Although the newspaper critics loved the performance, the harshest critics of all, the other kids in my class at school, thought it was hilarious and I was ribbed mercilessly.

School life had become quite tough, but in the midst of all the fun being had at my expense, I had made some really close friends who didn't care a jot about what I did. The best of them was called Neil Houston. He was so confident and mischievous that we became joined at the hip.

David Hughes Comprehensive was a big, tough school. The main interest in the lives of me and my mates was playing football, which we did at every available opportunity. The highlight of the week came if we had hot dogs for lunch. Other than that, I would usually spend my dinner money in the tuck shop on ice lollies, Chocolate Dib-Dabs and cans of Coke. These highly nutritious meals would be consumed while we sat on the branches of a tree overlooking the playing fields. I was always getting into trouble for misdemeanours, but the worst punishment I ever received came about in a biology lesson, where we were dissecting animal organs.

I put a tiny piece of pig's heart that had been left lying on a bench into a girl's pencil case. When she opened it up during the next lesson, she let out an ear-splitting scream. I received a severe earbashing from the biology teacher, who banned me from her lessons for a week. Instead I was given a knife and told to spend the time scraping chewing gum off the floor of one of the mobile classrooms, which has to rank as one of the worst jobs I have ever had to do.

The documentary people even came to school, but I had been adamant with Angela that I did not want my classmates to know that the subject matter of the programmes was me. So our teacher told my class that the crew was there to make a programme about maths. The cover was blown almost immediately by the fact that every time the camera panned across the room, it would end up zooming in on me. The whole class sussed it when they caught sight of the clapperboard, on which were written the words 'Aled Jones – The Treble'.

Mam and Dad tried hard to make sure that I missed as little school as possible, although sometimes it was difficult as there were some very tempting offers starting to land on our doorstep. One of the oddest jobs came just a few weeks after the Stuart Burrows concert. I was asked to record 'Sing a Song of Sixpence' as part of the backing track to BBC1's *Miss Marple* drama. It sounded exciting, so off we went to London on the train for what turned out to be the most boring time-consuming thing that I have ever done in my life. I spent a whole day in the studio with these guys watching a screen with the *Miss Marple* pictures playing on it over and over again. I sang 'Sing a Song of Sixpence' repeatedly until it was timed exactly to the pictures, although I never got to sing the very last word of the song because my voice was drowned out by the sound of a gunshot as the murderer in the story provided the great detective with her case to solve.

If there is one single moment in my career as a boy soprano that I could point to and say, 'That's where things really started to happen for me,' then it would have to be the Easter weekend of 1985. On Good Friday, *The Road to the Cross*, the second of the programmes we had made in Israel, was shown nationally. BBC Wales also gave *Voices from the Holy Land* its first airing. After the programmes were broadcast, our phone lines were jammed for hours with friends and relatives calling to offer their congratulations.

Three days later, the concert performance of Handel's *Jephtha*, which I had recorded with Neville Marriner the year before, was finally given its first television broadcast. I also appeared on the BBC's *Breakfast Time* and *Pebble Mill at One*. Princess Anne was one of my fellow guests on the latter and Dad was very pleased to have taken a photo of us together. It was the first of what became regular visits to Pebble Mill in Birmingham. I was asked to judge the school carol competition that they held every year – on one occasion the winners included a youngster called Gary Barlow, who later earned worldwide fame and fortune as a member of the pop group Take That. It turned out to be a very happy-go-lucky programme, being broadcast live every day, although I later realised that it was a little different on the first occasion because of the royal visitor – the posh china and nice sandwiches were very much in evidence.

Just a few days after Easter, I recorded a video with the eminent choral conductor, Sir David Willcocks. Called *Carols for Christmas*, it was shot in Bury St Edmunds, of all places, and was released in time for Christmas 1985 in both Britain and America. I was very proud of the review it was given by the *New York Times*, which called it 'classy'.

I was asked to London shortly afterwards for an audition for a very different sort of project – a full-length performance of Handel's oratorio *Athalia*, conducted by Christopher Hogwood for Decca Records. Chris had narrowed the contenders for the boy soprano's role down to me and another lad called Nicholas Silitoe, who was a soloist at the Royal Opera House and very experienced at this sort of work. I was particularly apprehensive, never having auditioned for anyone before. When I arrived and met Nicholas, there seemed something odd about his hair – it turned out that he had decided to have a go at cutting it himself with his mum's nail scissors the night before. Although we were the same age, we looked poles apart. I was dressed in the very best that Burton's had to offer, while he was incredibly cool in a battered old baseball jacket. I was very conscious that I looked like a country bumpkin compared to this very funky London boy.

Nicholas sang first and then it was my turn. I had the added pressure of Angela Pope and her film crew, so there was a very genuine risk that my failure to get a role would be recorded and shared with the nation on television. Afterwards, Christopher said nothing to either Nicholas or me and it was weeks later when the letter arrived with the news I had been waiting for. I sat on the big desk in my bedroom and Mam waited beside me as I opened the envelope. Yes, I had got the role. I screamed in delight and threw my arms around her. I felt so elated. When it came to recording the album, I worked alongside such musical luminaries as Dame Joan Sutherland, Emma Kirkby, James Bowman and Anthony Rolfe Johnson.

There were plenty of other records to be released during 1985 as well, the first of which was *Voices from the Holy Land*. Originally, the BBC only made a thousand copies, but it went on to sell three thousand copies a day, reaching number two in the pop charts and only being kept from the number one spot by Bruce Springsteen's album *Born in the USA*.

My second BBC album, *All Through the Night* hit the record shops three months later and the BBC released *The Best of Aled Jones* just a couple of months after that. To top it all, *Voices from the Holy Land* was also in the shops as a video. They knew that I only had a finite life as a boy soprano and were obviously keen to make the most of it.

I was appearing on television with increasing regularity and made the first of many performances on Terry Wogan's eponymous chat show. In the end, I appeared on the show more times than any other guest and on one very special programme I even turned the tables on Terry and actually asked the questions. It got plenty of laughs from the studio audience, although at one stage I confessed, 'This is really hard.' Terry was hugely supportive of me as a boy and is a genuinely lovely man. I don't see him that often these days, but whenever I have had contact with him he has always been a great friend to me.

My first performance on *Wogan* was to promote *The Treble*, which was being broadcast later that week. One of the best things about the programme getting an airing was that I would no longer be followed about by a film crew. Although Mam, Dad and I missed the individuals in the team, and the banter during the countless fun-filled evening meals out, it was great to finally get our house back to ourselves – it definitely wasn't big enough to have an extra nine people camping out in it every day.

A few months later, we were at home listening to the eight o'clock news bulletin on the radio one morning and the newsreader said, 'And good news for the BBC last night: it scooped three Emmy Awards in America, including one for *Aled Jones: The Treble* in the Best Documentary category.' This was news to us as nobody from the BBC had even mentioned that it was nominated. A few weeks later, I was asked to take part in a five-minute photo session in London, where my picture was taken with the award before it was whisked back to the BBC. That was the last I ever saw of it. I suspect it's now sitting unloved and forgotten in a dusty cupboard somewhere in the BBC – I'd love to give it a much better home. Recently I bumped into Melvyn Bragg and he told me that I was the bane of his life. Apparently, he had been offered the idea of making a television documentary about my life for ITV. He said that he always regretted turning it down – especially when the one that the BBC made picked up an Emmy.

I also appeared regularly on the Gay Byrne show on RTE in Dublin. At the time, Gay was to Irish television what Terry Wogan was to our screens in Britain. Just like Terry, he was a highly professional interviewer. He always remained very cool under pressure on screen and this seemed to be a characteristic that he had in real life too. On one of the occasions he interviewed me, he told me that a plane he had flown to Dublin on earlier that day had been forced to make an emergency landing because a flock of birds had flown into the engine. I thought that his composure was remarkable and I am sure that I would have still been a gibbering wreck. The other thing that always struck me about RTE was the level of security around the television station. This protection even extended to the drinks cabinet, which was kept locked and bolted before the programme and was only ever unlocked after the show had gone out. They had obviously had one or two bad experiences over the years with guests who had taken advantage of the programme's hospitality before going on air.

The relatively relaxed experience of performing on a television show in Ireland was very different to the experience that I had when I sang on one in Germany called *Auf Los Gehts Los*, which roughly translates as 'Ready, Steady, Go'. I was due to sing 'Silent Night' in its original German form. We arrived five minutes late for the rehearsal and were told in no uncertain terms that this meant that there would now be no rehearsal at all. I was used to British television, which was far less rigid in its routines. The whole trip was a strange experience because virtually nobody spoke English to us. I ended up spending my whole time there playing table tennis in the hotel with my accompanist, Annette.

Back home, the BBC bosses were far more generous when it came to giving me awards for my records than they had been over the Emmy trophy. They wanted me to go to Cardiff to pick up a gold disc for one hundred thousand sales of *Voices from the Holy Land* and a silver disc for sixty thousand sales for *All Through the Night*. However, it would have meant missing a day of classes, and Dad was concerned that my schoolwork would suffer. So the BBC blew the budgets and decided to charter a helicopter to fly me from

Anglesey to Cardiff and back. The only place they could land near my house was a huge field in the middle of Llandegfan village. It was a brilliant adventure for Mam, Dad and me. We piled into the helicopter and after it had taken off, we looked down on our home as it became smaller and smaller.

When we arrived down in Cardiff about fifty minutes later, we were photographed and filmed landing. I was presented with my gold and silver discs and was interviewed by newspaper, radio and television reporters. My old friends from the BBC Welsh Symphony Choir were there to sing. After a quick reception and some more photographs being taken, we jumped back into the helicopter and headed home.

When we had left the field in Llandegfan earlier in the day, it was quiet and empty. On our return, we were shocked to see that hundreds of people were standing waving around the edges of Anglesey's makeshift helipad. The whole village had turned out to cheer my success, with the Girl Guides even making a banner saying 'Welcome home Aled!' Most people had never seen a helicopter up close before, let alone a gold disc. It brought home to me for the first time that even though I was singing choral classics, this was like rock'n'roll. It was a taste of what life would be like when I made it in the pop singles charts later in the year. But before that success, I would suffer the greatest personal humiliation of my career, live on stage in front of the Queen.

6. THE WORST PERFORMANCE OF MY LIFE

D ad and I were standing in a luxuriously carpeted lift in an exclusive apartment block in West London. When we reached the top floor, the lift doors opened on to an exquisitely furnished living room, which was dominated by an enormous grand piano. It was just like a scene from *Dynasty*. Sitting behind the piano, playing 'Memory', was the composer Andrew Lloyd Webber.

'Memory' was a song that I had heard many times before, but the moment I listened to him playing it, it was as if the music was coming from his soul. Here was a man whom I had seen many times on TV and now we were actually in his London home. He had asked me to record the song as a single for BBC Records and we were in his flat for a rehearsal ahead of the studio session.

Andrew was very friendly and quietly spoken and I was in awe as he took me through the piece. Once the rehearsal was over, we had a cup of tea in the rooftop garden above the flat with his mum, who was a fan of my singing.

The recording session the following day went extremely well and afterwards Andrew said, 'I'm going to a Nordoff Robbins Music Trust lunch now. Why don't you come along too, as my guest?' Turning to Dad, he added: 'Sorry, Derek, but there's no room for you on the top table, but I'll put you on another one instead.' I was so proud when it turned out that Dad was going to be on the Radio One table, sitting with famous disc jockeys.

We went to the lunch and I saw so many stars in the first few minutes that I found it almost overwhelming. Rod Stewart was sitting with me on my table, alongside Andrew Lloyd Webber and Tim Rice, who were being given the Lifetime Achievement award. Dad's table included Radio One stars such as Mike Smith and Peter Powell.

During his acceptance speech for the award, Andrew Lloyd Webber almost made me choke on my lunch by mentioning my name. 'I am honoured to have with me as my guest, Aled Jones,' he said. 'And the great thing is that there are all of Britain's top musicians here today, but I bet none of you have had two albums in the Top Five of the charts at the same time, and that's something that Aled has achieved this week.'

We had heard that morning that my first BBC album, *Voices from the Holy Land*, was at number two with the follow-up *All Through the Night* at number five. Dad's new friends from Radio One had encouraged him to celebrate this success with particular vigour, helped by the three extra cases of wine they had stashed away beneath their table.

The next time I met Andrew Lloyd Webber was a far less happy experience for me. I had been asked to end the first half of a Royal Charity Gala in Edinburgh in the presence of the Queen by singing 'Memory'. It was a very prestigious event, packed full of Hollywood stars and with the Welsh legends Tom Jones and Shirley Bassey also on the bill. Sarah Brightman and another boy soprano, Paul Miles-Kingston, would be on stage before me singing 'Pie Jesu' from Lloyd Webber's *Requiem*.

It was the first time that I had performed 'Memory' in a concert and I seemed to be more nervous about it than usual. I had used the music copy in the rehearsal in the afternoon, but the director had asked me not to sing with it in the evening, because it would spoil the shots for the television cameras. Andrew Lloyd Webber said that he did not mind if I had the music in front of me, but the director persisted, saying it made me look stupid. I was unsure but, against my better judgement, I agreed to his demands.

That evening, I walked on stage and sang the first verse perfectly. Then, during the two-bar instrumental break between the first and second verses, I looked down the hall and saw an exit sign, the crowds of people, the Queen and her family sitting in the Royal Box . . . and my mind went blank. I thought, 'I haven't got a clue what comes next.' My legs had gone wobbly, my mouth was dry and my voice cracked a couple of times as I sang a completely bogus set of words, which I had made up on the spur of the moment: 'Memory, all alone in the moonlight, I can hear the choir singing, they are singing alone, I can hear them the choir singing beautiful songs, and the memory lingers on.' I felt terrible. Thankfully, for the third, fourth and fifth verses, my own memory came back and I reverted to the normal words.

The moment the curtain came down, Andrew rushed over to me, put his arm around my shoulders and said, 'Your words were better than the original. Don't worry, nobody will know.' Many of the other performers realised what had happened and came over to me and told me that the important thing was that I had carried on singing. To this day, I still cannot believe that I did.

It was the single worst moment of my life as a performer. You only ever have one of these, though, and it taught me the lesson that I should have prepared better and learned the words absolutely perfectly. It also taught me that as a performer you are out there on the stage on your own, and you should never allow somebody who wants to create great shots for television to put your performance in jeopardy. Even today, two decades later, if ever I am doing something significant for the first time, I always have a recurring nightmare about 'Memory' just before the big day. In this bad dream, I always stop, look up at the Royal Box, mouth the words, 'I'm sorry, your Majesty,' and run off stage. I always hear the Queen booming down from above, 'Off with his head!'

The possibility of my voice breaking was fascinating journalists by this stage in my career and, following the uncertainty of my performance at the Royal Gala, one paper said that it would be broken 'by the end of the week'. Two years later, I was still singing.

Andrew Lloyd Webber asked me to take part in the annual Sydmonton Festival, which takes place at his country home in Hampshire. I was completely gobsmacked when I received the invitation because the other guests read like a Who's Who of the arts world. With typical generosity, Andrew invited Mam, Dad and me to stay as guests in the house he shared with his then wife, Sarah Brightman.

The weekend began on the Friday evening with a recital followed by a sumptuous dinner. On the Saturday morning, we were treated to the first performance of the musical *Aspects of Love*. Andrew Lloyd Webber wrote the music, with the lyrics being provided by Don Black and Charles Hart. There was a real sense of anticipation as we all gathered together in the theatre in the grounds of Sydmonton to hear this major new creation. One of the lead roles was taken by Michael Ball and as soon as we heard his voice, everyone there knew that he was destined to become a star. I felt very privileged to be one of the first people to hear Andrew's amazingly powerful romantic music and it is an experience that has stayed with me ever since. It was at that particular moment that I was bitten by the musical-theatre bug. Even though I was sitting quietly in the middle of the auditorium, I felt an overwhelming urge to get up on to the stage so that I, too, could sing alongside Michael. It was almost a feeling of desperation to perform, and I suppose that hearing *Aspects of Love* that morning may have sown the seeds for the career choices that I made in my early twenties.

After the performance we were treated to a delicious lunch themed on the cuisine of the French Pyrenees, which was followed by a demonstration of hot-air ballooning. Unfortunately, there was quite a bit of wind so the balloon was tethered to two very sturdy cars and we all took it in turns to be ballooned about fifty feet in the air before being hauled back down to earth by our fellow festival-goers. Problems that other people regard as being insur-mountable never seem to be an issue for Andrew. He always triumphs in the face of adversity by coming up with a new plan, so a little bit of wind was certainly not going to scupper his intention for us all to go ballooning. I learned a lot about how to deal with what life throws up at you from watching how Andrew operated.

On the Saturday evening, we had dinner and I sat in pride of place next to Andrew and his daughter. And rather than sing for my supper, I was invited to take part in a debate. The motion put forward was: 'Sydmonton believes the Welsh can sing no better than anyone else.' The other speakers were the comedian Max Boyce, the politician John Gummer and the great Welsh rugby player and broadcaster Cliff Morgan.

As might be expected, I was on the Welsh side of the table with Max Boyce and Cliff Morgan. My argument centred around the fact that Welsh voices singing 'Men of Harlech' had defeated the Zulus in the film *Zulu*. I am not sure quite how factually correct this was in terms of either history or science, but it seemed to be greeted warmly by the audience. Unfortunately, John Gummer, who was on the opposing team, had gone one better by producing from under the table a set of specially doctored X-rays that he had brought with him from London. He claimed that these showed a typical Welsh throat and oesophagus, with a huge Welsh leek embedded where the voice box should have been. He went on to argue that without the leek, the Welsh were no better at singing than anyone else. The audience lapped it up and it breaks my heart to have to admit that we lost the debate. It felt as if Max, Cliff and I had let down our nation on a point of honour.

That particular weekend was the first time that I met Clive Anderson, who was booked to perform his stand-up comedy act for the guests. Back then, he had not become famous on television and was still working as a barrister. Once I had heard his act, I became quite convinced that he was the funniest man alive.

I was now being invited on to television programmes aimed at kids my own age, as well as those for older people. One of my favourites was Roland Rat on TV-am. The first time I was a guest in his sewer, he insisted on calling me 'Alec' throughout the interview. I didn't mind too much because the other guest was the Page Three girl, Samantha Fox. Sitting next to her was every teenage boy's dream.

Roland Rat was actually operated by two puppeteers. The man who did his voice operated his head and one arm and his assistant operated the other arm. The cameras recorded the programme from below the puppets, so when you watched it on screen at home, it seemed very lifelike. I found it a very bizarre experience to be sitting there holding a conversation with a stuffed toy and I struggled to remember to look at Roland rather than the puppeteers when I was supposed to be talking to him.

I was also invited on to Roland Rat's Christmas Special, which featured Errol the hamster, Kevin the gerbil and Roland's little cousin, Reggie, who blew me up as part of the show. As I sang a song, all the puppets were behind me getting ready for Christmas. One dragged a Christmas tree across the room, another put the lights on it, and then Reggie switched the lights on and at that point, there was a massive explosion. When the smoke had cleared, I was left covered in soot, with my hair standing on end and my clothes in tatters. To create this effect, they first recorded me singing the song in normal clothes before I went into make-up and changed into a new set to give me the 'blown up' look. I then had to stand back in the studio in exactly the same position, so that they could record me after the explosion. It took hours but I loved every minute of it.

My experience of appearing on television alongside puppets did not end there. I started to become a regular guest on the children's programme *Saturday Superstore*, which was presented by Mike Read and Sarah Greene. Their co-presenter was a large black crow, who often interviewed me. One week, I was part of the panel who were reviewing new pop videos. We watched the new release from the band Curiosity Killed the Cat and, when asked for my views, I said, 'Oh, the best part was when they walked off at the end.' My comments were taken in the studio as being highly critical, when in fact I had been trying to get across the message that the final scene of the video was my favourite part. I bumped into the band's lead singer, the glamorously named Ben Volpeliere-Pierrot a few weeks later in another television studio and he said, 'Don't worry. I understood what you meant.' I was very relieved not to have been lynched. I think I did upset Fergal Sharkey, though, on the same show by saying, 'His voice is good, but it's not as good as a classical singer.' He rushed on to the set and pretended to attack me, much to Sarah Greene's amusement. I loved appearing on *Saturday Superstore* because I was in awe of Sarah, who ranked alongside Terry Wogan as the ultimate television presenter as far as I was concerned.

Increasingly, I was becoming more involved in light entertainment, as well as performing classical music. It was definitely more fun for me because I was appearing on programmes that I myself would watch. To go on *Saturday Superstore* and meet my pop-music idols was so exciting, although I never really had time to dwell on it because my feet hardly touched the ground. The minute I finished the programme on a Saturday morning, there would be a plane waiting to take me back to North Wales, where more often than not I would be performing in a concert that night. It was nonstop.

1985 and 1986 were the really busy years in my childhood career, but when you are fourteen or fifteen, it is very easy to cope with the physical demands of such a busy schedule. Every day was such a roller-coaster ride that I was having too much fun to get tired. It's only now, twenty years later, if I have two or three concerts in a row, that I have to have a sleep in the afternoon, which would never have happened as a kid. Everyone was so nice to me. There had never really been any successful teenagers in the classical-music world before and, because of that, people always treated me brilliantly. Only Luciano Pavarotti and Nigel Kennedy were selling huge numbers of classical records, so I was definitely the exception to the rule in the classical world.

During this two-year period, we were shuttling back and forth from North Wales to London every weekend by train. I would finish school on a Friday afternoon and we would catch the ten-past-five train from Bangor to London Euston. We would never travel first class, travelling standard class instead, which I used to hate because everyone would look at me, nudge each other and whisper, 'There's Aled Jones.'

Now, I would not want this to sound churlish or ungrateful in any way, because without the people who came to see me at concerts or who bought my records, I would not have enjoyed any of this success. It's great when these people come up to you and talk to you. They often have incredibly kind and generous things to say and I find meeting them a wonderful experience. What is awful, though, is when people recognise you and whisper to each other as if you are some kind of freak, because you don't know whether to acknowledge them or not.

Sitting in those cramped train carriages, I often felt uneasy when I realised that somebody had recognised me and would be staring at me for the next few hours. Occasionally, there was a restaurant car on the service, and the staff were always absolutely lovely. Eating a meal in there meant that we could effectively sit in the comfort and privacy of first class and I remember trying to stretch dinners out to last for the whole journey, much to the dismay of the train guards. I would take refuge in my personal stereo and by listening to so much music as we made these trips week in week out, I learned every single word to my favourite musical *Les Miserables* from start to finish.

When I was at home, much of my spare time was spent learning new material with my music teachers, Robert and Julie. Most people in the music world release one album a year at most, but because my soprano voice had a relatively short life expectancy, I was recording four albums a year, so there was always a huge amount of new material for me to learn.

Julie would accompany me on the piano in these coaching sessions and Robert was very much the teacher. They were both incredibly knowledgeable about singing and were both great musicians. If you are a fantastic singer it does not always follow that you will be a great teacher, but Robert and Julie were very good at sharing their knowledge with me. They would always come to the house to give me my lessons and Mam and Dad would make themselves scarce for an hour or two while we went over the pieces.

Choirboys have a tendency to develop bad habits and I was no different. I used to put my finger in my ear and hang my head to one side when I was rehearsing so that I could hear myself singing. This used to drive Robert mad and he would shout, 'Perform! Take your finger out! You look ridiculous!'

Gradually, I became more proficient at learning new pieces of music; when I was recording later albums, I would be given the musical score just a couple of hours before recording it. The organist who always accompanied me on my albums, Hugh Tregelles Williams, would maybe change the key so that it suited me and then we would record it straight away.

I only ever fell out with Julie and Robert once and that was over 'Memory'. Robert advised me against doing it at the Royal Gala in Edinburgh because he felt that the song was too low for me and did not suit my voice. In hindsight, I wish I had listened to him because then I would not have forgotten the words on stage in front of the Queen.

Mam and Dad trusted Robert and Julie completely because they were old family friends. On one occasion, they accompanied me down to Cardiff when I was appearing on *The Margaret Williams Show*, a Welsh television programme presented by a lady who was Wales's equivalent to Lesley Garrett at the time. Margaret is such a lovely lady to work with and I was really proud to appear recently on a television show celebrating her fifty years in show business.

After we recorded the show, Robert and Julie introduced me to what became my favourite restaurant in Cardiff, called Champers. I had never seen anything like it because you don't find many restaurants in North Wales that have sawdust on the floor and just serve big juicy steaks. Every time I have been to Cardiff since, I always try to make time to visit Champers. If there's a Welsh rugby international on, the place is always heaving, but because I have been such a regular customer over the years, Tony the manager is always able to find me a table.

We were back in London a little later in 1985 for a very special concert at the Royal Albert Hall, one of my favourite venues. I was the soloist alongside a thousand-strong Welsh choir. We sang

'David of the White Rock' and 'How Great Thou Art'. It was a very uplifting experience to stand on stage with a thousand other people. I have often been asked in interviews over the years about the difference between being a soloist and being in a choir and I find it a very hard question to answer. I suppose that to be a soloist you have to be a show-off and to be gregarious and, by definition, that's what I must be.

As a youngster, I loved walking on stage and seeing a choir of a thousand people standing up ready to sing. It made me feel very safe. Nowadays, I would be a bag of nerves the day before a big concert like that, but you never have those worries as a child – you just get on and do it.

Mam and Dad wanted to watch the concert as part of the audience, so after I had performed, I was on my own in the labyrinth of corridors backstage. I was a little taken aback when a big man rushed up to me and thrust a piece of paper into my hand. He was sweating profusely and crying his eyes out.

'Your performance was so mesmerising. Thank you. You've helped me so much,' he stammered. I looked down at my hand and saw what I thought was a five-pound note.

'Thank you, but I can't accept this. It's very generous, but singing is what I do,' I said, handing the note back to him.

He pushed the money back into my hand and ran off down one of the corridors. It was only then that I realised that, rather than a fiver, he had actually given me two fifty-pound notes. I had never held one in my hand before, let alone two. Needless to say, we were at Hamley's toyshop in Regent Street as the doors opened the following morning.

I loved taking part in the Concert of One Thousand Voices because it was Welsh. I strongly believe that being from Wales has helped me to keep my feet on the ground. If I had been born in London, I think I would have been a totally different sort of person. I wasn't like cool London kids, with their spiky hair and trendy baseball jackets. I would not have known where to buy a baseball jacket in Bangor, even if I had wanted to. I suppose that this meant that I was quite naïve as a teenager; we were certainly from a different generation to kids now. For us, it would be quite brilliant to go to W.H. Smith on a Saturday afternoon and amuse ourselves by looking at the latest Scalextric. Now, kids seem to have far higher expectations of how they should spend their time.

The artists Sir Kyffin Williams and William Selwyn capture the essence of Wales brilliantly for me in their landscape paintings through their use of colour and texture. Kyffin's paintings often include a very special kind of green, which you see in the North Wales countryside because of the quality of the light there. Nearly all of the paintings I have on the wall of my house in London are by these two artists, because they never fail to bring back memories of Wales for me whenever I look at them.

Everyone always thinks of Wales as being the land of song, so the fact that I was Welsh gave me a clear identity to the wider British public. During the 1990s, I think that Wales may have seen its musical distinctiveness being eroded, but I am delighted to see that it's coming back now. Recently, I went to a Welsh rugby international at the Millennium Stadium in Cardiff and it seemed the most natural thing in the world for thousands of people to join together singing the Welsh hymn, 'Calon Lân'. I think it's what makes us unique as a country – 'Swing Low Sweet Chariot' just does not have the same heart and passion as far I am concerned.

7. 'WALKING IN THE AIR'

The story of how I ended up signing to Virgin Records is rather bizarre. In truth, I would not have been on the label at all had Richard Branson's dad not wanted to give up smoking. Every time he got wound up behind the wheel, rather than reaching for a cigarette, he put my BBC cassette *Voices from the Holy Land* on his car stereo to calm himself down. He managed to kick the nicotine habit and phoned Richard shortly afterwards to say: 'You should do something with this boy because his music has a special quality that can soothe people.' So Richard did his homework and the first we knew about the story was when a personal letter from him arrived at home in Llandegfan, inviting me down to London for a meeting at his head office, a barge moored on the Regent's Park Canal.

So Dad and I beat the now well-trodden path to London. After trudging along the canal towpath in pouring rain, we arrived by the boat and gingerly stepped on board. A secretary was working behind a desk in one of the outer rooms. She looked up as we came in and said, 'Hello. Richard's expecting you. Just go in, he's there now.'

We walked into the adjoining cabin and Richard was sitting in one of the armchairs. The office looked like a very plush living room. There were computers on the desk, but it was still very homely. I had the sense that it was somewhere where he hung out, rather than it being an office, although it turned out to be the centre of his business empire.

Richard was an incredibly nice man, very warm, but surprisingly shy when we first met. After some small talk, he came straight to the point. 'Listen, I want to sign you to Virgin Records because your music cured my Dad's smoking.'

It seemed incredible to me that this man, about whom I knew a lot because he was always in the papers, would want me to join his record label – the same label with artists like the Who, Boy George and my personal favourite, Phil Collins, already on the roster. Up until that point, I had made records for Sain, the BBC, Decca, EMI and Telstar, but I had never considered being signed exclusively to one particular record company. I just worked for people when they asked me.

After we listened to what Richard had to say, we left the boat in a daze. Dad turned to me outside and said, 'We are going to have to think very hard about this offer.' But by the time I had got back to Wales, I had already made my mind up. I wanted to be on Virgin Records, because it was just the place to be. After all, what was good enough for my hero Phil Collins was certainly good enough for me. I practised writing the Virgin logo on a napkin from the train's buffet car all the way back from London Euston to Bangor. It seems ironic that this service is now operated by Virgin Trains.

As soon as we said 'yes' to Virgin, the difference to our lives was amazing. I was introduced to Richard Griffiths and Pete Price, who ran 10 Records, one of Virgin's labels. They knew so much about the music business and were able instantly to answer all of our questions and to look after all of our needs. I loved going to visit them in their office, where there was a very real pulse, an energy. I felt a genuine excitement at knowing that this was the place where the pop albums, which I listened to on my personal stereo, were actually made. I was particularly delighted to see my LP bundled up on the floor alongside those of their other artists. The biggest difference in working with Virgin was that they were a pop-music label and so they operated very differently from the classical-record industry at the time.

In North Wales back then, *the* thing to have if you were a teenage boy was a shiny zipped Nike jacket. I was really excited when Pete and Richard gave me a special limited-edition jacket with the guitarist Gary Moore's logo on it.

Just after I joined Virgin, my old friend Andrew Lloyd Webber asked me to take part in a series of concert performances of his

Requiem at the Palace Theatre in London's West End. My first two dates were alongside the soprano Jane Gregory, and then Paul Miles-Kingston and Sarah Brightman did a couple of performances, with the final Saturday night show being sung by Sarah and me. Just being backstage at the Palace, which had been home to many great musicals including my favourite, *Les Miserables*, was such a thrill. For Uncle Arthur, the highlight of the early part of my career was when he walked past the Palace and saw my name up in giant lettering outside the theatre.

After the first performance, Richard Branson came backstage to my dressing room with Richard Griffiths and Pete Price. The first thing they said to Mam and Dad was: 'Have you got any booze in the fridge?' We all went out to a Greek restaurant in Soho. I was told to sit next to Richard and was made to feel as though I was the guest of honour. We were chatting away when suddenly I felt a strange tingling on my arm and I noticed that he was taking my watch off my wrist.

'What are you doing to my watch?' I asked.

Richard erupted in mock indignation and everyone else from Virgin roared with laughter, because nobody had ever stopped him performing his party piece before. It turned out that he had the ability almost to hypnotise you and while looking you straight in the eye, could remove a watch or bracelet from your arm without you feeling a thing. Then later on in the evening, he would give you your watch back. He quickly forgave me for stealing his thunder and we had a fantastic evening, packed full of laughter. Richard was very excited about his next adventure, which was due to happen the following morning: he was abseiling down the side of the Centrepoint tower in London, dressed as Spiderman. As he told me about his plans for the next day, I knew that I had signed for the right record company.

Very early on in my time with Virgin, I was invited to perform on a single with Mike Oldfield, who was the first artist signed to the label more than a decade earlier. He had had an enormous hit with *Tubular Bells*, but I am afraid to say that, at that time, I had never heard of him, so Pete Price sent me a copy of the record. I was blown away by it. Vincent Price's chilly voice at the end still sends shivers down my spine. One afternoon just after I had first heard the record, I noticed that there was a Vincent Price film on television later that evening. Mam and I videoed it and were petrified when we watched it the next day, because it turned out to be the horrific and gut-wrenching *Theatre of Blood*.

Mike had heard one of my BBC records and it had inspired him to write a song called 'Pictures in the Dark'. Pete took Mam and me to Mike's home in Denham. Now when I say home, I am not doing his mansion justice – it was more like a palace and certainly the largest house I had ever seen. His kitchen walls were covered in dozens of gold and platinum discs and every room was packed with the sort of gadgets that made my eyes pop out on stalks. As far as I was concerned, he had the ultimate bit of kit: a glass-covered table that was actually a Space Invaders game. The two players would sit either side while they competed to save the universe. I played on it for hours with Pete, who of course won every game, as he had become an expert on it over the years.

Pete had brought his young son, Joe, along with him and we were all perplexed as to why he kept on singing 'Plasticine in the dog' to the tune of 'Pictures in the Dark'. The confusion was cleared up when we realised that he had spent the morning feeding Plasticine to Mike's dog. A mild panic ensued as Mike and Pete discussed whether a quick trip to the vet was necessary. The dog seemed fine, so in the end they decided to let nature take its course.

Mike recorded and played every note of his music himself without any other musicians or engineers, and he had one of the most advanced recording studios in the country actually in his own home. His high-tech gear included a keyboard called a Fairlight, which could sample your voice. It seems a fairly run-of-the-mill thing now, but back then it was revolutionary. Mike had the only one in Britain and it had set him back £45,000.

After we had recorded my part of 'Pictures in the Dark', Mike turned to me and said, 'Now, you'd better go back downstairs for a couple of hours while I work on the computer to harmonise your voice with the soprano we've got singing on the track as well.'

'Oh, I'll do it now,' I replied. So he played the middle section of the song to me once and I sang a harmony for a whole verse.

'That's unbelievable!' he shouted. 'We'll record it now.' Little did he realise that for somebody who had been singing as a cathedral chorister for years, it was actually a fairly unremarkable thing to be asked to do. I was very proud afterwards to think that I had created that part of the song by myself.

When I had finished the recording, Mike said, 'Can you go and stand in front of that blue screen in the other room and just mouth the words to the song?' I did as I was asked, although I couldn't think why he wanted me to do this. It turned out that Mike was one of the few people in Britain to have a brand-new sort of special-effects computer, made famous by Peter Gabriel in his song 'Sledgehammer', and which eventually became very commonplace in the production of pop videos. In the final video that was shown on TV, he had me whizzing through strange environments and at one stage it even rained small Aleds. The reality though was that I just stood in front of a blue backdrop in an empty room. For me, this was truly cutting edge and a glimpse inside a magical world. Here was a guy who was seriously rich, but who deep inside was a child who loved gadgets, just like me. I was very chuffed that he had decided to write 'Pictures in the Dark' just for me.

There is one song more than any other to which my name is most often attached, but I was only given the opportunity to sing it in the first place by complete chance. I owe it all to the American chain Toys 'R' Us, who were opening their first shop in Britain. Their advertising agency had decided that the TV ads would feature a small boy flying down the aisles of the shop flanked by mountains of shiny new toys to the soundtrack of a song from *The Snowman* by Howard Blake. The track, 'Walking in the Air', which was first recorded in 1982 by another chorister, Peter Auty, had not been a hit in its own right at that stage. The animated film had been shown on television and there was a full-length album out featuring David Bowie, Bernard Cribbins and Peter Auty. The TV producers rang up Sony, the record company behind the album, and asked to use their version of 'Walking in the Air' for the ad, but they were refused permission. So the producers went directly to the composer, Howard Blake, who was keen for his music to be used.

'I tell you what,' he said. 'There's a great boy soprano around at the moment who I heard on television the other night. Get him to record it.' The rest, as they always say in stories like this, is history.

I particularly loved the idea of doing an advert for a toyshop and I was taken to a big fancy London studio to make the recording with the conductor, John Altman. The music had already been recorded the day before, so all that I had to do was get my vocals down on tape. I have never admitted this before – it is something that only those people present in the studio have known up to now

– but I had terrible trouble singing 'Walking in the Air' that day. Finally, in desperation, we recorded the song in tiny chunks, line by line. Funnily enough, I sang it dozens of times live afterwards and never had a problem, but that day, for some reason, I just could not get it right. So I sang, 'We're walking in the air,' over and over until I got it right and then we stopped recording. I then did the next line: 'We're floating in the moonlit sky,' and we repeated the process right through until the last line. I found it tortuous, but it was the only way that I could manage to get the song right. The process is often used by pop singers, so that every line is perfect on a record, but it was totally alien to me with my choirboy training and it's something I still cannot stand now. However, on this particular occasion, I was relieved to have the choice of using the technique.

EMI decided to release my version of 'Walking in the Air' as a single because it was getting so much exposure on the Toys 'R' Us TV adverts. When Sony got to hear of this, they decided to release Peter Auty's version as a single on the same day. My version started to get a lot of radio airplay, probably because I was already in the public eye. It gradually climbed up the charts until it reached number five in the week before Christmas. So when people say to me now, 'But your version of "Walking in the Air" wasn't the original,' I reply, 'I've never said that it was.' But my version was the only one that was a hit in the pop charts. I have never met Peter Auty, but he does pop up occasionally on Christmas programmes talking about me. I wonder if 'Walking in the Air' haunts him more than it does me. He is now a professional opera singer with a fine tenor voice.

'Walking in the Air' was being played everywhere in the run-up to Christmas 1985 and it allowed me to realise the lifelong ambition of appearing on *Top of the Pops*, which was a programme I had watched religiously on Thursday nights for my entire life. Dad and I travelled to London on the Tuesday afternoon, ready for recording on the Wednesday. I would be miming to a backing track on the programme, as nearly all of the acts did in those days. The BBC had re-recorded the music with their own musicians so that it would be cheaper to broadcast than if they used the original recording with a full orchestra. They were then planning to mix the original vocal from my first recording with the new accompaniment, but this time there was a hitch. The Musicians' Union representative had objected to the original recording of me being used, so the BBC had to re-record it or else 'Walking in the Air' would not be appearing on *Top of the Pops* that week.

Dad and I were fast asleep in the hotel when the phone rang at about half-past eleven that night. An engineer at the studios apologetically asked us to come in there and then to make the recording. A taxi was sent to pick us up and we made our way bleary-eyed across London. As you can imagine, Dad was not happy that I had been woken up in the middle of the night. It was one of the quickest recordings I ever made and certainly the only one I ever did wearing a pyjama top. I sang the song through once and the engineer's voice came through to the recording booth on the intercom: 'That's great, Aled. Thanks very much. We're only going to use this version once on *Top of the Pops* and then it'll never be heard again.' Relieved, Dad and I staggered back to the hotel. Considering how difficult I had found the original recording, it was ironic that this version had been bang in tune all the way through and had been completed in just one take. Despite the engineer's promise, it turned out that this particular clip of me singing has now been played more often in more countries in the world than any other.

In the run-up to the programme, I had other sleepless nights – this time about the performance itself. It was not the singing or the being on television that worried me, but instead I was very concerned about the *Top of the Pops* studio audience. How on earth would they dance to a song like 'Walking in the Air'? It was not exactly a disco floor-filler. As it turned out, I need not have worried.

The first people we met when we arrived at BBC TV Centre in West London were the four dance leaders. It was their job to work out the moves for the audience to each of the songs being performed on the show. I must have looked panic-stricken as I asked them what they were going to do for 'Walking in the Air'. In reply, they simply got out their lighters, held them in the air and started swaying gently. I was so relieved and was then able to get on with enjoying the whole experience of being on Britain's best-loved pop programme. I had not realised how much work went into the build-up to the show. There were rehearsals in the morning, a break for lunch and then more rehearsals in the afternoon.

EMI had decided to splash out on some new clothes for my performance – in the shape of two jumpers – even though Mam had packed an outfit for me as usual. Secretly, I was delighted that EMI had been shopping on my behalf. I chose the jumper that I liked best and wore my jeans and trainers for the recording. The director wanted me to look as relaxed as possible – it was a pop show after all – so I sang with my hands in my pockets. Andrew Goodwin back at Bangor Cathedral would have been very disapproving if I had performed like that when I was in the choir, but this was showbiz. Everything went without a hitch until after I had finished singing, when I tried to move my feet and found that my trainers had been sealed to the stage by the dry ice that had been swirling around me during the song. In the end, a stagehand had to come on and chisel my trainers off the stage.

This was another occasion when we had to fly back to Anglesey so that I could go to school the next morning, and it was the most hair-raising flight I have ever experienced. The plane was a four-seater and I sat alongside the pilot. After taking off from Denham, we had to fly very low to avoid aircraft taking off and landing at Heathrow and Gatwick and it appeared as if we were only just clearing the houses below. We then flew into the teeth of a gale so strong that we were being bounced out of our seats. The pilot held on to my knee to try and comfort me and not a word was heard from Dad in the rear seat. We were so relieved to land at Valley Airport, although even that was not a smooth experience. The pilot had to bring the plane in at a forty-five degree angle to the runway to be able to get it down safely on the ground.

Around the same time, I finally met Howard Blake, who wrote the music for *The Snowman*. He is a very creative and vibrant man. Alongside his biggest hit, he has written many other wonderful pieces of music, for which I always feel he deserves greater recognition. Over the months that followed 'Walking in the Air', he became a good friend to me and we worked together in a series of live concert performances of *The Snowman* produced by the impresario Raymond Gubbay at the Barbican Centre in London. Ian Lavender, who played Private Pike in *Dad's Army* and has recently shot back to fame as Pauline Fowler's friend Derek in *EastEnders*, was the narrator on each occasion. The concerts proved so popular that an extra performance was squeezed in at St David's Hall in Cardiff. On the train from London to Cardiff, Howard wrote a special song called 'Make Believe', which he dedicated to me. I gave it its world premiere at the concert that evening.

Without a shadow of doubt, singing 'Walking in the Air' changed my life. It certainly propelled me to the forefront of public attention. People ask now whether I have a problem with always being associated with the song and I can honestly reply, 'No, I don't.' It's a great song written by a great composer and I am very proud to have sung it. However, back at school in 1986, its success did mean that I came in for some fairly hefty ribbing, with virtually all of the younger kids running up to me every break and lunchtime and singing the opening line at me, but thankfully the novelty had worn off for my peers by that stage and they never really mentioned it.

As an older teenager, it still followed me around, with some bright spark tending to put it on the jukebox within five minutes of me walking through the door of a pub. I suppose that when I was nineteen or twenty I did find it a little uncomfortable because it harped back to the past. At that stage, I had not really done anything to prove that I had a future as a performer, so it was unnerving to be reminded of my early success. I certainly never worried about it being the pinnacle of my career, though, because I never sang to be famous – I sang because I loved singing.

Perhaps the belief that I would succeed again was arrogant and maybe I should have worried more. But today, with a whole new career as a singer and broadcaster in front of me, I regard 'Walking in the Air' much more as an old friend than an annoyance. Just recently, I was in a pub in Aberdaron in North Wales after a day's filming with a *Songs of Praise* camera crew when a group of lads sitting in the corner stuck it on the jukebox. They sat staring at me, sniggering. They obviously thought that hearing the song would somehow annoy me.

The first thing that went through my mind was: 'What on earth is this record still doing on a pub jukebox nearly twenty years after its release? And it's a Christmas song, so why is it still around in March?'

One of the guys from *Songs of Praise* asked, 'Does this sort of thing upset you?'

'No, not in the slightest,' I replied, before adding, 'I've never realised before how great the orchestration is.'

I still don't understand what effect the lads hoped to provoke. Maybe they thought that I would be embarrassed by it, but of course I'm not. It was quite simply one of the highpoints of my career – 'Walking in the Air', that is; not the trip to Aberdaron, beautiful as the village is.

My first professional acting experience came in the summer of 1986. By that time, 'Walking in the Air' had firmly established me in the public's consciousness. The writer, actor and television presenter Gyles Brandreth got in touch and asked if I would like to play the part of Christopher Robin in a stage show called *Now We are Sixty*, which was based on the life and work of A.A. Milne. Gyles had written the show with Julian Slade, who in turn worked with H. Fraser-Simpson on the music. Although I was a little apprehensive about turning my hand to acting, I thought that it looked like fun and so I said yes. I particularly liked the idea of being part of a band of actors. It took up nearly all of the summer holidays, but Mam was able to stay with me throughout because we shared the same holidays – one of the great advantages of having a Mam who was a teacher.

I had first met Gyles a few months earlier, when he had asked me to be a model for a knitting book he was working on. It certainly ranked as one of the stranger requests that I have had over the years, but I instantly hit it off with Gyles, who is a very charming man. He has an extraordinarily quick wit and I always sensed that a dangerously subversive sense of humour was lurking not very far from the surface. I loved doing the modelling session for the jumpers because the stylist spiked up my hair and made me look quite funky for the time.

Gyles always used to wear entertaining and original jumpers on his regular slot on TV-am's *Good Morning Britain*. Most of these sweaters were created by a designer called Linda O'Brien. Gyles and Linda decided that they would write a book that would share the knitting patterns for her creations with the public at large. Other models in the book included Lionel Blair, Lynsey de Paul, Nanette Newman, Paul Jones and Su Pollard. I modelled two sweaters, the first of which was called 'Pond Life' and featured fish, frogs and reeds. The second was themed around Halloween with a witch, bats and spiders. They even had me riding a broom for that particular shot. A few years later, there would have been a Harry Potter connection, but back then he was just a twinkle in J.K. Rowling's eye.

The chance of working with Gyles again was another reason why I agreed to take part in the play. The first thing that I had to do was to learn how to lose my Welsh accent when on stage. So I was taken to the home of the play's director, James Roose-Evans, and given elocution lessons. It was similar to the scene in *My Fair Lady*, where Professor Higgins teaches Eliza Doolittle how to lose her accent. In my case, a very pleasant and well-spoken lady taught me how to say 'how now brown cow' in received pronunciation.

I had never spent time with actors before and found them fascinating. They even seemed to speak in their own language. I was struck by how confident they appeared and how different they seemed to the people I had met so far in my life.

That morning in James Roose-Evans's house, I experienced for the first time a wave of excitement that repeats itself every time I am in a similar situation. It is a real thrill and it happens for two reasons: the first is the sheer buzz of seeing for the first time the small scale model of the set that we are going to be acting on; the second is a shot of nerve-induced adrenaline just before the first read-through of a new play.

The play was being rehearsed in a room above a theatre in Islington called The King's Head. Mam and I went down to London a couple of days before the school holidays had begun to stay with Uncle Arthur. We were a little unsure where Islington actually was, so we went to the theatre by taxi on the first day. Meeting up with the cast gave me a real kick and they all made a fuss of me because I was the only child in the production. If I was nervous at the first read-through, this was nothing to what I was feeling now. Suddenly, my anxiety levels had trebled. I knew that I was not an actor and that the only significant experience I had in this area was playing Joseph back at Llandegfan Primary School. I was scared that I would be ridiculed first by my fellow cast members and then by the people who came to watch the play. But my fears were misplaced and I need not have worried. The entire cast were incredibly supportive from start to finish and we had such a good time in rehearsals.

Very quickly, actors such as Rosalind Ayres, Ian Gelder, Sarah Crowden, Peter Bayliss and Allan Corduner felt like part of my family. I became very close to Rosalind and Ian, who played my parents in the play. I was in awe of them both and, looking back now, I do hope that I wasn't an annoyance to them.

During rehearsals, I always walked around with a Dictaphone in my pocket, as I found that recording my lines and then playing them back helped me to get them firmly lodged in my memory. At every available opportunity, Peter Bayliss would bound over to me and grab the Dictaphone from my hand before proceeding to recite a risqué limerick or joke into it. He became one of my favourites – when you are a boy that age, anyone who is a little bit rude and gets away with it has a magnetic pull. Mam had just as much fun wandering around the antique shops of Islington while I was working. She also endeared herself greatly to the cast by once again making endless cups of tea.

Soon it was time to move on to Cambridge, where *Now We are Sixty* was to have its main run at the Arts Theatre, a beautiful little building in the heart of the city. It was a perfect summer and I loved Cambridge and its sense of history. Mam and I stayed at the University Arms Hotel and we spent our days off sightseeing or punting on the River Cam with Peter Bayliss.

The actual performances went down a treat. Gyles was thrilled and seemed to spend the whole summer with us, which was unheard of for a writer. I know that many actors exaggerate about the level of camaraderie in their profession, but this really was one big happy family. During the second half of the performance each night, Gyles and Mam would prepare Pimms with all the trimmings for the cast. As soon as everyone walked off stage following the final curtain call, all of the actors and the backstage crew would congregate outside the dressing rooms to share a drink. It seemed like paradise to me: good friends together at the end of a barmy play on a balmy summer's evening.

Although I loved the acting, I was still keen to get back to singing, so I jumped at the opportunity of recording a special song to celebrate the wedding of Sarah Ferguson to Prince Andrew. The words were written by the then poet laureate Ted Hughes, with the music composed by my old friend Howard Blake. The song was to be performed for the very first time on Terry Wogan's television show on 23 July, just hours after the royal couple had been married and had become the Duke and Duchess of York. Nobody was allowed to see the words or to hear the music before the performance. By now, I was a regular on Terry's show, but all of the secrecy made me far more apprehensive than usual. I was accompanied by the Finchley Boys Choir and we all shared a sense of history being made that afternoon during rehearsals. Howard recently played me a video recording of the live performance we gave that night and I was pleased to see that I sang well and that the song suited the occasion.

Away from music, I have always enjoyed playing tennis so I was thrilled to be invited to perform at the Wightman Cup at the Royal Albert Hall. This event, which ended in 1989, saw the cream of American women tennis players battle it out with Britain's finest. The organiser, Mike Sertin, asked me to sing a solo in between two of the matches. By then, I was very familiar with the layout of the Royal Albert Hall, but I was unable to believe my eyes when I walked in to where I thought the stage would be, only to discover that the entire ground floor of the hall, including the stage area, was now a brand-new tennis court. I sang my solo from the centre of the court and was then dumbfounded to be asked to watch the remainder of the day's tennis from the Royal Box as the guest of the Duchess of Gloucester. She was a charming lady and even held my hand. It was an incredibly memorable day for me, not only because I was able to see many of my tennis heroes in the flesh, but also because I am always excited to meet members of the royal family. I met the Duchess again many years later at a 'Story of Christmas' charity concert in London. She bounded up the stairs and told me how much she had enjoyed the edition of *Songs of Praise* that I had presented the week before. She then asked me if I was married, because she had decided that I would be very suitable for one of her daughters.

8. BOB AND PAULA'S WEDDING

I was delighted when Virgin invited me to the 1986 Rock and Pop Awards. Getting to the event was always going to require some planning because I had been working on a television programme in Rome the weekend before. We were due to fly back on the Monday in good time for the ceremony that evening. But when we pulled back the curtains of our Italian hotel room, we were shocked to see a blizzard raging outside the window. We struggled downstairs and found what must have been the only taxi in the city with snow chains fitted. There was complete chaos on the roads and we passed more than one accident on our way to the airport. Unsurprisingly, our flight home was delayed and I was worried that I would miss out on seeing my pop-music heroes altogether. Finally, we took off from Rome and arrived at Heathrow late in the afternoon. We took a train into central London and got changed into our evening clothes in the public toilets at the station.

Dad had no more time off available, so he jumped on a train at Euston station. Meanwhile, Mam and I arrived late at the Grosvenor House Hotel in Park Lane, where things had already got under way. The Radio One DJ Mike Smith, the off-camera presenter in the hall, said into the microphone, 'Everyone, if you look up now, Aled Jones and his mum are walking in late. Say "hello" everyone!' All of these pop stars and record-company bigwigs looked up. I went the brightest possible shade of red and Mam needed a stiff drink to calm herself down when we finally found our table, which was right at the front by the stage.

Mam and I were sitting with Richard Branson, Roger Daltrey and Boy George. We never quite got the hang of what clothes to choose for these events. She was wearing an old-fashioned flowery dress and I was in my favourite leather bow tie and sparkly jacket. My only excuse now for this sartorial inelegance was that it was the 1980s.

Pete Price was fast becoming my hero because he seemed to know everybody in the record industry. The highlight of the night was when he introduced me to Paul Young. Having learned all of the words to his hit 'Wherever I Lay My Hat, That's My Home', I was ecstatic to actually shake hands with him. Many people presumed that I was a classical-music nerd, but in fact I idolised these pop stars, so I was on cloud nine. At that time, the music industry was not full of kids aged between fourteen and seventeen, contrary to how it has seemed to be in some of the years since. My unique position seemed to attract other artists, who tended to make a beeline for me rather than vice versa. It meant that I was able to meet and chat to everyone from Eric Clapton down. I was in awe and would always take my autograph book to these big industry occasions, which was very much 'not the done thing'. Probably because nobody else did it, the stars seemed to love being asked to sign my book. Neil Tennant from the Pet Shop Boys wrote 'Sorry that we spoiled your number one', because they were ahead of me in the charts with their hit 'West End Girls', when I was there with 'Walking in the Air'.

I had another encounter with pop music and pop musicians after Mam and Dad received a call from Jess Yates asking if I would be interested in singing at the wedding of Bob Geldof and Paula Yates. For me, this was the equivalent of being invited to sing at a royal wedding and I struggled to believe that these two massive stars actually wanted me to be a part of their big day.

We travelled to Kent the day before the ceremony and stayed in a little hotel just down the road from their home, Davington Priory, in a village just outside the town of Faversham. We visited them for a rehearsal that afternoon and they were so lovely. I was accompanied on the organ by Jess Yates. Bob particularly wanted me to sing the hymn 'Dear Lord and Father of Mankind'. The second line is 'Forgive our foolish ways' – something I think Bob especially liked.

We spent the morning of the wedding with the family in the kitchen while they were making the final preparations. Their daughter, Fifi Trixiebell, was tiny and kept running after me saying, 'Sing "Walking in the Air".' At lunchtime, I changed into a grey suit and bow tie and Mam and Dad put on their smartest clothes. Bob and Paula made us all feel so welcome. On the way into the service, the best man, Simon Le Bon from Duran Duran, complimented me on my white socks. At least, I took it as a compliment at the time, although I am not quite so sure now.

When the moment came for me to perform, I looked out at the congregation, who had gathered together in the chapel attached to Bob and Paula's home. It was mad. There was Midge Ure, Billy Connolly, Lulu, David Bowie, George Michael, Chrissie Hynde, the Boomtown Rats and Spandau Ballet. They were a very generous audience and I could tell that they were paying close attention to my performance. At the end of the service, Simon Le Bon walked up to me and was almost crying.

'Thanks so much for singing,' he said. 'You probably don't realise it, but even though most of these people are in the music business, they'll never have heard music that beautiful.' His wife Yasmin had a tear in her eye.

Looking back on it now, I cannot quite believe that I was included in the official wedding photograph. Bob and Paula sat in the centre of the shot and I stood with my hands on David Bowie's shoulders. He was a very quietly spoken man, unlike Midge Ure, who was one of the many larger-than-life characters there that day. As the photographer took the picture, Midge lifted up his kilt. Suffice it to say, Midge upheld Scottish tradition in this department. It marked the end of the formal part of the wedding and seemed to be the cue for widespread riotous behaviour for the rest of the day.

After the official photos had been taken, there was a magnificent lunch in a marquee on the lawn. I sat next to the Spandau Ballet band members, whom I had been almost stalking for the whole day. I must have become very annoying, particularly to the saxophone player who was my favourite because of the bright orange suit he was sporting that day. Once again, I was on a mission to fill as many pages of my autograph book as possible. On my other side was Billy Connolly, who had me in stitches throughout the meal. During the preparations that morning, one of the chefs had chopped off the tip of his finger. Billy kept saying, 'You might find it in your soup.' I knew that he was probably joking, but it didn't stop me from surreptitiously checking every spoonful to make sure there wasn't a finger floating on the top.

After lunch, we all played baseball. I was very pleased to have been picked to be on Bob's team. As it gradually became dark, we started to have trouble seeing the ball. This problem was quickly overcome when one of the guests took off his fluorescent green socks and tied them around it.

That evening, there was a disco where Paula, who was still wearing her bright-red wedding dress, danced with me, much to my intense embarrassment because I was a hopeless dancer. Halfway through the evening, many of the musicians got their guitars out and did a turn on the stage. Particular highlights were Lulu singing 'Shout!' and Tony Hadley from Spandau Ballet performing an Elvis number. Everyone else stood around the stage cheering, as star after star got up to sing. I was able to just enjoy it as part of the crowd, as my performing for the day was done. After the disco, it was back outside for the finale to the evening – a massive fireworks display that culminated in a huge set of fountains spelling out the words 'Congratulations Bob and Paula'.

It was a completely exhilarating day with the highlight for Mam being the goodbye kiss she received from George Michael. There were crowds everywhere, with heavy security around the edge of the grounds. And there we were, Mam, Dad and I, slap-bang in the middle of it all. It was unbelievable, the most glamorous and glitzy event to which I have ever been invited; I doubt I will ever experience anything quite like it again. I cannot say enough positive things about Bob and Paula. They were very kind, generous people who were under no obligation to treat me nearly as well as they did on their special day. They also went out of their way to make sure that Mam and Dad were looked after and were involved in every aspect of the day's events. Bob is a far gentler man than the media's portrayal of him would sometimes suggest. When I bumped into him a couple of years after the wedding when we were both at the opening of the new HMV store in London's Oxford Street, he gave me a big hug and was just as nice to me then as he was on his wedding day.

I was devastated when Paula died some years later. She was a hugely intelligent woman who had an enormous amount to give and, towards the end of her life, she had a really hard time of it and was very misunderstood. Her death was a terrible waste. She and

Bob were extremely happy on their special day and I feel very privileged to have played a small part in it.

Harry Secombe is another person whom I met and worked with as a boy, but who sadly is now no longer with us. In real life, he was just the same as he was on television – always with a twinkle in his eye and a sense of mischief. When he laughed, his whole body shook. I was asked to record a special edition of his ITV religious programme *Highway* which was coming from Rome. While the television show was filmed, we would be miming, just as I had done in Israel two years before, so all of the songs we were singing on the programme were pre-recorded at CTS studios in Wembley. These were the best-equipped sound studios in the country and were every gadget-loving choirboy's dream. My own particular favourite piece of technology was the enormous mixing desks, which were so long that the technician had to zoom along the edge on a chair with casters, so that he could physically reach all of the buttons and knobs. As a bonus, all of the faders lit up and moved up and down automatically, without any human help. It was a far cry from the truck parked around the back of Bangor Cathedral that Sain Records had used for my first album and I was in seventh heaven just watching the technician at work.

A couple of weeks after recording the music, Mam, Dad and I flew to Rome. We met Harry in the Winnebago that accompanied him on each of the *Highway* filming sessions. Harry was an extraordinarily professional broadcaster and I have heard many stories about him over the years since. For instance, he always had two sets of trousers for every programme. The first pair he wore whenever he was being filmed sitting down. As soon as he was required to stand up on screen, filming would stop while he changed into his 'standing-up trousers' – that way, he was never seen on television with even the slightest crease in his suits.

We recorded the programme inside the Vatican – Mam and Dad were disappointed that, because we were miming, I would not actually get to perform there. So, just for them, I sang unaccompanied. The acoustics were unbelievable and my voice soared around the empty chapel.

Once filming was over, we all went for dinner together. Afterwards, Harry, his musical director Ronnie Cass and I gathered around the piano in the hotel and sang songs. When Mam and Dad were not looking, Harry gave me my first-ever glass of red wine. He was such a great character that I always feel it is the biggest compliment people pay me now when I present *Songs of Praise* and they call me 'Junior Harry'.

I went to the memorial service held just after Harry died and met again his wife Myra, who is a lovely lady. During the service, Michael Parkinson and Jimmy Tarbuck both paid very moving tributes to their friend. There can have been few people like Harry who managed to rise to the top of the musical and comedy worlds and to stay there for so long.

By this stage in my career, international air travel was becoming a familiar experience for us as a family, although Mam was still a nervous flyer. Panic-stricken dashes to the loo were the norm; as were last-minute calls for the Jones family over the Tannoy just before our flights were due to take off. These days when I am travelling I am always early.

Mam managed to overcome her fears to come with Dad and me to California, when I was asked to sing in the spectacular final concert in the Hollywood Bowl summer series. The big attraction of the trip for me was a visit to the Universal Studios and Disneyland theme parks while we were there.

We arrived safely on American soil, where there was a limousine waiting to take us to the Roosevelt Hotel on Hollywood Boulevard. As we approached the Boulevard, we were confronted by scores of police cars and a helicopter overhead. The driver, who appeared to be completely unfazed, explained that it was 'only a heist'. I thought, 'Anglesey it ain't!' By the time we reached our suite late at night, all three of us were starving, so Dad went out across the road for a takeaway from the Pink Panda Chinese Restaurant. The meal seemed far more glamorous in its smart cardboard boxes than the takeaways we were used to. We were intrigued by the fortune cookies, which we had never come across before. So intrigued, in fact, that Mam has kept hers to this day.

After we had gorged ourselves on the delicious food, Mam and I stood in the window of our room looking down on Hollywood Boulevard below. The noise, movement and bright lights were almost intoxicating. It was a Friday night and people were hanging out of their car windows and honking their horns. We were captivated by the sights and sounds and stayed there watching and listening for ages. I had an excited, nervous feeling in my stomach because everything seemed so much more glamorous than anything

I had experienced before. Our hotel was just opposite the Mann's Chinese Movie Theater, which hosted many of the big film premieres. On the pavement outside were the hand and footprints of the big stars set in concrete. I was so seduced by the whole place that I began to dream of seeing my name there among them one day – not a dream that has any likelihood of ever coming true.

The next day, I had my first sight of the Hollywood Bowl – a huge open-air auditorium and far bigger than anywhere I had sung previously. The last night of the series of concerts is marked by a grand fireworks spectacular. After I had run through my four songs, a mean-looking pyrotechnics guy wandered over to me. He fixed me in a piercing gaze and nonchalantly drawled, 'When you finish "Where e'er you walk", you've got thirty seconds to get off the stage, otherwise you'll be blown to pieces by a rocket.' Consequently, all I could think about throughout my four songs that night was getting off the stage as quickly as possible at the end. I certainly wasn't going to hang about to see if the pyrotechnics man meant exactly thirty seconds or roughly thirty seconds, so I rushed off almost as soon as the applause started at the end of the Handel.

Apart from my rapid departure, the performance went without a hitch. Funnily enough, it wasn't the size of the place that struck me as I walked on stage, but rather the strange sounds echoing around the Bowl. It took me a moment to work out what it was – the American audience had brought huge picnics, so my singing was accompanied by nearly 18,000 sets of jaws munching and glasses clinking.

We were just about to go back to the hotel after I had successfully made my escape from the stage when a smartly dressed man walked up to us. As soon as he started speaking, we realised that he was English.

'Hello, Mr and Mrs Jones,' he said warmly. 'I did enjoy your son's performance tonight.' He introduced himself as Harold Lodge, the butler to Louis B. Mayer's daughter. He offered to take us back to her house to have a look around. Mam and Dad jumped at the chance of seeing inside a real Beverly Hills mansion, so instead of going back to the hotel, we were driven away in a huge limousine towards Beverly Hills.

As the car slowed down, Lodge the butler, as he called himself, pointed out Barbra Streisand's house and then gestured towards Frank Sinatra's home in the distance. The car pulled to a halt outside the imposing mansion between the two megastars' homes. We walked up the driveway into the house and were bowled over by the opulence. The only metal on show was solid gold – and it was everywhere – even the cutlery was nine-carat. I felt as though I would drown in the carpet, so luxurious was the pile. Room after room was ornately decorated. The highlight for me was the private cinema, complete with about twenty deeply padded leather armchairs. The butler flicked a button and a whole wall moved to become a cinema screen. I was amazed – this house had even more great gadgets than Mike Oldfield's place, and that had been amazing in itself. He pressed another button and a cabinet opened up to reveal a group of gleaming Oscar statuettes inside.

'Would you like to hold one?' he asked.

'Yes, please,' came the reply, as I gingerly picked up the Best Film Oscar that was awarded to *Grand Hotel*. The statuettes were much heavier than they look on the television.

We wandered out to the beautifully landscaped garden and could see the lights shining out from the windows of the many famous stars who lived there. I could not help wondering to myself what they happened to be doing at that very moment. Visiting the house was a unique experience. When else would we have got the chance to see inside a genuine old-style Beverly Hills mansion? I went to bed that night dreaming of all the big stars who had reclined in those big leather armchairs watching previews of the great Metro-Goldwyn-Mayer movies.

During the interval at the Hollywood Bowl concert, two American television researchers came to see us. They asked if I would be prepared to stop over in the States for another four days, as there was a strong chance that I could appear on *The Johnny Carson Show*. Both Dad and Mam had only arranged time off work to suit our original schedule, so we were forced to turn them down. This did not pose a problem to me, as to be honest I had no idea who Johnny Carson was. I was also missing my girlfriend at the time and was keen to get back to North Wales. Added to that, the school football team was playing the day after we were due to arrive home and I was really looking forward to the game. So we said 'Thanks, but no thanks' and turned down any chance of appearing with Johnny Carson.

It's not something I regret now, although when I tell people in the music industry the story, they always look at me in horror, because he was one of the most influential talk-show hosts in American television history and one appearance on his programme could put a singer on the pathway to generating millions of record sales. But what is the point in beating yourself up about what might have been? For all I know, I might have sung terribly on the show and nobody in America would have bought any of my records anyway. I always think turning down Johnny Carson is the sort of thing that the cartoon character Homer Simpson would have done. Therefore, the best way of getting over it is to react as he would, by saying 'D'oh!' and carrying on with life as normal.

The closest I ever did come to making my own appearance in the annals of Hollywood history happened when I was hired to sing the opening song on the soundtrack to *Santa Claus – The Movie*, which starred the great Dudley Moore. The director Ilya Salkind asked me to sing the song in my most childlike voice. He was delighted with the end results and turned to his assistant and bellowed, 'Get the knife! We'll do the operation now.' For a moment, I looked at Mam in terror, before I realised that he was only joking and I was not destined to spend the rest of my days as a castrato.

I had another, even stranger, experience recording a song for a film soundtrack not long afterwards. This time, the movie was *The Mission*. I had been recording the Rod Stewart song 'Sailing' for my album of the same name at a studio in Cardiff. We jumped on a train straight after I had finished singing to get to London for the film soundtrack recording. I was more than a little nonplussed when I arrived to be asked to sing the song into a bucket. It wasn't a special bucket either – just a normal plastic household one. I have recorded many songs in my time, but never before or since has a bucket been involved in the process. I still don't know to this day if my voice actually features on the final version of the soundtrack or not.

One of the technicians at that recording walked up to me at the end of the session and said, 'You're my hero, mate. You were on *Spitting Image* last night.'

At the time the satirical Sunday night programme featuring latex puppets provided many of the Monday morning talking points in schools and offices across the country. I – or rather a puppet purporting to be me – appeared on the show on quite a few occasions. To my intense consternation, the producers always gave me curly ginger hair and a South Wales accent. I was prepared to overlook this transgression because I was secretly very proud of the show. It was the only thing I ever did on television that earned me universal kudos among my school friends. In the first skit, a very trendy record producer puppet was sitting at a studio mixing desk, snorting cocaine, and I had just finished singing a song.

'Yes, brilliant Aled, brilliant, brilliant,' he says. 'How long have we got? Ten minutes before his voice breaks. That's thirty-six albums. Right, get in there!' He then walks up to my puppet and kicks it very hard where it hurts.

On another occasion, a Phil Collins puppet was singing a Christmas song at a piano before my puppet walked on, sang one line and was then unceremoniously yanked off screen with a shepherd's crook. The jokes were never complex, but they appealed enormously to my schoolboy sense of humour, as did my appearance around the same time 'singing' in cartoons in the brilliantly outrageous *Viz* magazine and in the far gentler *Beano* comic.

As well as television and film work, I was regularly appearing on the radio, often being interviewed by Hywel Gwynfryn, the main presenter on BBC Radio Cymru, the Welsh-language radio station for Wales. I spent a lot of my childhood visiting the studios of BBC Bangor at Bryn Merion before and after school to give interviews from the tiny unattended studio, where I would sit with crib sheets of answers in front of me. My favourite radio interviewer of all was Chris Stuart. When first I talked to him for his early-morning BBC Radio Wales programme, it was the first interview I had ever given in English and he instantly put me at ease. We chatted about all sorts of topics and he seemed very interested in my everyday life, which was a very odd experience for me back then. It was the first of many interviews with him and Chris would always let his listeners know what I was doing.

Chris is a fine broadcaster who was regularly on television and radio in Wales. He became a large part of my choirboy life, even acting as compere at many of my concerts. He presented a programme for BBC Radio Four called *Aled Jones: A Musical Portrait of a Teenage Superstar*, which collected together songs and interviews.

On one occasion, when I appeared on his BBC Wales television show, Chris wrote 'Aled's Song' especially for me. He said that he felt it summed up my hopes for the future:

Give me a song, the kind that young boys sing,
A song of open road and rustling spring.
Give me the time for sport and fun and joy,
For all work and no play maketh dull the boy.
These are the things I ask,
Were I to get them, happy would be my lot.
But above all, there's one more plea
Most important that, I very near forgot.
Give me the thing for which my young heart aches;
Give me a tenor voice when this one breaks.

The last word of the tune is belted out on a top G, which created a very funny effect. Although this song was very light-hearted, Chris was also capable of writing far more serious music, including a beautiful ballad called 'Tell Me, Boy', which I recorded because I had a few minutes to spare at the end of a studio session. I gave it its first public performance at a concert in the North Wales Theatre in Llandudno and revisited it some fifteen years later, this time duetting with my choirboy self. I have always found it very poignant, with the words describing life through the eyes of both a child and an adult.

I also worked with Chris recording the theme tune to a cartoon called *A Winter Story* for the independent Welsh-language version of Channel Four, S4C. It was about a very popular character from Welsh children's books called Sion Blewyn Coch. The cartoon was made in Wales by a company called Siriol Animation. It was the follow-up to the very successful children's series, *SuperTed*. Chris provided the music and two sets of words were written for me to sing: one version in English and another in Welsh. We all met up at the Loco Studios in Caerleon, Gwent to record the tracks. It was another of those days from my childhood that I remember with great affection. Although I was the only youngster there, everyone else treated me as an equal rather than a junior. When you are a teenager, you respond so positively to being shown respect that it means that you find yourself automatically acting more maturely. I owe a lot to Chris Stuart; he is one of those people with whom I worked as a boy, who have remained a family friend ever since.

9. MY MUSICAL HERO, LEONARD BERNSTEIN

One evening, I sat at home with Mam and Dad watching a documentary about *West Side Story*, the musical written by the legendary American conductor and composer, Leonard Bernstein. It was easy to see that the great man had a fiery temper and was not afraid to use it to get what he wanted. During the course of the programme, he virtually annihilated the tenor José Carreras, shouting and ranting at him during a rehearsal. He would then immediately switch on the charm when he spoke to the soprano Kiri Te Kanawa, before once again castigating Carreras in front of the whole orchestra. The word in the classical-music world was that you never messed with Leonard Bernstein. If you did, he would absolutely hammer you.

Just two weeks later, Lydia Connolly, my agent, received an offer for me to sing Bernstein's *Chichester Psalms* at the Barbican Centre in London with the London Symphony Orchestra and Chorus in front of the Queen. All of that, I could take in my stride. What totally petrified me was that the conductor would be Leonard Bernstein himself.

I practised and practised the piece over and over, learning the Hebrew text phonetically. Then the day came when I would finally meet the maestro. We were in a rehearsal room in the Barbican: Mam, Dad, Lydia, a pianist and the choirmaster Richard Hickox were all sitting down next to me. The entire London Symphony Chorus was lined up along the edge of the room. You could cut the tension in the air with a knife. Everybody knew about Bernstein's reputation and he was due to join us any minute.

Suddenly the doors burst open and into the room walked this whirlwind of white hair, long black flowing cloak and bright-red jumper.

'Hey, you're the London Symphony Chorus. You guys are great!' he boomed at the choir, smiling warmly. Then he walked over to me. I stood up and put my hand out, but instead of shaking it, he grabbed me in a headlock and tapped my head repeatedly with his conductor's baton, saying, 'And you, little fella – I've been listening to you and I've been wanting to work with you for ages.'

My brain was almost paralysed by an overwhelming mixture of fear and relief. All I could think to myself was, 'Leonard Bernstein's not supposed to say things like that.' He seemed more like a friendly grandfather than a tyrannical ogre.

The choir sang through their part and he complimented them on their performance. Although he changed one or two things, he seemed very pleased with the work that had already been done by Richard Hickox. Almost as soon as I started to sing my part, though, he stopped me. For the next hour and a half he proceeded to give me the most astounding masterclass on the Hebrew text and how exactly he wanted the piece to sound. The hundred-strong chorus looked on, enjoying every minute. I cannot remember another rehearsal where there was so much laughing and clapping from a choir. The atmosphere was electrifying and the feeling continued right through the week.

By the Thursday, security was very tight ahead of the Queen's visit, with sniffer dogs all over the Barbican. During the afternoon, we had a full-length rehearsal so that nothing would be left to chance while Her Majesty was watching us. I was singing away at my solo and Bernstein was conducting the orchestra with massive sweeping movements and huge energy. He gave the impression of a man who loved his job. Suddenly, he leaned over to me in the middle of my solo and boomed, 'Haven't you learned it yet?'

'Yes, I know it,' I replied between sung phrases. He grabbed the score out of my hands and carried on conducting. I continued singing without a glitch and after five phrases he handed back the score to me with an indulgent smile. Still talking between the bits where I was supposed to sing, I said cockily, 'No, I don't need it. I know it, don't I?'

He thought this was very funny and threw his hands in the air in mock indignation, saying 'Oooh!' in a very camp voice. The choir and orchestra were by now laughing out loud. Without warning, he charged over to where I was standing and, in the middle of the piece, put me in a headlock. So I stood on stage singing my solo while he had my head jammed under his arm. He continued to conduct the orchestra without missing a beat and I continued to sing my heart out. Even though that very evening we were due to be singing in front of the Queen and a packed house, with a full orchestra, a hundred-strong choir and soloists the calibre of the pianist Christian Zimmerman and the violinist Gidon Kremer, he was still relaxed enough to tease me.

When we did the performance that night, the piece finished and Bernstein did not pause for even a moment to acknowledge the audience's enthusiastic applause. Instead he rushed over to where I was standing, kissed me on the cheek and grabbed my hand. He turned to the audience and tapped me gently on the head with his baton – the crowds were loving every moment. I still have two photographs of this point, both of which he signed with the words: 'With great hopes for your future and all love, Lenny.'

Working with him influenced me like nobody else. I would hang around backstage during the concert watching all the musicians walking on and off stage. I was intrigued to see Bernstein's personal assistant standing just off stage with a glass of scotch in one hand, a towel in the other and a lit cigarette in a holder in his mouth. But as soon as there was a break in the music, the reason for his being there became clear. The maestro would rush off stage sweating like mad; he would grab the towel and wipe his face, down the scotch in one and then take a huge drag on the cigarette, before turning on his heels and charging back into the hall to rapturous applause from his adoring public.

There are plenty of performers who have a presence about them, but here was a true star, for whom I was full of admiration. When he walked into a room, people would stand back in awe. It was like Moses parting the waves. I had worked with many brilliant conductors before and since, but he was by far the greatest of them all. Added to that, he had actually composed the *Chichester Psalms* and that increased my respect for him even further. I had never heard music like it before and it made me realise how special he was – he could write a musical like *West Side Story*, but he could also compose a complex modern work like this as well. Because the music was his and came from his soul, getting it right meant everything to me.

To watch him conduct was astounding; even when I was not singing I could feel the energy radiating from him as he drove the choir to ever-greater heights. Despite being a man of mature years at that point, he would put in a hugely physical performance and the sweat would pour off him. During the Friday night performance, I started to panic that he was going to die on stage because he appeared to be foaming at the mouth. I realised moments later that he was actually eating a polo mint while conducting and, because he was getting so worked up, that was causing the white froth.

Truly great musicians are a breed apart and, as with all of their number, Bernstein had passion, heart and guts. To my mind, the greatest musicians don't hide – they're not afraid to sweat or look odd on some occasions. There are so many singers these days who give performances that are polished and effortless, but personally I want to hear something with a little more guts. If you listen to the recordings of the great Maria Callas, they are not always perfectly polished, but they have a very real edge and are electrifying for the listener. She would sit alongside Bernstein in my list of all-time greats, sharing that sense of charged energy when she performed. In the case of Bernstein, he was completely transformed into another world when he was on that stage. The moment he pointed his baton at you as a performer, it was like a Harry Potter wand, and his little bit of magic would bring out the best in you.

After the second concert at the Barbican, Bernstein gave me signed copies of every album he had ever made. Rather embarrassingly when I look back on it now, I decided to return the favour on the second leg of the concert series, in Rome, taking with me signed copies of all the albums *I* had ever made, although he had released a few more than I had.

Dad and I flew to Rome on the same plane as the orchestra and I enjoyed watching all the instruments being packed away in the hold. Taking an orchestra to a foreign country is a massive logistical exercise and we were both relieved finally to slump into our seats next to one of the horn players. Shortly after we had taken off, the cabin crew starting walking frantically up and down the aisle, opening the overhead lockers and checking the hand luggage. Very quickly, we realised that something was seriously wrong and eventually we were told by the pilot that telephone calls had been received in London and Rome saying that there was a bomb on board the plane, which would detonate on landing. Obviously, the airline had no choice but to take the threats seriously.

Everybody on board was deathly quiet and ashen-faced as we came in to land. I had already written a note to Mam telling her that I loved her, which I had left in the seat pocket. I gripped tightly on Dad's arm. The second that all three wheels touched the tarmac at Rome airport, the plane skidded off the normal runway. All that we could see through the windows was a sea of flashing lights from fire engines, ambulances and police vans. The plane's doors were opened and the stairs were attached to the side in record time and the cabin crew bundled us out on to the tarmac. We then had to wait for hours in the airport baggage hall while every piece of luggage and every musical instrument was checked by the police. The emotional turbulence of the flight had left us all drained. The leader of the orchestra actually fell asleep on the baggage carousel, as he waited for his violin to be returned to him. Now, whenever I stand around in airports waiting for my luggage, I always get the urge to jump on the carousel and just lie there.

The bomb scare turned out to be a hoax, which was probably aimed at Leonard Bernstein. However, he was the only person involved in the show not travelling on the plane, touching down in Rome safely some hours later.

The concerts in Rome's Santa Cecilia auditorium passed off without any further incidents. Afterwards, there was a sumptuous buffet laid on at an estate about half an hour's drive from Rome, but after such a roller-coaster few days, all I really wanted was a dose of normality. So Dad and I sneaked off with a few guys from the orchestra to a small restaurant just by the concert hall, where I had a proper thin-crust pepperoni pizza baked in a wood oven. It was a very tasty end to an exciting week.

That night in Rome was the last I ever saw of Lenny Bernstein. We exchanged home phone numbers and he asked me to give him a call and sing for him once my voice had broken. He died just a few years later. Working with him ranks as the most enriching musical experience of my life, and he joined Andrew Lloyd Webber and Richard Branson as one of the three people who had more impact on me than any of the countless other great talents whom I was privileged to meet as a boy.

10. THE BIG BREAK

I continued to record albums right through until my sixteenth birthday. It was great to work regularly with the old team of Hefin Owen and Mervyn Williams. It seemed only natural that we should carry on together, even when I joined Virgin Records. Hefin was the 'doer' and Mervyn was the 'thinker' of the partnership – and I am not intending to be disrespectful to either man by saying that.

We would record in a church in Penarth, just outside Cardiff, and they would give me a list of music a couple of weeks before each session, which I would then learn. By the time that I arrived at the church, they had always set up the microphones and would be sitting waiting in the van outside. I would then have a quick run-through with Hugh Tregelles Williams, who remains one of the most outstanding organists I have ever come across. Then it was time for the red light to go on and recording to start. I would sing each song through a few times until everybody was satisfied and then it was straight on to the next one. People often used to tell me that they thought that I must spend hours working on pieces, but I have to admit that I only looked at some of them a couple of minutes before recording them. The whole process of completing an album never took more than a couple of days.

Mervyn was a smoker and would spend the days pacing up and down outside, puffing away on endless cigarettes. You could always tell where he had been because all the plant pots in the vicinity would be littered with stubbed-out cigarette butts. One night, as we were locking up, Mam looked down and saw a lit cigarette discarded on a pew.

'Mervyn, is that your cigarette?' she asked reproachfully.

'I could have burned the whole church down!' he exclaimed with concern etched on to his face. It was only when he picked up the offending item that he realised that it was a fake glowing cigarette, which I had mischievously bought from a joke shop earlier in the day.

It became something of a ritual that whenever we finished recording an album, we would have dinner with a big group of friends, which usually included Hefin, Mervyn, their wives, the BBC Radio Wales presenter Chris Stuart and Hugh Tregelles. We would take up a large part of the Happy Gathering Chinese restaurant in Cardiff, where we became very regular customers. Without fail, we would gorge ourselves on a huge banquet. Everyone would drink plenty of wine, except for me, who would be quietly sipping Coke.

During the course of the meal, Mervyn would always ask, 'What do you fancy recording next?'

I would then reply with a musical theme, such as 'hymns', and he would then say, 'Well, you write down some of your favourite hymns on the tablecloth and I'll do the same. Then we'll see what we come up with.'

Everyone else around the table would have their say and by the end of dinner, we would have the track listing for the next album, which would usually be recorded in exactly the same place about a month later. There would, of course, be another Chinese banquet at the end of the session, and so the cycle went on.

I had never intended the recording session on 29 December 1986, my sixteenth birthday, to be my last as a boy soprano. It just happened that way. I arrived in the church as usual, having learned all of the pieces of music. I do remember having a slight cold, but my voice was unaffected. In fact, the top part of my voice was the best it had ever been – absolutely crystal clear, and I was happily able to belt out top Cs. There was one hymn that I wanted to record again with my boy soprano voice – 'Dear Lord and Father of Mankind'. In the old days, I would have had no problem singing it and had performed it live in concert many times. But on this particular frosty December morning, I was having trouble with the middle of my voice, which was particularly breathy. The session was proving to be hard work. I had successfully recorded four pieces during the morning, but throughout the session I kept asking, 'Is it sounding all right?' because things didn't seem normal to me.

'Yeah, it sounds fine,' replied Hefin on the intercom from the van outside.

'No problems at all,' echoed Geoff Atkins, the sound engineer.

'Is Mam there?'

'No, she's just this minute gone shopping,' said Hefin. Mam was, in fact, sitting next to him in the van with tears in her eyes because she had realised, just as Hefin, Mervyn and Geoff had, that my voice was no longer sounding the same.

We took a break for lunch and headed off to a very smart Italian restaurant in Penarth. Mervyn and I went on our own in one car, with Geoff, Hugh Tregelles, Hefin and Mam in the other.

Once we were on our own, I turned to Mervyn and said, 'Listen, I know you're set up and everything, but I'm not really enjoying it. Do you mind if we don't go back and record the rest of the album?'

'I'm so glad you said that,' he said very gently. 'Let's leave it as it is.'

As soon as we arrived at the restaurant, Mervyn and I announced to everyone that we were stopping. At the end of the meal, the waiter brought over a cake, which we shared out before having a toast to say: 'Well, that's it. It's done.'

Suddenly a huge wave of panic spread over me and I stammered, 'But we haven't recorded the album. That means we won't go for a Chinese this evening.'

'Don't you worry,' replied Mervyn with a broad grin on his face. 'This Chinese is going to be momentous.'

That evening, I arrived at the Happy Gathering to discover about forty people waiting for me on the top floor. Virtually everybody I had worked closely with over the years had come to say goodbye to my boy-soprano days. They were all there: from Mam, Dad, Hefin and Mervyn to people such as Chris Stuart and his wife Megan. Everyone had an enormous laugh and it was not a sad time at all. We spent the evening reliving moments and it was a very happy occasion. After the party, we went home on a high, but I had no sense of fear or worry about the rest of my life. I knew that I would sing again – but whether I would sing publicly was another matter.

My overwhelming emotion over the next few days was one of relief. I wanted to be a normal person who played football, went out with girls and, most important of all, didn't sing. By this stage,

I felt as though I was on breakfast television every week justifying why I was still singing. The obligatory question became a standing joke between me and the TV-am presenters Anne Diamond and Nick Owen. The papers had been predicting my demise as a boy soprano ever since that Royal Gala in Edinburgh, but here I was nearly two years later, still singing. The difference now was that I was starting to feel the pressure of continuing to do what had previously come naturally to me.

Looking back, I cannot be sure whether my voice started to change when I was fifteen, or if I could have kept on going until I was seventeen, because a large part of my singing was down to technique. I used to sing all of the time, so my voice was a very strong instrument and I had far greater control over it than the average boy of my age. I spent so much time training that I was like a 100-metre sprinter in his prime – I would never get a sore throat because my voice was always in a state of readiness.

The morning after my decision in the church in Penarth, the world was told. The public-relations person spun the line: 'He's retiring on a high note to concentrate on his O levels. He's looking forward to the break.' I went into the BBC studios in Bangor and spent a few days sitting there doing interviews for the BBC, ITN, HTV, TV-am and numerous radio stations and newspapers. My voice breaking had become national news and I was the 'And finally . . .' item on all of the major bulletins. It even made the national news as far away as the USA and Australia. There was one slight anomaly though: my voice had not actually broken. I was still singing, but only at home and only in private. I could still belt out the top Cs and sing with a pure boy-soprano voice. I never went through the period that often happens with boys' voices, where they can never predict whether they will speak in a high- or low-pitched voice. One day, quite a few months after I had officially retired, I was standing in my bedroom brushing my hair and singing. The note that came out was a low one rather than a high one. My voice had changed.

Quite soon after I had stopped singing, I went back to the Barbican in London to perform *The Snowman* in a Raymond Gubbay production. This time, though, I was the narrator rather than the singer. It was a totally new experience for me and I was racked with nerves, despite the fact that I had been singing in the very same hall just a few months before without any worries at all. I was back in the same dressing room, but this time I was petrified and I threw up before going on stage. The audience were in their seats and the house lights had dimmed and I stopped dead for a moment, just before walking on stage. I said to myself, 'Listen, this is not natural. If you're this nervous, don't do it.' I took a deep breath and walked on. It went much better than I had hoped and I quickly regained the confidence that I had when I was a boy. It's like everything else really – the more you do something, the better at it you become. I do still suffer from nerves on occasions, though. Ever since I can remember, I have bitten my nails down as far as they can go without drawing blood. I still do it today, although Paul McKenna has promised that he can cure me of the habit through hypnosis.

Life slowed down quite a bit once I was no longer singing, but it still had its excitements. The second member of the royal family to contact us was Prince Edward. He said he was planning a massive charity version of the cult television show *It's a Knockout*, featuring teams led by members of the royal family. He wanted me to be involved in the show.

I was over the moon because throughout my childhood I had loved the programme – and particularly the hilarious commentaries of Stuart Hall. We had trouble understanding exactly how everything would work. It all sounded so bizarre and it was not until we received the written briefing document that we were able to comprehend the magnitude of the event. The list of people taking part was like nothing I had ever seen: Princes Edward and Andrew, Princess Anne, the Duchess of York, Christopher Reeve, John Travolta, Kevin Kline, Anthony Andrews, Cliff Richard, Tom Jones, Sheena Easton, Rowan Atkinson, Barry McGuigan, Jackie Stewart and Steve Cram, to name just a few.

The hosts were to be Les Dawson, Su Pollard and me. I would play the role of the royal pageboy who announced the details of the games that were about to be played. With the opportunity to meet so many famous people, there was no way in the world that I was going to turn down the offer, which was even more attractive because the whole event would take place at the Alton Towers theme park, somewhere I had long wanted to visit.

The recording took place over two days, with a rehearsal for the presenters on the first afternoon and then the actual games being played on the second day. I had a problem though – the rehearsal day clashed with the final examination paper for my Maths O level. It was a subject with which I had always struggled and Dad had spent many evenings coaching me through all of the sciences. During my O level year, I had missed a lot of time at school because of recording or performance commitments, but Mam and Dad had filled in the gaps in my learning. The headmaster, Mr Dafydd Whittall, was very far-sighted in believing that I was getting a schooling by doing all of my extracurricular work. Many other headmasters would have made life difficult for a pupil in my position, but he saw a real long-term value for me in what I was doing.

We had worked out that it was possible for me to complete my Maths O level and still get to Staffordshire in time for the rehearsal. I arrived at the school gym knowing that as soon as the two-hour exam was over, Dad would be waiting for me in the car outside and we would head straight off to Alton Towers. I sat at my desk and spent the time while we waited for the papers to be handed out mulling over the very precise instructions that our Maths teacher had given us. We were to spend the first quarter of an hour reading the paper, marking the questions which we felt able to answer quickly and which ones we were going to really concentrate on. Above all, we were not to rush through the paper. All of this advice was running through my head. I had the added pressure of knowing that I had to be out of the gym at midday, otherwise I would not be at Alton Towers in time for the rehearsal, which was vitally important because the next day we were going to be making an incredibly complicated outside broadcast.

The invigilator told us to turn over our papers. Immediately, my heart sank. I had made a terrible mistake. The second part of the Maths exam was a three-hour paper and not the two-hour one that I had been expecting. That meant the exam would not be finished until one o'clock and we would have no chance of getting to the rehearsal on time. My mind went into overdrive. I instantly forgot all of the instructions we had been given and rushed through the questions on the paper. I got up and left the room and ran to the car outside. Slumping down in the passenger seat next to Dad, I confessed what I had done. He felt terribly guilty and spent the following weeks worrying about whether his decision to allow me to take part in the 'Royal It's A Knockout' during my O levels would result in my failing Maths. In the end, though, he need not have worried – I passed with a grade C, which was all that I needed to do.

Once we arrived at Alton Towers, we were transported to another world. A morning spent among lines of silent schoolchildren slaving away over simultaneous equations was instantly replaced by an afternoon in the hustle and bustle of the television world. Producers wearing earpieces and carrying clipboards ran around everywhere, cameramen were practising the angles of their shots and technical people were making adjustments to the sets. To add to the sense of chaos, it was pouring with rain. We were ushered into one of the many marquees that had been especially erected for the show and I was introduced to my co-presenters, Les Dawson and Su Pollard. I became great friends with Les over the next couple of days. He was a very genuine and grounded man and he made me laugh during the rehearsal. He looked after me right through the recording, probably because he had kids himself and could sense that the whole experience was very new to me. Su was charging around, never stopping to pause for breath. I have never met anyone with such energy; she must have been absolutely exhausted when she went home in the evening.

The next day, things got more serious. The production was so large that the only way it would come together would be if all of those taking part followed a rigid timetable. I was in awe of the stars I kept bumping into. I met Rowan Atkinson when I was just leaving make-up and he was on the way in. I had a great chat to the star of *Superman* Christopher Reeve, who sadly died in 2004, and to the boxer Barry McGuigan, who was a particularly nice bloke. My favourite contestant was the American football star, Walter Payton. He was enormous and towered over everybody else. He did so well in one particular game that Princess Anne pretended to knight him. As normal, I was the only child taking part so I was utterly spoiled by everyone.

After make-up, it was time to get changed into my costume and I was not in the least bit happy when I saw what I was obliged to wear: grey tights, a very frilly skirt and an ornate pageboy's hat. It was excruciatingly embarrassing and all I could think was, 'What will my mates in Llandegfan say, when they see me dressed in this lot?' I found out the answer not long afterwards, when I watched the programme with my girlfriend, and her brother and sister. They were rolling around the floor of her bedroom in hysterical laughter as soon as I made an appearance on the screen.

The day went by in a complete blur and I was rushed from one part of the theme park to another as we recorded each of the madcap games. I had been hoping to sneak off and enjoy some of the rides, especially the massive roller coaster, but we were far too busy for that. The royal family faced a lot of criticism for the programme once it was broadcast, but there was no sense of that for those of us taking part at the time. It raised a huge amount of money for charity and all of the royals were charming when I met them. Prince Edward, in particular, went out of his way to thank all of us who were taking part.

I bumped into the Duchess of York again a few months afterwards when we both took part in a charity book called *One Day for Life*, where the participants were asked to photograph whatever they were doing at one particular moment of the day. My picture was of Gloria Hunniford with her feet up on the desk at BBC Radio Two, shortly after she had interviewed me. That morning I had been in a recording studio in North London where I was narrating an audiobook version of Charles Dickens's *A Christmas Carol*. It was a strange experience to be asked to read a book out loud from start to finish. In the end, it took three days to record the whole thing and was a mentally exhausting experience, although it is something I have done again recently for Classic FM with an audiobook called *The Story of Classical Music*.

Even that particular job did not prepare me for being asked to take part in a recording of *Under Milk Wood*, written by the legendary Welsh writer Dylan Thomas. It was overseen by Sir George Martin, the man responsible for producing the Beatles. The session took place at Air Studios in Oxford Circus in London. I played two different roles, 'Little Boy Waldo' and 'One of Mr Waldo's', which sounds impressive, but in fact I only had a total of two lines, one of which was 'Wee wee wee wee all the way home'. Imagine my surprise when I turned up in the studio and saw more famous Welsh faces gathered together in one place than I thought possible, including Jonathan Pryce, Windsor Davies, Sian Phillips, Ruth Madoc and Nerys Hughes. I was even more surprised to find that I would be recording my lines with Sir Anthony Hopkins, who was 'First Voice'. He was a delightful man and gave me a masterclass in wringing every dramatic nuance out of saying 'Wee wee wee'.

11. AFTER THE SINGING STOPPED

Just a few days after I stopped singing, we were sent a letter at home saying that JVC Victor was releasing all of my albums in Japan. This was good news, because in a sense I was going to be able to relive my boyhood career, without actually having to do any singing. The decision by JVC Victor turned out to be all down to two girls – one just a couple of years older than me called Reiko Kunitani, and another called Norie Masuyama, who was one of the biggest classical-music journalists in the country. Reiko often travelled to London, where she had bought all of my CDs. She loved them and passed them on to Norie, who in turn reviewed them very positively in her magazine. JVC Victor picked up on the reviews and decided that there would be a market for my records, so they released every one of them in chronological order. Each of them went to number one in the Japanese charts.

We were asked to go out to Japan to take part in the first of two promotional and concert tours in the summer holidays after my O levels. On both trips, I would be narrating Humperdinck's opera *Hansel and Gretel* in Japanese, with the music being performed by the Vienna Woods Boys Choir. I was completely unprepared for the reception we received once we had touched down on Japanese soil. As soon as we walked off the plane, we were mobbed by hordes of screaming teenage girls. Wherever we went, we were surrounded by young fans. Dad even had his hair pulled as he tried to stop me from being drowned in a sea of Japanese girls.

The workload on the trip was incredibly high, but it was great fun because it was so different from anything we had experienced before. We stayed at the very stylish Takenawa Prince Hotel in the centre of Tokyo. On our first morning there, JVC Victor's representative Mr Nishimura arrived to see us. He was a real gentleman and was always immaculately turned out. As we got to know him better, he became my tennis partner on our trips over there. We were taken to another suite in the hotel and I was introduced to Masako Watanabe, who was going to be my interpreter. A very Westernised trendy woman in her early forties, who had spent time in both New York and London, she was very different from many of the other Japanese people we met and I loved working with her.

Masako and I chatted away as if we had known each other for years while we waited for the first interview of the day to begin. On the dot of nine o'clock, there was a knock at the door and in walked a reporter. He bowed and presented me with a gift, which was some sort of electronic equipment. I continued to talk to him until just before ten o'clock, when there was another knock at the door and the person running the interviews told the journalist that their time was up. The interviewer thanked me profusely for talking to him and then walked out through the door while still bowing to me. At ten o'clock precisely, the same thing happened, but with a different interviewer and a different gift. By the end of the first two-week trip, Dad had to buy three new suitcases just to transport all my new gadgets home.

The interviews happened solidly for six or seven hours a day for the entire fortnight we were there. In the downtime, between interviews or over lunch, Masako would teach me *Hansel and Gretel* in Japanese. The first time I was there, I learned it phonetically, but by our second trip, I had a better idea of what I was actually saying. Doing the whole of the opera in Japanese was a very brave thing to do really, because it could easily have been a total disaster. Masako was a very kind and patient teacher, who bribed me to learn the words with chocolate cake. She spent so much time schooling me that by the time I got around to performing the opera, I sounded Japanese.

In the evenings, we would either go out for dinner or I would narrate the Vienna Woods Boys' concerts. During the first year we were there, the concerts tended to pass without incident, but by the second year, the performance of *Hansel and Gretel* would finish and thirty or so girls aged between eleven and seventeen would storm the front of the stage with flowers and gifts. Much to the disdain of the Vienna Woods Boys, their chaperones and conductor, it would then take me about twenty minutes to fight my way off stage. It was like being a pop star. There were always a dozen Japanese girls camped outside our hotel. I would go down to talk to them and, on one particular night, I sneaked out to play *pachinko* with them. This was a game where thousands of ball bearings would move about in front of you, from which you could win all sorts of prizes. When the concert promoter found out, he was very angry with me, because it was simply not the way that 'stars' were expected to behave in Japan.

Whenever we were taken out to dinner, it would usually involve a photo shoot for the press or some filming with a television crew. One night, we were taken to one of the most famous sushi bars in Tokyo. When we arrived, plastic versions of the meals were on show in the window. There seemed to be a large amount of very exotic-looking seafood and I could sense that Mam was already getting a little nervous about what exactly we were going to be eating. We sat on stools along the edge of a glass counter, which was stacked full of the ingredients for making the sushi, including huge slabs of raw fish. Our hosts told us that the food was top quality and that each portion was very expensive, but this was totally lost on Mam, Dad and me. Mam was already starting to feel queasy. Dad prodded me in the side and whispered, 'We've got to eat this, because otherwise it'll really insult them.'

We took a deep breath and watched the woman behind the counter prepare our food. She moulded the rice in her hand and then a ginger cat jumped up on the counter. She stroked the cat, got a sponge out of a nearby bucket of brown water, wiped the top and slapped the rice down. She stroked the cat again and then reached down for a big white fish, which she sliced thickly on top of the rice. An unidentifiable red thing was added to the dish and then a piece of tentacle was cut up and sprinkled on top. This culinary masterpiece was then presented to us with a flourish.

Mam immediately had a coughing fit as soon as she picked up a piece of sushi. Thinking quickly, Dad said, 'My wife has not been well and has lost her appetite.' Our hosts said that they understood and that she was not to worry. That increased the pressure on Dad and me. I picked up a lump of sushi and was almost overcome by its smell. Rather than eat it, I put it in my mouth and kept it crushed in my cheek. Dad manfully ate his first piece, but from then onwards, I could tell that he, too, was keeping the food in his cheek. The photographer was gleefully snapping away. When he had finally finished the shots inside the restaurant, the three of us trooped outside for more photographs – this time, next to the front door of the restaurant. It was a good few minutes later that Dad and I were finally able to spit the remnants of our dinner into a litter bin. He turned to me and said, 'That was the most horrendous thing I've ever had to eat in my life.' It's strange how people's tastes change, because these days I am often to be found willingly eating mountains of sushi, which is now one of my favourite foods.

We did, however, make one food discovery that we absolutely loved while we were in Japan, called *shabu shabu*. All the diners sat around a huge bar with their own pot of boiling water, into which you put very thin slivers of Kobe beef. We were told that this meat is created by feeding beer to the cattle and massaging them so that their fat is evenly placed throughout the meat, giving it a marbled effect and making it incredibly tender. After using your boiling pot to cook vegetables and meat, you were left with a delicious casserole as all the juices mixed together. At the end of the meal, we were congratulating ourselves on having finally found some authentic Japanese food that all three of us liked – then the dessert arrived. It appeared to be a long, stringy jellyfish and Mam recoiled in horror. Our hosts told us that it was actually derived from the root of a plant. Dad tentatively took the first mouthful and, with a look of mighty relief on his face, said, 'Oh, actually it tastes OK.' We never managed to relax when we were eating out in Japan because we were always a little unsure about what was coming next.

My two trips to Japan were a complete bonus at the end of my boy-soprano career. The screaming girls made it a very different world from how life had been in the UK, but the great thing was that when I came back home, I could escape from it. Although it was great to have so many young girls chasing me all the time, it would have been a nightmare to be the object of such adulation for a sustained period. My fans in Britain tended to be altogether more genteel. During interviews back home, I would often use the standard line: 'Everybody who wants to be my girlfriend is over sixty.' It's a line that Terry Wogan claims he invented for me.

When my O level results came through, I discovered that I had six B-grades and three C-grades, which meant I was able to go on to the sixth form to do my A levels.

By this stage, my only performances were the occasional narration or small parts in plays for BBC Radio Four. One of my favourite roles was playing a teenage King Arthur in *The Sword and the Circle*, which was part of the children's radio show *Cat's Whiskers*.

I was asked to interview various guests for the legendary BBC Radio Four programme *Start the Week*, which was presented by my old champion, Richard Baker. My most memorable interview was with the Hollywood star, Donald Sutherland. I also talked to the playwright Alick Rowe about his television drama series *A Sort of Innocence*. The central character in the programme was a thirteen-year-old choir boy whose voice was breaking, so the production team of *Start the Week* obviously felt that I would have some common ground with the drama's main character.

I presented two editions of the long-running BBC Radio series, *Down Your Way* – one from Anglesey on my seventeenth birthday and the other from the Barbican Centre in London. In the first one, I had a canoeing lesson and was lucky not to drown. I also had my first driving lesson taped for the programme. I seemed to have a little trouble keeping the car on the tarmac part of the road and, much to my embarrassment, the whole of Britain heard my driving instructor say to me in exasperation, 'It would be nice if the tiny trees you're driving over were allowed to grow up to be big ones.' In the second of the two programmes, I was the only person lucky enough to be granted an interview with Prince Edward, who was at the Barbican narrating *Peter and the Wolf*.

I love working in the medium of radio, but being interviewed by broadcasters such as Gloria Hunniford or Chris Stuart and my work for BBC Radio Four were not my only experiences of the wireless in this period. Looking back, I would say that I learned the most as 'junior reporter' on one of Britain's more bizarre radio programmes called *Radio Brynsiencyn*, which was broadcast twice a week on BBC Radio Wales. The scriptwriter and presenter was a very experienced journalist and broadcaster called Ian Skidmore. He fronted the programme along with his wife Celia, who was also a prolific writer. However, they eschewed fancy recording studios and instead recorded the programme in the parlour at their home in the village of Brynsiencyn on Anglesey.

The *Radio Brynsiencyn* staff also included Rose the Cleaning Lady and Goronwy Generator, who powered the station with his bicycle pedalling. Marmaduke the cat and Miss Kipp the dog also made regular appearances. The programme was recorded on an ancient reel-to-reel recorder and, even though it was satirical, it contained real interviews and tackled serious local issues. I was coached to conduct interviews by Ian and Celia and undoubtedly learned a great deal from them during this difficult period after I had stopped singing.

Tennis became more important to me as a means of letting off steam during this time, and I was delighted when Mike Sertin invited me back to introduce the whole of the Wightman Cup at the Royal Albert Hall in front of Her Majesty the Queen. Much to my embarrassment, he made me wear a bright-maroon velvet jacket. I suspect this was so that I would blend in with the colour scheme of the Royal Albert Hall, but it simply had the effect of making me look highly comical. I have forgiven Mike for what he inflicted on me and he has since become a good friend. Over the years, he has regularly berated me about my favourite tennis players and football teams, although I know that he liked the idea of a choirboy not only being passionate about music, but also about sport. He still teases me about the occasion when we visited Wimbledon to watch the men's final. Pat Cash won the match and I was one of the few people who refused to stand up and cheer. He had beaten Ivan Lendl, who was in my view a true champion and one of the sport's greatest heroes. As Pat Cash celebrated by climbing on to the commentary boxes in order to embrace his family, I was sulking – not least because had Lendl won, I was due to go back to his dressing room to meet him. Pat Cash played the better tennis on the day and dashed any hopes I had of fulfilling that particular dream.

One morning while I was hosting the Wightman Cup, I turned up early and watched a couple of the American team members warming up on court. At such close quarters, I was amazed at the consistency and accuracy of their powerful shots. All of a sudden, one of America's real stars at the time, Zina Garrison, asked me if I would like to have a hit around with her. My jaw dropped open and I could not believe my luck. True, my voice might well have broken and true, I would no longer be able to sing as a boy soprano. But at that precise moment in time I had forgotten any concerns I might have been feeling about that particular issue, because I was playing tennis at the Royal Albert Hall with one of the finest players in the whole world. Those few days were so different to anything I had ever experienced before in my life. The icing on the cake would have been if the British team had actually won, but sadly that had not happened since Virginia Wade's time. Disappointing as that might have been, I was having the time of my life mingling with such sporting greats and I felt very honoured when Virginia presented me with two brand-new professional tennis rackets.

Later, Mike asked me to take part in a Cliff Richard pro-celebrity tennis tournament in Brighton, which was held in front of 2,000 of the great man's most ardent fans. I was teamed with the British player Julie Salmon. Our opponents were Cliff himself and Jo Durie, Jimmy Tarbuck and Annabel Croft, and Mike Read and Virginia Wade. It was a serious event with all the trimmings: ball boys, umpires and even physiotherapists on standby. My highly competitive streak came to the fore and I was determined that Julie and I would win the whole thing, particularly because many people had written us off due to our relative youth and inexperience.

We had great fun playing against Jimmy Tarbuck and Annabel Croft. He was hilarious and insisted on playing with a huge joke racket that gave him a far better chance of actually hitting the ball. We still beat them and then took on Cliff and Jo. We were victorious, much to our opponents' displeasure, because like us, they really wanted to make it through to the final. Even when I bump into Cliff now, he still reminds me about the time when I beat him at tennis.

That meant that we were due to meet Mike and Virginia in the final. By this stage I had managed to convince myself that I was a serious contender as world number one, but I had the rudest of awakenings, because Virginia simply was not going to let us get anywhere near winning. She was a truly awesome player who ran rings around me. During one rally, she took pity on me and just before she hit the ball, she shouted out exactly where it would go and I was still unable to return it. By the end of the match, we had been trounced and I felt gutted to have lost. I had run about so much that the physio had to give me a massage to relax my muscles.

Virginia thought it was hilarious that I wanted to win so much, but I think she actually shared my mentality completely. I have never played tennis with anyone before or since who was so graceful and accurate and yet so committed to being a champion. I now value the lesson she taught me that day. In the end it boils down to one thing: whatever you do, whether actor, singer or sports star, strive to do it to the very highest possible standard and to the best of your ability. I have always respected people who want to be champions and nowhere is this characteristic more apparent than in the cut-throat world of sport.

After I had licked my wounds, we all went back out on to the court for a traditional Cliff Richard sing-along. After he had performed a few of his hits, he invited everyone to join in some Christmas carols. Mike, Jimmy and even the tennis players joined in with gusto. Although I mouthed the words, my voice remained completely silent, because I was no longer a boy with a nice soprano voice. I had started my foray into other areas of the entertainment world, becoming a jack of all trades. The other people standing next to me on the court could not quite believe that I was silent because they still thought of me as a singer, but I was adamant that nobody would hear me sing in public for a very long time to come.

During my A-level years, I wasted a lot of time messing around. I suppose that I had become bored with school. I started playing tennis for up to five hours a day and would often avoid going to lessons altogether, which was easy to do in the sixth form. Looking back, I don't think that I would have made it through to my A levels without the release that playing tennis gave me. I was studying English, Music and Computing, with the latter the only subject that I really enjoyed at the time. To my eternal shame, I realise now that I was particularly disruptive in the music classes, where I was always made to sit on my own, because if I was with somebody else then we would get no work done at all. The only explanation I have for this behaviour is that for the preceding seven years, every moment of every day had been taken up without me having to think about it and now I was having to get used to being far less busy.

Questions were starting to form in my mind about what I would end up doing as a job in the long run. I was starting to think that it would be something in the entertainment industry – I certainly never considered doing a proper job that involved sitting behind a desk all day.

I developed a taste for presenting television after being invited to front an ITV children's programme called *Chatterbox* by Peter Murphy, the man who went on to discover Ant and Dec when they played the roles of PJ and Duncan in the children's drama *Byker*

Grove. Peter was working on a new format, which was to be made by HTV in Bristol and networked across Britain. It would be a discussion programme for kids tackling the serious subjects that were important to them. I was involved from the start of the development process, when a few aspiring presenters who were all near my age got together in a big empty room in Bristol and helped Peter and his team to brainstorm ideas. There were around a dozen other kids and we all started talking. Peter listened and put together a show that covered the topics that we all cared about.

From this came a pilot programme, in which I worked with three other presenters – a guy called Michael and a girl called Vanessa, who both introduced the features, and a guy called Von from Cardiff, who was a bit younger than us and presented some of the more wacky elements. I did the interviews with guests and involved members of the studio audience, who were all kids, in the discussions about topics thrown up during the show.

The series was commissioned, but Vanessa and Von left the show along the way. I bumped into Von more than a decade later in his job as a security guard at the Welsh Assembly. We had a great chat reminiscing about old times and he proved to be just as nice a bloke now as he was back when we were kids. Vanessa was replaced by another girl called Josie, who was great fun.

On the morning that we were making the first proper programme, I had the old feelings of excitement mixed with nerves, which I used to get before performing a solo in Bangor Cathedral. I desperately wanted to get everything right on the show, so I went to the empty studio two hours earlier than everyone else, just so that I could walk through each of my positions in front of the camera. It turned out to be great experience for the future, because I learned how to keep talking on screen while simultaneously listening to instructions in my ear from the very suave, Rolex-wearing director called Ken, whom I idolised. It's a bit like getting the hang of patting your head with one hand while rubbing your stomach with the other.

We presenters were given every possible luxury and were treated like stars. The show was important to HTV and it was well staffed. I must admit that we all felt that we had really hit the big time. We had people looking after our wardrobe and make-up. We were taken out to dinner every night and special parties were laid on for us. I interviewed some of the big stars of children's television at the time on the show: Michaela Strachan, Gary Wilmot and even the very naughty Gilbert the Alien, who was operated by an extremely talented puppeteer called Phil Cornwall. The programme also covered some tough issues such as bullying, drugs and glue-sniffing.

Not long afterwards, I co-presented the ITV Telethon in Wales with Arfon Haines Davies, who was the main local-news anchor, and Ruth Madoc, famous for her role as Gladys Pugh in *Hi-de-hi!* Michael Aspel was the main network host for the 27-hour fundraising event in London. It was my first-ever live television and I was very glad of the experience I had gained on *Chatterbox*. Everything had to be timed to the second because most of the programme was broadcast across the whole of the UK with shorter segments originated in the local regions. We were reading words from Autocues, which were being written just moments before we had to say them, so it made things a little hair-raising.

The first time that I had to present a link without another presenter alongside me on screen, I heard the director shout in my ear, 'The tape's gone down. Aled, you're going to have to fill for the next two minutes.' I kept on talking and just out of the corner of my eye I could see the Welsh comedian, Owen Money, sitting in the audience. I ran over to him and started a completely unplanned interview. I noticed he was wearing funny socks, so live on air, I asked him to take them off. Turning to the camera, I said, 'Anyone who fancies Owen Money's socks, give us a call right now and make a bid. Remember, it's all for charity.' I managed to keep it going until it was time for us to cross back to London. Afterwards, I was hailed as the saviour of the programme, which was something of an overstatement. One of the more memorable opportunities I had on the evening was dancing with Catherine Zeta Jones, who was then just starting her West End career. She was wearing a beautiful 1940s sequined dress and dance shoes. She did her solo number and I could hear the director saying in my ear, 'Why don't you do a dance with her?' I did as I was told, but unfortunately I was completely unprepared for the occasion with a pair of clumpy trainers on my feet. I am not sure if the sight of Catherine teaching me how to tap dance was good television or not.

School continued throughout the time I was recording *Chatterbox*, although I was still not enjoying it. I was having a drink with some friends in a pub called the Belle Vue in Bangor on the night before one of our English exams. They were all testing each other on the set texts. I knew that I hadn't even read one of the books about which I was going to be asked to write an essay the following morning, and I wasn't even the slightest bit bothered. My class-mates were talking about characters whose names I didn't know. Thinking back now, it's not something that I feel proud about, but for some reason right then, I simply didn't want to revise. Maybe this was my teenage rebellion, although it didn't manifest itself in any other way – I never reacted badly to Mam or Dad or went out clubbing every night. I think that basically, I had big adjustments to make to my life and am grateful to my then-girlfriend, who helped me through that transition period, because I had her as a constant companion.

During our time in the sixth form, all of our thoughts started to drift towards what we would do next. University or college? Some time off? Or maybe straight into the world of work?

I decided that I would like to get back into music, so I had some lessons from Yvonne Mathias, the wife of the eminent Welsh composer William, who was probably best known for writing music for the wedding of the Prince and Princess of Wales. The hours I spent with Yvonne were always great fun as halfway through, Bill would invariably emerge from his study having written some masterpiece or other. He would take over at the piano while Yvonne and I sang along. Then he would suddenly stop and say, 'Tell you what we need. Gin and tonic.' So the three of us would have a drink, before carrying on with the lesson. He was a true genius and his larger-than-life characteristics were matched by those of his wife. She helped me a great deal with getting back into the swing of disciplined music. I loved going for lessons in the Mathias household and the world lost a unique composer far too early when Bill died in 1992.

When I was a boy, Dr George Guest, the Organist and Master of the Choristers at St John's College, Cambridge, wrote a letter to Andrew Goodwin after he had heard me singing. In it he said that I had the three qualities that all good boy sopranos should possess: a very good voice, an innate musicianship and the ability to give a public performance without showing any nerves. George was himself a native of Bangor and so it seemed logical that I should consider going to St John's.

George arranged for me to attend one of the formal interviews and Dad drove me down to Cambridge. We were on our way into the college, when the porter stopped Dad and said, 'Oh no, sir. This is just for the boys.' So Dad spent the whole day wandering around Cambridge, not knowing what was going on. I was very self-conscious when I walked into a room full of other boys, because they all knew who I was and what I had been doing over the past few years. The surroundings seemed very austere and antiquated to me. We were given a talk about how the day would progress and a sheet was handed out containing a list of all the applicants' names. Almost everyone was double-barrelled and they attended the Premiership of the finest public schools in the land. Right at the end, next to my name, were the words 'David Hughes Comprehensive'. It stood out more than ever because it was such a long name compared with 'Eton' or 'Harrow'.

I sensed that George understood my unease and he did everything possible to quell my fears. He put me with the college's organ scholar, Andrew Nethsingha, who is now Director of Music at Gloucester Cathedral. He was a great guy who did everything possible to help me. The first part of the entrance test was a sight-reading, which I was very nervous about because it was something I hadn't done for a very long time, whereas it had been second nature to me back in my Bangor Cathedral days. We were asked to sing a motet in front of all of the other applicants and the existing students. George played the piano and I could hear him helping me along by banging out the note for me. My pre-prepared piece came next. Foolishly, I had chosen 'How Lovely Art Thy Dwellings'. George gave me quite a few opportunities to get it right before stopping and saying, 'It's too big for you, isn't it?'

'Yes, I'm really struggling,' I replied.

'I don't know if it's the right time for you to be doing this, you know. I don't think that your voice is ready. Why don't you come back again in a year's time?'

I was despondent on the long car journey back from Cambridge to Llandegfan.

Before he retired, my Uncle Arthur had been in charge of the London office of the music publisher Riccordi and he knew absolutely everybody in the classical-music scene in the city. He suggested that I go to see Ken Bowen, the Head of Voice at the Royal Academy of Music. Yvonne taught me some pieces for the audition and I was invited down to London for the afternoon with instructions to bring my accompanist with me. Uncle Arthur arranged for the renowned Nina Walker, who used to be the *répétiteur* for the Royal Opera House, to accompany me for the day. When I turned up at the Royal Academy, the lecturers were far more impressed to see Nina than they were to see me. I sang my pieces, which I had chosen more carefully this time, and then I was given half an hour to get to know a sight-reading piece. Nina and I went over it and I found that I had time to learn it completely, so I was able to go back into the room and perform it without the copy, which, looking back, seems a bit flash. They didn't seem particularly impressed and obviously thought that I had learned the piece somewhere else beforehand.

The next stage of the entrance test was a poetry reading. 'Do not go gentle into that still night' by the great Welsh poet Dylan Thomas was chosen for me. Afterwards, one member of the selection board told me that my reading was disappointing. I left the Academy feeling disheartened once again.

The Academy got back in touch and suggested that I join the intermediate course, which is attended by people in their late teens, who come to the building every Saturday for lessons. Many famous musicians have been through the course, including Sir Elton John. But I had got it into my head that I would either study on the performance course, which lasted for four years, or I would not go to the college at all. My persistence paid off and I was offered a place at the Royal Academy. It meant that I would be leaving home, moving from Llandegfan to London. It also meant that, in my mind at least, my childhood was behind me and I was an adult. As it turned out, my second childhood was just beginning.

12. THE MUSIC STUDENT

When I say that I was leaving home, I am almost telling the truth. Mam and Dad were certainly back in Llandegfan, far away from London. But I was moving into the spare room of Uncle Arthur's flat in Baker Street, which was remarkably close to the Royal Academy of Music, so it was more 'home from home'. Mam came down on the train and I didn't seem to have packed much stuff – just a couple of bags. I think she wanted to prolong for as long as possible the time before she actually had to say goodbye and acknowledge that I had left home.

On the first morning, I walked into the Academy in a state of great excitement. I had the sense of being surrounded by history, but at the same time, for me personally, I was about to begin something new, a sort of voyage of discovery. After we had signed in, all of the freshers were herded into Dukes Hall, where we heard speeches from the Principal, David Lumsden and from the President of the Students' Union. It was riotous because many people in the crowd appeared to be armed with water pistols. If college is like this every day, then I'm going to love it, I thought to myself.

After the speeches, all of the new students were gathered together for coffee. This was our opportunity to size each other up for the first time. Everyone was in the same situation, knowing either nobody at all or just a few other people. The questions were always the same and are probably common to all such occasions in universities and colleges everywhere: 'Where do you come from?'

and 'What A level results did you get?' There was one added
question at the Academy: 'What's your instrument?'

Considering how many people were there in the room, it seemed
as though fate had a hand in propelling me towards three particular
people who were to become my best friends throughout my time at
college. The first to introduce herself was a girl called Heidi
Moulinié, who came from Sidcup. 'I'll play the piano for you if you
need anyone,' she said. It turned out that she was both an amazingly
proficient pianist and had a terrific personality too. Added to the
fact that she confessed to having liked my singing as a boy, what
more could I have asked for? We instantly became firm friends.

The other two people I met were a countertenor called Charlie
Humphries and a double bass player called Dominic Seldis. Charlie,
who had bleached blond hair, bonded with me instantly because he
was a fellow singer. Dominic had studied at Chetham's in Manchester, one of the finest music schools in the country. He seemed to
already know everyone at the Academy. We spent the rest of the
day together going from room to room to hear talks about how we
would be spending the next few years.

I was on the Performance Course, which meant no degree or
anything like that. We were there to learn how to become
professional musicians and nearly everything we did was centred on
actually performing. They did manage to slip in a history of music
class and a theory class, but most of my time was spent studying
with Kenneth Bowen, who was a fellow Welshman and the Head
of Voice at the Academy at that time. My second instrument was
piano, which was something of a joke, because I was pretty useless
at it. I think I only managed to learn one tune in my first year – a
Chopin nocturne.

We were given a guided tour of the Academy and I noticed the
older students I came across in the corridor were nudging each other
and pointing at me. It was something that I had grown used to.
Mam had stayed with Uncle Arthur for the day and we were due to
go out to dinner to his favourite restaurant, a family-run little
Italian called Anacapri in Dorset Street, which is almost his second
home. It has since become one of my favourite restaurants in
London and still has photographs of me on the wall. Before the
evening meal, Charlie and I decided that we would nip into the bar
at the Academy for a quick drink. It turned out to be a hellhole,
with very little lighting, broken furniture and hundreds of people

squashed into a very small space. We walked in and looked around the sweaty mass of bodies. Very quickly, Charlie and I realised that we were the only first-years in the room. 'Oh, no. This is going to be awful,' he said.

We bought ourselves drinks and wandered over to where some students we had met earlier were sitting. You can always spot a singer at music college a mile off – they are the ones wearing scarves to protect their voices even when it's sunny, while talking in a 'frightfully loud fashion'. They are the exact opposite to brass players, who are far more likely to be downing pints or pouring them over each other's heads.

I didn't feel that I belonged in the group at first because all of the second and third-years started to make fun of me. Someone thought that it would be good sport to make me drink a yard of ale, as a sort of rite of passage into their number. The special glass was brought down from its home above the bar and I was handed it, brimming full of beer. This could so easily have been my undoing, but luckily I knew what to do with a yard of ale. You must twist the bell of the glass because otherwise, when you are nearing the end of the drink, the bubbles will suddenly shoot all over your face. I successfully drank the yard and at that moment, I became one of the crowd. I was left alone and felt as though I fitted in, although I have to say that we were an odd bunch. Many kids at school are teased for studying classical music, so by being together in the Academy, we gained the confidence that comes from being in a huge group of people who have all endured the same thing.

The Academy bar very quickly became the centre of our college lives. I became good friends with a couple of violinists from Singapore who lived around the pool table drinking snakebite – a heady mixture of lager and cider. Many of my fellow singers stopped visiting the bar because it had become very dilapidated and smelly, but I loved it. I became friendly with a percussion player called Colin, who ran the place. He in turn was mates with the feisty Students' Union president, Peter, who spent his days writing long agendas for the regular meetings at which he would berate the Academy's governors. Peter was a great character: very well spoken and always dressed in a pinstripe suit. He drove everywhere in his beloved MG. He was hyper-efficient, a rarity for any student, and it made him one of the best presidents the Academy ever had. I became his vice president in the second year and got to know him very well.

I suspect that in my early days at the Academy, the other singers mothered me a little bit. Some of them were very interested in what I had done as a kid. There was a strange irony in my studying 'performance' there, though, because in the whole of my three years at the Academy, I never once sang solo in front of anyone except my singing teacher and accompanist. I simply wasn't confident enough of my new voice at the time. I felt that there was a great deal of pressure on me to be able to sing well as an adult and that pressure turned me into something of a singing recluse. I had the sense that everyone was waiting to listen to me and pass judgement. However, I was unworried about being heard singing as part of an ensemble, so very early on, Charlie and I auditioned for the Academy's chamber choir, which was run by a very extrovert teacher called Geoffrey Mitchell and was acknowledged to be the best choir in the college. My sight-reading was back up to scratch because I had done so much practising in my attempt to get into Cambridge, but even I was unready for the bizarre audition piece that we were given. We were asked to sing 'Jack and Jill went Up the Hill' to a totally different tune and rhythm to the nursery rhyme that everyone knows. It was very testing, but both Charlie and I made it through into the choir. I found that it was great to be one of sixteen people, rather than a soloist at the front. I simply didn't have the guts at the time to sing on my own.

When the opportunity came later on to go to Paris with the Academy's orchestra, I seized it – but not as a singer. I went along as the roadie, with responsibility for wheeling the piano on and off stage and for packing the musical instruments into the van. The vice principal turned to me and said, 'Every time I see you in a dinner jacket, I think you're going to be performing. I can't believe you're just here to push the piano around.' I, however, was very happy with my new-found anonymity.

I was not quite so anonymous, though, when I made my first trip to Highbury to watch Arsenal. People always seemed to believe that I was a Liverpool supporter when I was a kid, but I have always followed Arsenal. One or two people in the crowd had recognised me as I stood cheering on the team and there was some good-natured banter. All of a sudden, the whole of the North Bank and part of the Clock End started to chant – and it literally was hundreds of people. The tune was familiar – from the hymn 'Guide Me, O Thou Great Redeemer'. It's often sung at football grounds by victorious fans when the supporters of a losing team fall silent. Then the words became clearer: 'Aled Jones, Aled Jones, You're not singing any more, You're not singing any more.' I went bright red, but inside it felt brilliant and I didn't have to buy anyone a pint that night. It was so great that it happened in Highbury of all places. I have developed a particularly strong affection for the place. It was a dream come true when I was invited to sing at the Millennium Stadium in Cardiff many years later, but it remains an even bigger dream of mine to sing on the hallowed turf of Highbury in front of a capacity crowd, before the stadium is redeveloped. I really do love Arsenal so much.

There is no question that I had a great time at the Academy, living life to the full and doing everything that you would expect a boy from Anglesey to do once he had been let loose in London with no parental control. I was adamant that there was a life for me outside singing. I had enjoyed a great innings as a boy soprano and had been given musical opportunities beyond most people's wildest dreams. Now, I was more interested in going to pubs and chatting up girls and I am not ashamed to say that I was a party animal throughout my time at the Academy. It was something I had to do.

We would go out on the town most nights – a particularly favourite haunt was a pub called the Devonshire Arms which had the words 'Full price + + Half Price + + Free + + 2-for-1' scrolling along a computer display along the bar. You were given a remote control and whichever the screen stopped at when you hit the button, that was what you paid. I always made sure that we had my good mate Joe, a percussionist, with us because his timing was so precise that he could always make sure that it stopped on 'Free'. We never paid for any drinks there at all. Countless days were spent at the Trocadero, just off Leicester Square. Charlie, Joe, Mark (a huge viola player), George (a jazz pianist), good old Heidi and I would play on the dodgems and would zap each other in the Laser Quest. When I think of the Academy now, it makes me smile. It was a wild time, when I was very much the normal student.

I was elected on to the Academy's bar committee during the first year and by the second year, I was running the whole thing. It was a job that I took seriously, even coming back a day early at the start of the first term to try to spruce up the bar, so that it was a little less daunting for the first-years. The security guard and I found some old furniture and replaced the broken tables and chairs. By the end of the evening, it looked a little better but was in desperate need of the complete refit which it finally received after I had left the Academy.

At the beginning of the third year, I decided to stand to be president of the Students' Union. I was up against a girl called Sophia, who received all the votes from the serious musicians who never went to the bar. I, on the other hand, had all the votes from those people who were regular drinkers. My campaign was led by an influential friend called Rachel, who walked around wearing a big home-made sandwich board bearing the legend 'Vote Aled'. I won by a healthy margin and took on the presidency. I decided not to take the wage normally paid out for doing the job, as the Union was in debt when I took it over. It was in exactly the same amount of debt when my term of office was over a year later.

My lasting legacy as president was to arrange social evenings, because I believed that quite a few of the musicians there had no life but music, which was not at all healthy. Having said that, maybe I had a little too much of a life and not enough music. But that did not stop me from organising a cracking ball at the Grosvenor House Hotel and jazz and Halloween nights in the bar.

I did do some proper work while I was at the Academy and ended year one by winning the Arthur Burcher Prize for gaining a first. Each week, I would learn four new songs with Heidi, which we would then go through with Ken Bowen. But by this stage, much of my time was being spent in a pop group I had set up with a group of mates.

Going by the name of A2Z, we were the busiest band in the world. I don't mean busy in terms of the number of gigs we had, but rather in the style that we played our music. The idea for the band came from my bass-playing friend Dominic Seldis and George Muranyi (the jazz pianist from our Trocadero exploits), who introduced two friends of his: Tony Lopez, who played guitar like Jimi Hendrix, and a drummer known as Ginger Skellern to his friends, because he had ginger hair and looked like a skeleton. Other band members included Orefo Orakwve, who always looked particularly stylish, helped no doubt by the discount he got on clothes from his part-time job in Next in Hammersmith. He has since played bass on many hit records.

Over time, we also added a brass section, led by Gareth Small, who is now assistant principal trumpet with the Hallé Orchestra in

Manchester. He was joined on saxophone by Nathan 'Jonnie' Webb, a student across town at the Guildhall School of Music and Drama, and Dave Holt, who was a superb classical trombonist in the Academy.

Our weekly rehearsals were punctuated by creative differences, which often turned into full-blown rows. The rehearsals took place in a dive in King's Cross called The Playground, which was the most inappropriately named venue in the world. It was used as a rehearsal space by the Shamen, a group who had a hit with a record called 'Move Every Mountain'. Everyone else who rehearsed there belonged to loud, rocky, Goth bands. We looked and sounded completely incongruous with our well-scrubbed appearance and our delicate blend of jazz and pop. At the time, though, this was completely lost on us and we thought we were the bee's knees.

As well as playing in the bar at the Academy, where we always received a warm reception, we were the resident band at the Rock Garden restaurant in Covent Garden. But we also performed gigs in some very rough pubs, including one where we arrived on stage while the bar staff were still clearing up the broken glass from the riot caused by the previous act.

An intelligent loveable hippy-type called Andy, who was one of the people who ran The Playground, became our manager. He managed to secure us a gig in Oxford and hired a minibus to take us and our instruments there in style. Andy was an incredibly patient man and drove around London picking us up. When we arrived at the house in Heston where George lived with his Hungarian father, our pianist dragged a huge bin into the bus. It was packed full of ice and around a hundred bottles of beer.

We decided that no visit to the city would be complete without a trip on a punt. We all clambered into a boat and set off, with Gareth standing at the back propelling us along. Suddenly, George stood up and pushed the fully clothed Gareth into the river. The next thing we knew, half the band were swimming around in the water in the centre of Oxford. Tony the guitarist made his way to the bank, stripped off all of his wet clothes except for his underpants and marched away. A few minutes later, he arrived at Marks and Spencer, still wearing nothing but his underpants and asked a startled shop assistant, 'Excuse me, please, could you tell me where the underwear section is?' Once directed to the right part of the shop, he bought some dry underpants, put them on in a changing room and then marched out of the shop and back to the river.

In the meantime, we had met a group of girls on another punt, whom we had cajoled into coming along to our gig that night. When we arrived at the venue later in the day, they were all there, as promised. The only problem was that they made up the entire audience. As we went on stage to do our sound check, we hoped that things would get busier in time for the proper performance. As the lead singer, I took it upon myself to look as rock'n'roll as possible, so I was wearing dark glasses. Along with my smart leather jacket and chinos, I must have been a ridiculous sight. The sound check went well and we vibed ourselves up for the main event. We bounded on stage to discover that the six girls had left, thinking that our sound check was, in fact, the proper performance, and our audience consisted of an elderly couple who had arrived early for the folk act that was following us. George was in tears of laughter.

Our performance was inauspicious and the journey all the way to Oxford had not seemed that worthwhile. We polished off the rest of the beer in the minibus on the way home. By the time we reached George's house in Heston, all of the ice in the beer bin had turned to water. We helped George to carry it off the bus, but before shutting the back doors he turned around and, with a superhuman effort, lifted the bin and threw all of its contents into the back of the bus, soaking all of the other members of the band. Poor old Jonnie bore the brunt of the attack and I feared he had developed pneumonia by the time we dropped him off. Andy, our manager, delivered the minibus back to the hire firm and posted the keys through the office door. The next morning, it was booked for an outing by the Women's Institute. Unfortunately, it was still soaking wet and stank of beer. Poor old Andy lost his £150 deposit, so he made a huge loss on that gig.

The band made a couple of recordings in a studio we had hired for an hour or two in the middle of the night when the rates were at their very cheapest, but it was never our intention to take it seriously and try for a record deal. We did pay a visit to Bill Curbishley, who managed the Who, just to see what he made of us. He turned around to me and said, 'Listen, you don't need these guys. I'll sign you and try to get you some sort of record deal, but no way with the band.' But I didn't want to go down that pathway – I was having far too much fun with my friends.

The highlight of A2Z's career came when we played the legendary Marquee club. We were booked as the support act to the Goth heavy-metal group the Blessed, after their original support backed out. As we walked on stage, we were all aware that this was a big gig for us. The brass section walked on first and started playing, then the drummer walked on and joined in. He was followed by the bass player, the lead guitar and George on keyboards. I went on last and shouted, 'Good evening, London!' which was greeted with a resounding silence from the audience. Heidi, my accompanist, had dragged along a couple of other girls and, rather bizarrely, the Vice Principal of the Royal Academy of Music had come along to watch, too. Nearly all of the Blessed's fans were still at the bar.

We were awful, absolutely awful. The brass players were so drunk that they were all slightly out of tune with one another, so every time they played together it sounded terrible. Our set was only forty minutes long, but that didn't stop me from managing to forget not only the words but also the melody to at least one song, which was unforgivable. We made a recording of our performance and laughed hysterically at it afterwards, because I could quite clearly be heard wailing appallingly over the music. We must have been one of the worst acts ever to grace the Marquee's stage. To top it all, unbeknown to us, a reviewer from the *Guardian* was lurking at the back of the hall, waiting for the Blessed. When we walked on stage before them, all of his prayers must have been answered at once. He quite justifiably ripped us to shreds because we were so terrible. I was once again wearing my shades and leather jacket and he described me in print as 'an insipid Michael J. Fox lookalike'. A2Z disbanded pretty smartly afterwards.

My time at the Royal Academy was made even happier because I would often eat out with Uncle Arthur, who was in his early seventies, and his best friend Melville, who lived a couple of floors above him in his block. Because Uncle Arthur had been involved in classical music all of his life, there were often drinks parties in his flat involving all sorts of people from that world. I enjoyed spending time with Uncle Arthur and Melville, particularly because the pace of their lives provided a little respite from my frenetic college life. We would often sit drinking wine on the fire escape outside Melville's flat on hot idyllic summer evenings, looking out over the streets of London below. I consider these to be some of the happiest

I have spent in the city. I learned so much from Melville, who was a real maverick with a heart of gold.

In the middle of my second year at the college, an offer came through to my classical-music agent, Harrison Parrott, for me to do a play in Northampton. I liked the sound of it so I travelled up to meet the director, Michael Napier-Brown, with my manager, Lydia. He was putting on a new version of Richard Llewellyn's novel *How Green Was My Valley*, written for the stage by Shaun McKenna. He was interested in me playing the lead boy, Huw, after hearing me playing a small role in a play broadcast on BBC Radio Four. Michael asked me to read a few lines and then offered me the role. 'Why not?' I thought to myself. So I took six weeks off from the Academy and moved temporarily to Northampton.

Once again, I found the actor's lifestyle to be great fun, just as I had done when I worked with Gyles Brandreth in Cambridge. I stayed in the spare room of a house owned by a woman called Norma, who worked in the press office of the Royal Theatre. We had a good laugh together, but she was a very maternal figure who kept an eye on me throughout my time there. I loved the role, but in all honesty, there was very little acting required. I played the part of a young Welshman, which was something for which I was pretty well suited. I shaved off all of my hair so that I looked more like a miner. The most nerve-racking part of the role was a stage kiss, which I panicked about for ages beforehand. What would happen if I had bad breath? What would happen if *she* had bad breath? As it turned out, it was one of the more pleasant parts of the many roles I have had since.

I loved being in Northampton and away from London. The actors who were working beside me were all superb at their job and I learned so much just from watching and listening to them. Sometimes, when a group of people come together to perform in a play, there is a feeling of great camaraderie and this was one of those occasions. We were one big family in the story on stage, and off stage we were just the same, doing everything together and spending many a happy hour in each other's company.

Whenever I did anything new, it tended to attract the attention of journalists who had still not forgotten the mass of interest in my voice breaking. The big question for them now was whether I would have a strong singing voice again in the future. One of my favourite newspaper interviews, which took place just before *How*

Green Was My Valley began its run, was with Jean Rook, who wrote for the *Daily Express* and was known as 'the First Lady of Fleet Street'. When she came to see me, I was scared that I would receive a savaging; after all, she had made her name by saying what she thought. In reality, she could not have been nicer and the profile piece she penned included one of my favourite ever quotes about my voice breaking a few years before. She wrote that it was 'The Voice which caused the greatest crack since Humpty Dumpty'. It was at the time when I was not yet confident enough in my adult voice to sing in public, but nevertheless Jean was adamant about her feelings that I would go on to make a career as a singer. I wish that she were still alive today so that I could show her that her predictions have come true.

At the end of the run, I returned to the Academy and carried on from where I had been before, taking lessons from Kenneth Bowen and running the Students' Union bar in my spare time. At the end of my second year, Michael Napier-Brown asked me back to Northampton to take the lead role in *Martin Chuzzlewit*. I thought about it long and hard and decided to go back to the Royal Theatre, the scene of my acting debut a few months before.

This time, I hated it because I was dreadful. Everyone else was speaking in Received Pronunciation, but I was a Welsh Martin Chuzzlewit, which I am sure is not what Charles Dickens had intended. Michael had shown a lot of faith in me in giving me the part in the first place and I felt that I had let him down. When he asked me to do it, I should have said, 'No thanks, I don't think this one's for me.' I was foolish to take the part, although my mistake underlined to me that everything in a career as a performer is about choice – the difference between success and failure often centres on the choices that you make along the way.

We did all of the rehearsals and I was technically competent in the role by the opening night, but a few days into the run, I thought to myself, 'You're out of your depth, mate.' Usually a play gets better during its run, as the actors become more practised in their roles, but I wasn't showing any improvements. I was stuck and had taken the character as far as I could.

The reviews were all right, but they all said that the new production was nowhere near as good as *How Green Was My Valley* had been. I sensed the same feeling among the cast as well. There was a young boy in the play who forgot his lines a couple of times, forcing one of the other actors to shoo him off the stage with the words, 'Well, anyway, off you go.' This cut away a whole scene that explained many intricacies of the plot. The audience must have been very confused.

One night, about four weeks into the run, three of us were due to appear in front of the audience on a revolving part of the stage. We missed our cue, so the stage moved around to reveal just one of the three actors. The audience then heard a door banging and the two of us ran on to the stage. The one actor who had been there on time was sitting in a chair reading the newspaper. He slowly folded it up and said very pointedly, 'Nice of you to turn up.' Well, that was it, the three of us were totally gone, and we turned away from the audience, our bodies shaking with laughter and tears streaming down our faces. Eventually we carried on with the performance and thought no more of it, until we were out shopping the next day. A woman in the bakery refused to serve the other two actors when they tried to buy sandwiches for lunch, because she said that the play had been a disgrace the night before. We all promised ourselves that we would stop, but we simply could not control ourselves, so every night for the final two weeks of the run, we corpsed all the way through that scene. Michael was very angry with us and gave us a severe dressing-down.

During my second period in Northampton, I happened to say in a local newspaper interview that I would love to do some radio. One of the bosses at BBC Radio Northampton invited me into his office for a chat and offered me my own programme on Saturday mornings between nine o'clock and midday for six weeks. I had never done anything like it before so I needed some training – and fast. I worked first with one of the most experienced presenters on the station, David Saint, and then with a brilliant guy called Steve Taschini, who became my producer for the six weeks. I had three hours to fill every week with a mixture of interviews, competitions, music and phone-in chat with the listeners.

I had a very clear idea in my mind of how I wanted the programme to sound – basically something approximating Steve Wright's show on BBC Radio One, which I had always thought was a brilliantly produced programme. I am not sure I really appreciated the amount of effort that a professional like Steve has to put into his programme each day, but I decided to give it a go nonetheless. I set off to London with a Uher tape recorder, loaned to me by my very trusting boss at BBC Radio Northampton, to record a cast of characters who would become part of my programme. Uncle Arthur's neighbour, Melville, was the voice for the very well-spoken gentleman who would reproach me throughout the programme with mad sayings such as 'I don't like your tone'. I recorded him saying about thirty different things that my producer put on to tape for me, so that they could be played out during the programme.

Each week, I would interview a celebrity, pulling strings wherever I could. So Ruth Madoc did a turn for me, and Anne Charleston, who played Madge in *Neighbours*, was also pressed into service. I begged a favour from a comedian in South Wales, Nigel Crowle, who had been one of the writers for *Chatterbox*. He would ring me up at a different time each week, pretending to be my Uncle Alwyn. The conversations would basically be a string of very corny one-line jokes, such as: 'Aled, I'm disgusted with you. Your Auntie cleaned out your room last week and found two dirty magazines – *Farming Weekly* and the *Shepherd's Gazette*.' The jokes were truly awful, but the highlight of the programme was when I invited the listeners to take part in karaoke on the radio. I never ceased to marvel at the number of people who would ring up asking to sing a particular song, to which it would turn out they knew neither the words nor the tune, once they actually went on air.

I don't think that I came anywhere near mastering radio in that six weeks, but it certainly gave me a taste for the medium. It also rekindled my appetite for hard work because after three hours on air in the morning, I would have to rush from the BBC Radio Northampton studios to the Royal Theatre for the matinee perform-ance of *Martin Chuzzlewit*, before going back on stage all over again in the evening.

Even though I was having a lot of fun learning about radio, I was still getting no better at playing my role. Michael Napier-Brown would often be backstage during performances and he would sometimes come across to me sitting on my own. He could see that I was gradually becoming more and more worked up with myself as the run went on. I was desperately keen to learn how to act properly and I had instilled in myself a rule that if I was going to come back and do something in the public eye, I was going to be good at it. The last thing in the world that I wanted was to be 'little Aled, who used to sing, and now tries everything but isn't very good at any of it'.

My early childhood –
growing up on Anglesey –
was a very happy and
peaceful time.

▶ Performing on stage in one of my trademark bow ties, sadly no longer a part of my stage wardrobe these days!

David Redfern/ Redferns

▼ With legendary Welsh tenor Stuart Burrows (seated) and Finnish Soprano Karita Mattila

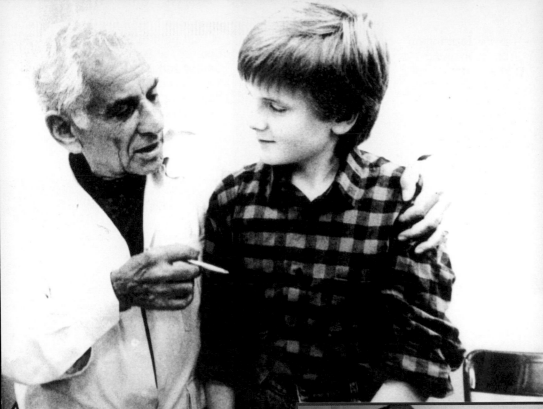

▲ Leonard Bernstein – a true star and my musical hero.

▶ With Sir Geraint Evans at the Eisteddfod.

▼ The light aircraft we hired so I could perform in a matinée at the Barbican in London and be back in time for an evening charity performance in North Wales.

◀ I sat next to Billy Connelly at Bob Geldof and Paula Yates's wedding. He had me in stitches the whole time.

▼ Thanks to 'Walking in the Air' I'll always be associated with this particular time of year.

▶ Leading the Welsh national anthem at Cardiff's Millennium Stadium.
Camera Press/David Williams

◀ I was a shameless autograph hunter in those days! Most people, like Linda Evans, were happy to oblige.

▼ On stage with Libera.
JM Enternational/Redferns

▲ With Cliff Richard at the Royal Albert Hall for a *Songs of Praise* fortieth anniversary concert in 2001. Whenever I see Cliff he still reminds me of the time I beat him at tennis.
David Fisher/LFI

◄ Welsh tenor Bryn Terfel at the Classical Brit Awards at the Royal Albert Hall.
Camera Press/James Veysey

► Claire and me at the christening of our daughter, Emilia, in St Paul's church, Covent Garden.
Getty Images

►► On holiday on Mustique – Emilia was eleven months old.

▼ Taking a break from my hectic dancing schedule in 2004 to support the Welsh team in a football international against England.
Joe Bangay/LFI

'What's the matter?' Michael asked me one night as I sat staring at the floor glumly.

'I know I'm bad at this and I don't know what to do,' I replied.

'Go to drama school,' he said emphatically.

'I suppose I could audition to go to RADA?'

'No, don't go there. Audition for Bristol Old Vic. I'll ring Chris Denys, the Principal, to see when the auditions are.'

It turned out that the auditions were happening soon afterwards and so I decided to give it a go. It was the toughest process I had ever been through. All of the tutors sat in a line in front of me and each of them asked me to do something for them. I started by doing a very powerful and moving scene from *How Green Was My Valley*, which is beautifully written. Huw, my character, is telling his mother how he has just witnessed the death of his father in a coal mine:

> Up against the coal face, he was. His head was on a pillow of rock. And sheets and bedclothes of rock covered him to the neck. And I saw if I moved one bit, the roof would cave in. Afraid, I was, to put my hands with tenderness on his face for fear my touch might be an extra hurt. But as the blood ran from his nose and mouth and the redness ran out of his eyes, I could see a shining smile in them that came from a brightness within. And I knew that he was my father, fighting still, and unafraid. And he smiled and went.

Then the singing teacher, Neil Rhoden, asked me to sing, which was one of the easier parts of the test. After that, I had to do a reading for Francis Thomas, the voice coach, before facing an interview from all of them, including Rudi Shelly, the Head of Acting and Chris Denys, the Principal. I told them that I wanted to go on the one-year course and they completely refused to countenance that, because it was for postgraduate students or those who had a lot of previous acting experience. They offered me a place on the two-year course instead. So, I went back to the Academy and talked through the offer with Ken Bowen. He agreed that it would be a good idea for me to take two years out from the Academy to go to Bristol, before returning to London to complete the final year of my singing course.

Before I left the Academy, I had one more important function to perform in my role as President of the Students' Union. At the end-of-year graduation, I had to make a formal speech to thank the guest of honour, who was giving out the awards. The thought of this worried me a great deal. So much so – and I have never admitted this to anyone before – that I gave my old friend Brian Kay a call. Brian used to be one of the King's Singers and now presents programmes for BBC Radio. I took him out to lunch and asked him if he would write the speech for me, because I felt that he would instinctively understand how to blend just the right level of humour with the sense of propriety necessary for the occasion. Needless to say, he wrote me an excellent speech, which went down very well with everybody except the brass players, who all thought it was a bit too posh. My career at the Academy ended with me being presented with the Princess Alice Award, which was given to the outgoing President each year. That evening, we all went to the Grosvenor House Hotel and the ball for which I had been bullying my colleagues to buy tickets for the past few months. I had discovered that attempting to sell tickets for anything to musicians is like trying to get blood out of a stone.

Although I was supposed to return to the Royal Academy two years later, in the end I went to the Bristol Old Vic and never went back to music college. The next two years would see me grow up enormously. Whereas I had spent three years at the Academy idling my time away, my years in Bristol were filled with twelve-hour-long days of hard work. We had no choice – either we did exactly what was required by our tutors or we were off the course. They were tough and demanding, but utterly brilliant at knocking aspiring actors into shape. I would learn more new skills and discover more about myself in the next two years than at any other time during my life.

13. JOCKSTRAPS AND JAZZ SHOES

A couple of weeks before I was due to start my course at the Bristol Old Vic, a list of essential items for all students arrived in the post. The set texts included the sort of thing that I had expected – *The History of the Theatre* and a vocal-exercises book – but I was more than a little surprised to see *Zen and the Art of Archery* there as well.

The other items were more on the practical side and I went to a dance shop in Covent Garden in the heart of London's theatreland. I chose some black tights and a pair of jazz shoes – these are small leather lace-ups for dancing. I then made my way to the counter, cleared my throat and asked nervously, 'Please could you tell me where the jockstraps are?'

The assistant, a matronly looking woman, asked, 'What size are you, dear?'

I had no idea how to respond. 'Er, large?' I stammered hopefully.

She looked me up and down and said, 'No, I think you'll probably be a medium. Here you are, why don't you go and try this on in the cubicle?'

I grabbed the jockstrap and rushed to the changing room. After I'd put it on, I stood looking at myself in the mirror and thought, 'What have I done?'

The drama school is made up of two huge houses on Downside Road in Bristol – the first for the stage-management students and the other for the acting students. There are one-year, two-year and three-year courses and the learning is very practical. Rather than concentrating on coming out with letters after your name, you hope to come out with an acting job.

I was apprehensive when I arrived in Bristol because I wasn't quite sure what I was letting myself in for. I knew that it was a very demanding course and I was worried about whether I would be able to stand the pace. My worst fears came true on the very first morning as we made our debuts in the dance class. It must have been quite a sight: a group of lads in their twenties and thirties, mightily embarrassed as they walked around the dance studio in the most ridiculous garb that you could ever imagine.

We looked dreadful in our white dance socks, black jazz shoes, flesh-coloured jockstraps, black tights and T-shirts. Very soon after we started, I made the discovery that I could not move for toffee – I was the world's worst dancer. Gail Gordon, the dance teacher, decided fairly early on that she was going to knock me into shape and would respond fiercely to my failures on the dance floor – slapping me across the legs and shouting, 'Point your feet!' I was not alone in earning Gail's disapproval. She would treat many of my male colleagues as if they were small children until they started to show signs that they could dance after all.

Later that day, I was put into a room with my thirteen fellow students on the two-year course. We were told to play a memory game. Sitting in a semicircle, the first person had to give their name and their claim to fame. The first person in the group said, 'Hello, I'm Charlotte and my claim to fame is that I can put a whole packet of bonbons in my mouth in one go.' Then came Dave, who had to remember Charlotte's claim to fame and add his own, and so the list would go on getting ever longer.

I was thirteenth out of the fourteen. 'My name is Aled. I'm from Anglesey and my claim to fame is that I used to sing a bit before my testicles dropped.' Everyone laughed. The person next to me was called Guy, who became one of my best friends at Bristol, but I had never spoken to him at this point. He rattled off everyone else's name and claim to fame faultlessly and then said, 'My name's Guy and my claim to fame is that I'm sitting next to my Granny's favourite singer.' The rest of the room collapsed laughing and nothing more was said about my boyhood career. That moment broke the ice completely, just as drinking the yard of ale had done at the Royal Academy.

Next we were given an exercise in trust run by John Hartock, who was a real character and a fine musician as well. His lessons were always high-octane and on this first occasion we had properly met, he told each of us, one at a time, to climb on to the mantelpiece above the fire. The rest of the group stood in a line with their hands linked together. The person on the mantelpiece then had to stand with their back to the group, close their eyes and fall straight back, safe in the knowledge that the rest of the group would catch them. It was all about building trust in each other. One by one, we all did it – although Chris Punter, who was a big chap, nearly wiped out an entire year of budding actors when he fell on top of us.

Chris Denys, the Principal, came to talk to us about what we could expect from the course. He explained that it would be hard work and that the teachers would make massive demands on us. We would have to learn and perform different audition pieces every week, which would be marked by the staff. The amount of learning and teaching was immense and I quickly came to understand why occasionally some people left the course because of the stress of keeping up with the expected workload. Chris ended his speech by telling us to make sure that we took care of ourselves. 'Some of you, especially the first-years,' he said, 'will no doubt find that you are living on nothing but baked beans.'

I have to confess that until this moment, my domestic thoughts had been limited to finding a house. My fellow student, Chris Punter, had a lovely house in the centre of Bristol and was renting it out to pay the mortgage, while he went to live with his parents. So I became his tenant along with a guy on the three-year course called Julian. I had a huge four-poster bed in my room and my new home was just a five-minute cycle ride away from the Old Vic – or at least it was before somebody nicked my bike.

Chris Denys's words made me realise that I hadn't bothered to go shopping, nor had I ever needed to go shopping before. In London, I had been looked after by Uncle Arthur, which basically meant going out to a restaurant for dinner every night. Most of the other students knew how to look after themselves because they had been away to university beforehand, unlike me. That evening, I walked back to the house and Julian was there, making himself toast and a cup of tea. 'What shall I eat?' I said to him. 'Well, I've got my cupboards here and I've left these ones for you,' he replied. I opened one of my cupboards and, of course, there was nothing in it. 'What do I do now?' I thought to myself. In the end I rang up for a takeaway pizza, but the next day I went and did my weekly shop, which was a whole new experience for me. Over the next two years, I became an expert in preparing ready-made meals, which was far easier than attempting to actually cook.

Very quickly, the Alma became our pub of choice and I became good friends with Richard, a Scot in my group who was exactly ten years older than me. After studying for a law degree at Cambridge, he had become a very well-paid lawyer in Hong Kong. He had done some acting on the side and eventually the lure of the stage became too strong, so he decided to turn his back on the law altogether and successfully auditioned for Bristol. We would have a pint of Directors' Bitter in the Alma each evening before going our separate ways. I would always take a couple of bags of Twiglets home with me from the pub and these became one of the main staples of my diet while I lived there.

We would have to go home to learn scenes from plays each evening, so we tended not to spend too long in the pub. I went to Bristol thinking that the actor's life consisted of a couple of hours' work a week – but this was far from the truth. We would often start at around half-past seven in the morning and we would still be in the school at six o'clock in the evening. Having experienced professional training for both actors and musicians, I can honestly say that actors without a doubt take everything far more seriously. As an actor, it's all about you, the individual. Your aspiration is that you will succeed on your own, while for the majority of musicians, hopes centre around joining an orchestra or playing as part of an ensemble. I think you have to be braver in acting because, for the average person, there is less money to be made than there is in music. Many of my colleagues at the Academy ended up becoming music teachers, while at Bristol very few people end up teaching acting, so you have to be good because the stark reality is that you get work as an actor, or you don't work at all. Very soon after I arrived in Bristol I realised that there was little chance I would return to the Royal Academy of Music.

We spent more time with John Hartock in the first few weeks building up our trust in the other members of the group and learning to use our senses – both vital if we were to become good actors. In one exercise, we would pair up and one person would be blindfolded while their partner guided them around Bristol city centre, crossing busy roads and going into packed shops. By the time I was there, the residents of Bristol were used to seeing these odd couples wandering around the town. In another exercise, two people closed their eyes and stood at either end of a room. One would play the role of the hunter and the other of the hunted. The hunter had to listen carefully and try to catch the other person using sound rather than sight. When it came to his turn, Chris Punter closed his eyes and charged to the other end of the room, bashing into the hunted, a very quiet Canadian exchange student. His head hit hers and split open her forehead. Needless to say, he was made of sterner stuff and there was not a mark to be seen on him.

Soon after we arrived in Bristol, there was a documentary on television about the Drama Centre in London, called *Don't Put Your Daughter on the Stage*. The initiation there was far stranger than the things we were asked to do in Bristol – very early on in the course, they made you walk into class naked in front of your classmates. One of the teachers came and spoke to us the day after it was shown.

'We don't agree with that sort of method of teaching,' he said. 'In our way of thinking, you will leave here and get a great job because you're in a top drama school. When you get a big role in a film, where you have to take your clothes off and you're earning millions, you don't mind doing it.'

Chris Denys is a remarkable man – in many ways he *is* Bristol Old Vic. He would always wear a checked lumberjack shirt and faded ripped jeans. It was very different to the Academy, where everyone who was in authority always dressed in a way that underlined this. At Bristol, teachers such as Gail Gordon and the Musical Director, Neil Rhoden, are brilliant motivators, but they are also hard taskmasters. They chip away at you as an actor, getting rid of your bad habits, whereas other drama schools seem to spend more time talking about your psychological problems to see if they can ultimately be used in your acting. At Bristol, they train you hard, giving you a better voice and making you fitter, but they also hold your hand as they teach you the other attributes as well, and that is something that I found so comforting.

A typical day for a student would begin, first thing in the morning, with a physical warm-up, which lasted about twenty minutes. It consisted of the stretching exercises that we did in dance classes and a little yoga. Our first lesson after that was usually a voice class with Francis Thomas. He taught us how to make all sorts of strange noises, while bashing our chests. Although this sounds odd – and looks even odder than it sounds – it had the desired effect, with everyone's vocal range changing dramatically within six months. I still use the techniques Francis taught us to warm up my voice before I sing on stage. His class lasted for an hour, which would leave us exhausted. We then went straight into an hour of dance class, which in the early days was all about learning to point and keep your leg up in the air, improving our basic fitness so that we would be able to tackle more complex routines in the future.

At the end of this lesson, it was only half-past ten in the morning and already we had done two and a half hours of very physical activity. We all changed out of our jockstraps and tights as soon as the dance lesson ended because they were so uncomfortable to wear for any length of time. We then went to Rudi Shelly's classroom for a History of Acting lesson, which was a chance for us to catch our breath. Rudi was a living legend, and had coached all of the greats who had passed through Bristol Old Vic's doors. He was particularly proud of the time he spent teaching Brian Blessed. Rudi would talk to us for an hour and a half about subjects such as the development of theatre, period costumes, and different methods of staging drama.

After lunch, we had another more practical lesson with Rudi, where he directed us in a scene from a play such as *School for Scandal* or some Shakespeare. One afternoon, he said, 'Today, we are going to waltz with a chair.' He picked up a chair and held it high over his head, instructing us all to do the same. After about three minutes, the girls started to flag and within ten minutes, so did the boys. My arms were killing me, but Rudi, who was at least eighty, stood in front of us without a care in the world with the chair still held high above his head. 'All of your postures have gone,' he said. 'You should pretend that you have a tangerine in your buttocks and you are wearing a bolero. Pull down your bolero and your posture will be correct.' We did exactly as he said and suddenly it was easier to carry the chair.

'Now we will waltz!' he said, before proceeding to teach the class the waltz steps. Suddenly he stopped and said, 'All of your postures have gone again.' This went on for an hour and we left the classroom feeling absolutely shattered. Our next class was about role-play under John Hartock's watchful eye. However, Rudi's day was not over: he spent another hour with a chair above his head teaching students from the three-year group how to waltz with it, just as he had done with us.

Role-play was one of my favourite classes, although on one occasion, which became infamous among my fellow students, I came a cropper. We all went to an imaginary bar in Bristol and were told to walk in one by one, each having chosen the status of the character we were playing. If your character was status level one, then he was arrogant and strong, while if you decided on status level five for your character, then he was as quiet as a mouse. We had to interact with the other characters in the bar and work out the status of the person we were talking to. I went into the bar like a bull in a china shop – very much status level one. 'I'll have a gin!' I bellowed at the barman. 'Come on, hurry up. What are you looking at?'

Guy came in straight after me and decided to knock me down a peg or two. He also chose status level one, but he was a better actor than me and said, 'Crap shirt you've got on.' Instantly, I panicked and said, 'What do you mean?' nervously. My status had collapsed back to a level five. Guy reached over and looked at the label in my shirt collar and said mockingly, 'Top Man, everyone!' People started laughing and I tried desperately to think of a way to regain my status and blurted out, 'It's not Top Man. It's *Topo Mano*. It's Italian.' The class had to stop because everyone collapsed laughing at me; John told us it was the worst status game he had ever seen.

As well as the voice and dance work, we also learned mime and puppetry during the first year of our course. I always thought that the mime teacher was very funny because after he had done anything he would say, 'Can you see it?' To which the correct answer was, of course, 'No!' because it was mime. We would learn how to walk up imaginary steps and how to fall over without hurting ourselves – even how to appear to be running up a wall.

My worst lesson was, without a doubt, yoga because I was somebody with so much energy. The thought of saluting the sun for half an hour was my idea of a nightmare. The girls on the course absolutely loved it and were all to be found at the front of the class, which took place in the dance studio in the basement of the house. It has been refurbished now, but in those days it looked a little squalid with mirrors all along one wall. We did yoga under the instruction of a teacher called Lynette, who was passionate about the benefits of her subject. Usually, Guy, Rich, Dave, Martin from New York and I had an outbreak of the giggles at some time during the class and Lynette would tell us off. The lesson always ended with a quarter of an hour of relaxation where we were told to lie on the floor with our eyes closed. The boys at the back often ended up punching or pinching each other. Everyone else left the dance studio saying how relaxed they felt, but we were like animals that had been caged for ninety minutes.

Music was an important part of the course and we had singing lessons with a teacher called Rita, who had a dog called Ben, the oldest, scabbiest animal I had ever seen. He seemed to moult at an alarmingly high rate and the floor of her room was always covered in dog hair. Although I went to her classes, the musical highlight of my day came when Neil Rhoden taught me songs from the shows in his room during lunch breaks. My mates all jokingly accused me of being teacher's pet, but I think that he saw me as something of a project and the work he did with me back then gave me a large repertoire of songs that I have relied on in auditions ever since.

Despite all of the hard work, there were plenty more fun times during the two years I spent in Bristol. For example, on Thursday evenings we would often all go down to Mrs Renato's, a pizzeria a few doors down from the Bristol Old Vic Theatre in King Street. Mrs Renato was a big Italian woman with a big heart. She ran the restaurant, which was a real family affair, with her husband behind the bar, her son waiting tables and her daughter in the kitchen preparing the pizzas. There was a piano in a corner of the restaurant and each week Mauro, a student on the three-year course, would sit at it and play. He was a fantastic pianist and could pick up any tune in moments. It became like a scene from *Fame*, with students singing show tunes together and each person doing their party piece. It was a great chance for us all to let our hair down. Needless to say, though, I never sang on my own, as I was still nervous about giving my voice a tryout in public.

Mrs Renato's pizzas had the uncanny ability to burn the roof of your mouth, no matter how long you left them on your plate or how long you blew on a slice before biting into it. The cheese always remained like molten lava, resulting in intense pain for many of the group every Friday morning, after they had injured themselves the night before.

One night, Richard and I were the only two people left in the bar at about two in the morning. Mrs Renato walked over to us and said, 'Boys, I have to go to bed. It's been a long day. I give you the key. You help yourselves to drinks and lock up if you leave. If you're here in the morning, I'll make you pizza for breakfast.' Richard and I decided that we would never be able to cope in Gail's dance class in the morning if we had no sleep, so we declined Mrs Renato's kind offer and wearily headed home.

On Saturday nights, I would spend the evening with another mate from the course, Martin, who was a very laid-back, very witty New Yorker. We would meet up at my house and eat sandwiches while watching *Baywatch* on the television, before heading out to sample the local ale on King Street.

On one occasion, Richard was giving a piggyback ride down this very same street to Jessie from the stage-management course, who also happened to be the daughter of the actress Jean Boht and the conductor Carl Davis. He tripped and fell on the cobblestones and smashed open his nose. There was blood everywhere and he was in shock, so we called an ambulance. Mrs Renato came out of her restaurant as he was being wheeled away by the paramedics and was famously heard to shout brightly, 'See you tomorrow night, then!'

I had my own injury from playing football during one lunch break. I was tackled and felt my ankle go weak. I went to hospital in Bristol and, after the obligatory three-hour wait, a doctor said to me, 'You've broken your ankle in two places. We'll put you in a cast for six weeks.' I was devastated – we had just started to learn how to tap dance and we were about to do a course on acting for television, where we would be filmed in a short cops-and-robbers programme. I had a really great part as one of the bad guys and Chris Punter was supposed to be the chief investigating officer. The television tutor had to recast everything and I became the chief policeman, which was terrible because it was totally unrealistic having someone who was only in their early twenties playing the role. I just couldn't pull it off.

I knew that I had to let Gail Gordon know, but I was terrified of having to tell her that I would be unable to take part in her dance lessons for nearly a whole term. I tried to pluck up the courage, but decided that hers was by far the scariest phone call that I had to make, so I called Chris Denys and Neil Rhoden first.

Chris's reaction was blunt when I told him what had happened. 'You're an idiot. If you were a professional actor, then you would be knackered now, unable to work. We'll just have to make allowances for you and change things around it.' Neil echoed his comments, telling me that I had let myself down and that I should not have been playing football. Later, Chris spoke to all of the other students and told them: 'You can do things like play football, but you've got to realise that if you had been cast in a film and broke your leg between casting and the start of filming, then you'd be out. That's it. And you might need that money to survive.'

During my call to Neil, he kept asking, 'Have you spoken to Gail yet?' It took me another hour or so to finally pluck up the courage to call her.

'Hello Gail, it's Aled.'

'I know, you've broken your leg, you idiot.' She had already found out and was absolutely lovely on the phone. She did, however, get her revenge, by making me go to every dance lesson and sit in the corner watching everyone else working. She could tell that I hated the fact that I was unable to join in and this helped me to develop a very strong rapport with her over the six weeks I was in plaster.

A couple of nights after I had broken my ankle, there was a barbecue at another student's house. We all spent the evening racing down a hill on my crutches. Funnily enough, I was faster than everyone else, so Guy decided to pour half a bottle of red wine into my cast to slow me down. It was completely invisible until a nurse cut off the plaster six weeks later. My leg was stained red and covered in mould. She was shocked.

'What the hell's happened here? You've been bleeding,' she exclaimed.

'Ah, no. I'm afraid it's wine,' I replied with some embarrassment, my face quickly turning the same shade of red as my leg. The nurse smiled as her initial shock and concern turned to amusement.

14. STAGECRAFT

A very important notice board in one of the corridors in the theatre
school suddenly became the centre of our universe towards the
end of the second term. This was where the castings would be
pinned up for each of our productions. It was the first time that a
competitive element entered into our group, with each of us looking
out for ourselves because we wanted to get good parts. We had
become so close by this stage, but there was always a little distance
between us around the time that castings were announced. Having
said that, Dave, Guy, Richard and I still gave each other a lot of
support.

It was not until the end of our first year in Bristol that we put on
our first proper production, *Alice in Wonderland*. I had two parts:
in the first half I was the Griffin, wearing a large, brown costume,
which virtually boiled me alive. I decided that the character was
nuts and should be played as energetically as possible, so I ran on
stage and bashed straight into a tree at the start of my performance.
From then onwards, it was physically very demanding and I would
walk off stage at the end of the first half dripping with sweat. After
the interval, I played the knave of hearts who stole the tarts and
Neil Rhoden wrote a song for me, which I sang as a camp cockney.
I was so exhausted at the end of each performance that if we had a
matinee and an evening show, I would have to go home for an
hour's sleep between the two.

Each week throughout the course, we auditioned two fresh pieces
of work – one had to be a classic such as Shakespeare and the other

would always be a modern piece. The idea behind this constant auditioning would be to widen the breadth of our repertoire. In the second year, we auditioned each week in front of professional casting directors and agents, but in the first year their role was played by members of the teaching staff.

Whoever was behind the desk, these auditions were always treated as being deadly serious. Chris Denys was absolutely ruthless, because he wanted to make the experience as realistic as possible. There was a time for each of us to be there written on a piece of paper in the corridor. We would check our time and then disappear off to a quiet corner for a final run-through of our pieces. When it was our turn, we would walk into one of the classrooms and Chris would be sitting with two other teachers behind a desk. You were even expected to dress as you would for an audition. They could throw absolutely anything at you and you would have to react accordingly. We would have to prepare a one-minute Shakespearean monologue, plus a one-minute modern monologue and often a song as well. Some weeks they would suddenly ask us to do a dance. They would even time the monologue and if you were over a minute they'd stop you and tell you to go. Sometimes they'd say hello and be welcoming – other times they would hardly look up and would ignore you, so you never knew how to react. Chris could be particularly demanding. The whole experience was very much focused on helping us to learn how to get jobs and we could see the pressure on those students a year ahead of us who were doing their auditions for real in front of casting directors.

Our next production was Shakespeare's *Twelfth Night*. I had never done any Shakespeare before and I found that it was very tricky, because it is impossible to ad-lib – you cannot make Shakespeare up. Performing in a modern play is easy by comparison. On the first night, I had a horrendous moment when I forgot a line – thankfully my mate Dave whispered it to me. I was fine after that and had no other dodgy moments in the entire run. It was the only time I had a problem learning words, apart from the 'Memory' incident in Edinburgh a few years before. I have always had a near-photographic memory and can scan words and learn them very quickly, which is handy as a television presenter because sometimes you are given scripts ten seconds before you have to do it live. However, there is no substitute for really learning something by going over it again and again. The more often you do it, the quicker it gets into your memory bank.

As we took part in more productions, there were patterns emerging and it was possible to start to see where different people would carve their niche within the industry. One would tend to be given comedy parts, another would always get the character roles; one would usually be the juvenile lead, another would always play the ruggedly handsome leading man. It was at that point that I understood why the teachers chose so carefully who would get into the school in the first place; there is no point in having 25 actors in one year group who are all the same. People like me were clearly chosen because we would end up doing musical theatre, with a bigger emphasis on singing than those who were destined for more straight-acting roles.

All of this would be going on and we would still do our voice work with Francis, our yoga with Lynette and our dance with Gail. The rest of the time was spent working in groups on scenes from our productions. Just to keep the pressure on, we would do extra productions that would only be seen by the rest of the school, rather than the paying public. When we did *The Music Man*, rehearsal space was always at a premium, so we would use the garden if the weather was fine. It was quite usual to see final-year students practising a scene from one play in one part of the garden, while a couple of metres away, a set of first-year students were frantically trying to get a scene from their play ready for a rehearsal that afternoon. If you walked inside the house, you would hear banging and sawing, as the stage-management course made the sets for both productions. There was an enormous amount happening wherever you looked, making it a fantastically dynamic place to be. It was so much more real than normal academic institutions – with everyone working to full capacity all of the time.

I grew up during my time in Bristol because it was simply expected of me. Looking back, I think I must have been quite an annoying person when I arrived there. I had been used to spending my time in the bar of the Academy and generally messing around. In Bristol, there were people on my course a good ten years older than me, along with others who had come from university and who didn't want a little Welshman playing the joker all of the time. I was forced to adapt, although I don't think I ever lost my playfulness. Each one of my colleagues had their quirks and foibles, but the whole atmosphere of the place meant that we all took a more mature approach to our work. The great thing was that all fourteen of us in our year group operated as a team. Very quickly we had become a family.

In the second year, three groups of students on the course are allowed to put on a lunchtime show in a small performance area in the Bristol Old Vic, which seats around seventy people. The actors are extremely close to the front row, so it can be an incredibly powerful experience. It was up to the groups to come up with an idea and take it to Chris Denys, who would then say 'Yes' or 'No' to it. Rich and I were best friends by this point and he was keen to perform a Scottish play called *Dead Dad Dog* by John McKay. It's about a lad in his twenties whose dead father comes back to haunt him on one of the most important days in his life.

When Rich had the idea, nobody believed that Chris would give it the go-ahead because the lunchtime plays usually involve as many actors as possible, to give everyone a chance. This particular script needed only two actors – Rich and me. Chris surprised us all, saying, 'Yes, it's a great idea. Go on and do it, boys.'

We were very lucky that he even gave us a professional director to work with called Anne Adamson, who happened to live in Bristol. So, for two months whenever we had a free afternoon or evening, we would cycle down to her house and rehearse with her there. We needed a long preparation period because the roles were very intense – there was no set and no props, so everything had to be demonstrated either through the words in the script or through mime. It was very tricky, with even the simplest everyday action requiring a lot of thought on our part. For instance, in one scene my character was standing drinking a pint of beer at a bar in a disco. I had to make sure that I picked the imaginary glass up from exactly the same spot where I had put it down. Learning the mimes as well as the words made it a very difficult challenge for us both, but Rich and I really bonded during the process because we had to do everything to make the play happen – even down to making the flyers and handing them out around the city.

When it came to the performance, Rich was dressed in a white suit and had a huge moustache and a big wig because his character was stuck in the sixties. My character had not seen his dad since he was a little kid. The play begins with my character getting ready in front of the mirror, when all of a sudden the imaginary mirror says, 'Hello, son. It's yer wee Da'. How are yer?'

The play was a gentle comedy, but very touching. In the end, the father and son become friends and manage to have the sort of relationship that they never had when he was alive. The play ends with the two of them embracing and then the father disappears, leaving my character on his own again. The production was warmly received and it was one of my proudest moments in Bristol. Mam and Dad even came down from Llandegfan to watch it. For Rich and me, it was special because we were involved in every part of the process that made the production happen. We had taken a gamble and it had worked.

Another highlight of my second year in Bristol came when we were taught stage-fighting. First, we learned how to realistically punch and kick someone without hurting them. When you next see one actor punching another on television or on stage, watch very carefully, because the person throwing the punch never makes contact and the noise of fist hitting cheek is actually made by the person who is receiving the punch. Likewise, if you come across a scene where one actor appears to be kicking another, it will be the flat part of their foot that connects so that, again, the person who is being kicked does not get hurt. It seems simple when you see it written down, but a good stage fight owes just as much to excellent choreography as a stunning dance scene does.

After we had mastered unarmed combat on the stage, we moved on to working with swords. We started off by learning how to fence properly and then learned new moves from there. This is where it *does* get dangerous, because actors use real swords, which can do quite some damage if anything goes wrong. After months of training, the chief fight director from the National Theatre came to examine us and to award our official stage-fighting certificates.

We were all put into twos and had to pick a scene from a film or play to which we would choreograph a fist fight for two minutes followed by a sword fight that went on for the same length of time. I was paired with Guy, who was not known for his movement skills, but he turned out to be a great partner. We both understood the danger because we were working with real knives, so now was not the time to mess around. I came up with the idea of taking the song 'Anything You Can Do, I Can Do Better' and adding in the fight.

We were both wearing dinner jackets and after we sang each line, we would hit each other:

'Anything you can do, I can do better. I can do anything better than you.'

'No, you can't.' Whack!

'Yes, I can.' Whack!

And so it went on. At the end of the verse we did a couple of somersaults across the stage and then picked up daggers and did the same thing with the words changed to 'Anything you can kill, I can kill faster'. All of our movements were choreographed very quickly. The examiner said that he loved the idea because it was so different from what he usually saw. We both passed our fight tests and I was given the qualification at the advanced level, which made me very proud.

Halfway through the second year, a notice was pinned on the casting board that was far more important than any of the others. It gave the details of who would play which part in the final two shows of the year – one was a musical, *Salad Days*, and the other was a heavy straight drama, *Romans in Britain*. This moment was eagerly anticipated by everyone on the course, because the shows would be seen by people who could give us real jobs in the outside world. Neither Guy nor Rich were song-and-dance men, so they were relieved to find themselves in *Romans in Britain* and not *Salad Days*. In fact, they were so bad at dance that they were known as the 'Step Ball Change Brothers' after the dance moves that they struggled to perform. I walked up to the board to find out what I was doing and there were people crying and shouting with either ecstasy or disappointment all around me. I saw my name in the cast for *Salad Days*. It was written next to Timothy, the lead male role. I was completely over the moon, although my excitement turned to apprehension when I discovered that I would have to do a five-minute song-and-dance routine. I could not have got through it without a great actress and singer called Charlotte Collingwood, who was my leading lady.

Salad Days was directed by Chris Denys, who proved to be so efficient that by the end of the first rehearsal, we had read through the musical once and he had blocked the show. That is where the director tells each actor where they have to stand on the stage during each scene. It was not that we were competitive, but we were gratified to find out that the cast of *Romans in Britain* had not even finished reading through the play for the first time by that stage. We would be performing in the main house at the Bristol Old Vic in front of audiences of around eight hundred people a night.

We learned all of the songs with Neil – my biggest number was 'We Said We'd Never Look Back'. I quickly came to realise that I had the best role in the show, not just because I was the male lead, but because I did not have to do any of the dance routines except for this particular five-minute number with Charlotte.

I was absolutely determined for my big scene to be as close to perfection as possible. I worked on the dance every day in my own time and was always to be found in the dance studio. It started off with my character sitting on a park bench, when suddenly he hears music from a magic piano. His arms begin to move by themselves and he says, 'Look at me! I'm dancing!' Eventually, the routine develops into really high kicks and dramatic movements. To pull it off convincingly, Charlotte and I needed to dance to a high standard and the rehearsals were physically very intense. It was a far cry from that first morning in Gail's dance studio, when I stood there in my brand-new jazz shoes and pristine white socks, with my tights right down to my ankles. By this stage, my tights were rolled right up like a ballet dancer's and I wore no socks, just jazz shoes and I was so fit that my T-shirt fitted tightly over my muscles.

On the opening night, just before the curtain went up, Gail came into my dressing room with a good-luck card and gave me a big hug. She told me she knew how hard I had worked on the dance and that she was very proud of me. I walked out on to the stage on cloud nine. Gail was the toughest teacher in the school, who demanded the most from her pupils and it meant so much to me that I had earned her respect. Afterwards, Neil Rhoden came into my dressing room to tell me that I had sung superbly. To get his blessing along with Gail's made me feel that all the hard work had been worthwhile. I learned so much from them both and I still keep in contact with them today. They always come along to my shows whenever I perform in Bristol.

Before a student leaves the school having passed the course, there are various boxes that he or she has to tick. These include a clean driving licence, a fight certificate and some experience of horsemanship. By the end of the *Salad Days* run, I had managed the first two, but not the third. So a group of us were taken off to a field to gain some experience with horses. I was shown my mount and it was the largest animal I had ever seen in my life – a monster called Rocky, who towered above everyone else's trusty steeds. I climbed on to his back with some trepidation, but he turned out to be one of the gentlest animals anyone could wish to meet. After spending a few hours in the saddle and learning the basics of horse riding, I had ticked the final box necessary to pass the course successfully.

Once *Salad Days* and *Romans in Britain* had finished their runs, there was one more big task ahead of my group of students – a trip to London to perform in the Bristol Old Vic's annual showcase in front of agents, producers and casting directors in the Fortune Theatre. Each of us had to go to see Chris Denys with one of the monologues we had learned over the previous two years. It had to be exactly one minute long – if it was five seconds over or under, he would not allow us to do it. This was when Chris was at his toughest. When we were rehearsing, he would say, 'Crap! Change it!' to anything that he felt was substandard. He was brutal, but it was understandable considering the audience we were about to face. Chris was somebody we all came to rely upon and we trusted his advice completely. As well as individual monologues, we performed short scenes from some of the plays and musicals we had learned.

Chris chose an extra scene from a Shakespeare play for five of us to master in the week before our trip to London. I was cross with him when I found out.

'That's not fair, we don't have time to learn it,' I complained.

'Tough!' came the reply from Chris.

'Well, I don't mind not doing it.'

'You haven't got a choice. You've got to do it,' he said adamantly. I think he was testing us and wanted to make sure that we did not feel too comfortable. Once again, I chose for my piece Huw's monologue from *How Green Was My Valley* – the very same piece that helped me to get into the school in the first place, but by now I had learned how to give a much better performance.

We all travelled to London on a coach together. Each of us had brought a chair from Bristol to sit on while we were on stage. There was no other scenery or props. The show went well, although it was the most nervous that many people on the stage had ever been in their lives – their whole careers could rest on this one performance. It was especially important for those people who had still to find themselves an agent, because without some sort of representation, searching out any acting work would be almost impossible.

I was not under quite the same pressure as my friends because I had already signed up with the well-respected theatrical agency run by the husband-and-wife team of Scott and Denise Marshall. I was far more concerned about the day after our trip to the Fortune Theatre, because Scott and Denise had already come up trumps and got me an audition for the lead role in *Joseph and the Amazing Technicolor Dreamcoat* in front of the show's director, Steven Pimlott. We had finished at the Fortune Theatre by lunchtime and everyone else was due to go back on the bus to Bristol for a big end-of-term party that night. Much to the dismay of Chris Denys and Neil Rhoden, I decided to return with everyone else, even though I had to be back in London the next morning. I wanted to be with my mates because we had just done something momentous together and I wanted to share the final celebration. So, I went to the party for around an hour before saying my farewells and going home for an early night. The following morning, I got up first thing and headed back east on the train for my audition.

My student years, first at the Royal Academy of Music and then at the Bristol Old Vic, were a natural break between my time as a boy soprano and my emotional and practical need to find a new career. Frankly, I was grateful to have the space. But after two years in Bristol, I felt ready to go out to try to see if I could find a niche for myself in the entertainment world. That I went on to do anything else at all in acting is completely thanks to everything I learned at the Bristol Old Vic Theatre School. Recently, I went back to Downside Road and saw a 'Who's Who' of alumni on the wall. Alongside Brian Blessed, Daniel Day Lewis, Pete Postlethwaite, Jeremy Irons and Patricia Routledge, was a picture of me. I am by no means certain that I am worthy to be mentioned in the same breath as a group of actors as great as these, but I was very chuffed to see myself there anyway.

15. *JOSEPH AND THE AMAZING TECHNICOLOR DREAMCOAT*

However realistic Chris Denys had tried to make our auditions each week at Bristol, doing it for real was far more nerve-racking. I sat waiting in a corridor of the London Palladium, next to two very beautiful dancers, who had been in the original production of *Joseph* and who now wanted bigger parts. A steady stream of guys came into the room and then went through the doors to the auditorium. I just stared down at the plush red carpet, thinking how much more fit and handsome everybody looked compared to me.

At last, my name was called and I walked down the aisle through the stalls. I was surprised to see around thirty people sitting towards the front. They introduced themselves: the director Steven Pimlott; the casting director David Grindrod, who I knew was responsible for deciding who went on stage in just about every big musical in London and always seemed to be on my side; the musical director of the original production Simon Lee; the musical director of the new production Robert Purvis; the resident director Wayne Folkes; the original choreographer Anthony van Laast; and so the list went on, a mass of new names, faces and titles.

Steven Pimlott asked me to sit down in the empty seat at the end of the row, right next to him.

'So, what have you been doing?' he asked.

'I'm just finishing in Bristol,' I replied.

'What have you been doing there?'

'*Salad Days.*'

'Timothy?'

'Yes.'

'What else?'

As I rattled off all my acting roles, I started to relax because Steven seemed very pleasant and genuinely interested in my work. Little did I know that by this stage, they had already seen and rejected dozens of potential actors, singers and celebrities for the role of Joseph.

'So, what are you going to sing for us?'

' "Johanna" from Sondheim's *Sweeney Todd*,' I replied. It was the piece that I always used for auditions.

'Right, go on, then. But after you've done that, have you got anything more upbeat?' came the reply.

'I could sing other things – I could do something like "Being Alive"?' I was thinking on my feet and it was the toughest song that I could think of on the spur of the moment. It has a big finish on a top G.

'Go on, then. Go and do it with the music at the piano,' said Steven. I climbed up on to the stage and sang through both songs before he asked, 'What about anything from Joseph?'

I told them that I had done it many years ago as a boy at school and that I still remembered the words to 'Close Every Door' and 'Any Dream Will Do'. In reality, I had mugged up on the score on the way there that morning.

'Oh great,' said Steven. 'Do "Close Every Door".' I did as I was told. 'Great. Now can you do the other one as well please?' So I sang 'Any Dream Will Do' and was surprised when my small audience all sang the 'ah ah ah' part of the song without any encouragement from me. They actually seemed to be having a good time.

He beckoned me to sit back down next to him and continued to grill me, giving nothing away. 'So, what else have you been doing at Bristol?' I told him about some of my drama roles and he said, 'Do me a piece of that, then.'

I went back up on stage and did the one-minute monologue as Huw from *How Green Was My Valley* that I had performed the day before at the Fortune Theatre. It started with me at the back of the stage saying the words 'I am going down for my father', before I rushed to the front of the stage and fell on my knees. I then did absolutely nothing for as long as I could hold it before I started to say the, by now, very familiar words: 'Up against the coal face . . .'

'Thank you very much. Very powerful. Thank you,' said Steven. I walked back down into the stalls and shook his hand before waving goodbye to everyone else and walking out of the theatre.

I heard absolutely nothing for a couple of months, but I found out much later that after I had left the hall, Steven turned around to his team and said, 'Right, everyone agreed? We've found Joseph.'

In the meantime, I had to carry on trying to find other work. There was no point presuming that I had got the role just because I wanted it so much. The very first part I landed out of college was in a Ministry of Defence film for the army about alcohol abuse. I was the good soldier who turned his back on his drunken mates in order to become fit. I must have had no more than two lines in the whole film and spent the remainder of the scenes in which I appeared in the background in army gyms. I am sure that new recruits must have a real laugh when they are played this film shortly after signing up.

I was given a part acting in a Welsh-language drama for S4C called *Agoriad Llygad* which was written by the playwright Dafydd Huws. My character was an innocent research student who met up with his literary hero Dewi Burgess, played by Stewart Jones. I was made to look very geeky for the role, with small round spectacles and a college scarf. It was the first time that I had done any acting in Welsh and I relished the opportunity of working in my first language.

My next role could not have been more different: pantomime at the Yvonne Arnaud Theatre in Guildford. It was during this run that my agents Scott and Denise telephoned me to pass on the good news that I had won the lead role in *Joseph*. I was ecstatic, but I still had a job to do playing Prince Erik in *The Snow Queen* alongside Bernard Cribbins and Anita Dobson. Bernard was a genius, playing around ten different parts, all of which were brilliant. His talent really shone through. Anita Dobson was equally excellent as a very regal Snow Queen. I also enjoyed meeting her real-life partner, Brian May, the extraordinarily tall guitarist from my boyhood heroes Queen.

It has to be said that Prince Erik, unlike Bernard and Anita's roles, was not the greatest of parts. The highlight was singing 'Bring

Him Home' from *Les Miserables*, with the words changed to 'Bring Her Home'. As I sang, snow would fall – usually in clumps. Bernard came up to me in the first week of rehearsals and said, 'You've got to do something with your part or you'll die of boredom.' Pantomime is hard work and although I didn't have a brilliant role, I enjoyed my time in Guildford, but I was nearly bursting with excitement at the thought of playing the lead in *Joseph*. Every evening in Guildford, I would sit in my dressing room quietly learning Andrew Lloyd Webber and Tim Rice's songs.

At the end of the panto run, I had a phone call from Wayne Folkes, the resident director on *Joseph*. It was going to be his job to get me ready to take on the role and we agreed to meet up. As soon as I saw Wayne, I thought to myself, 'This man's an animal.' He looked like a bodybuilder and frankly he scared me a little. I knew that he had a long track record appearing in big musicals, including *Cats* and the original *Joseph*, but that this was his first time as a resident director. When we met, he looked me up and down and said forcefully, 'You're too skinny, so we've got to bulk you up. We'll start this week, so why don't you come along to my gym?'

Two weeks of intensive work-outs with Wayne followed. The pattern was the same every day. After warming up, I would attempt to lift up a weight and would say, 'I can't do it, Wayne,' and he would drive me onwards shouting, 'Lift it!' in my face. With a superhuman effort, I would then manage to do as I was told. After the gym, we always played squash, which gave me the opportunity to get my own back on him because I usually won. He would hate that because he was incredibly competitive.

I was secretly flown up to Edinburgh to have dinner with Wayne, Robert the musical director, Sheila the wardrobe mistress (who was a real hoot), and Jonathan the production manager, who looked after the finances and the day-to-day running of *Joseph*. They wanted me to see the show for myself and rushed me into the theatre at the very last minute just as the cast were about to go on stage. I wore a baseball cap so that it would be harder to recognise me – at this stage, nobody in the cast knew that I was taking over the lead and the producers were keen that it remained a secret.

I sat next to Wayne watching the show and kept whispering, 'This is amazing, amazing.' Suddenly a Scottish woman tapped me on the shoulder and I thought, 'Oh, no. She's recognised me.'

'Oi! You! Take your hat off. I can't see,' she hissed. I was just relieved that my cover had not been blown.

I fell instantly head over heels in love with the show and leaped to my feet along with the rest of the audience at the end. It was unbelievable – I had never seen anything like it.

The next morning, I was measured for my costumes for the first time by Sheila, who showed me around her empire with great pride. 'Just to let you know,' she beamed enthusiastically, 'everywhere we go, come down to wardrobe because we always have a bed made, so you can just relax with us.' I was starting to understand the scale of the operation behind the scenes. Sheila ran an army of fifteen other dressers and wardrobe mistresses and there was a battalion of ten washing machines lined up in the corner, which they took with them to each of the theatres on the tour. With a cast of around 35 and 60 local schoolchildren to dress each night, the task was huge. After Sheila finished measuring me, she said conspiratorially, 'See you soon.'

A few days later I was sent to an obscure room under a railway bridge somewhere in South London. I knew that I was going for a wig fitting, but when I walked inside I was astonished to see a man surrounded by thousands of wigs and samples of hair. He greeted me warmly with the words, 'Ah, Aled. Now, you're going to have the hair of a Polish nun.' He took some measurements and told me to come back in a couple of weeks' time.

When I next returned, the wig was made. He fitted it on to my head and, as soon as I looked in the mirror, I saw that I had suddenly sprouted very realistic shoulder-length hair. It fitted perfectly and he glued it on the gauze on my forehead and at the back of my neck. 'Now, how do you do your hair normally?' he asked. I gingerly ran my fingers through my new mane and discovered that it reacted just like normal hair. I could part it and it fell into place as if it was my own. When I pulled it, it stayed in place. I looked in the mirror and thought how bizarre it was that since breakfast I had grown fine, flowing blond locks.

Next, I went to another building in a backstreet in South London, where I was met by Sheila and five other very maternal women, who by then had made my costumes. It was time for me to try them on and I have to admit that, even though I had seen the show, I hadn't given much thought to what I would be wearing. They handed me a pair of silk panties and told me to change into them behind a screen. I came out wearing nothing else and they fussed around attaching various bits and pieces on to me.

'Right, there you go,' said Sheila triumphantly. 'That's what you'll be wearing for most of the show.' I looked in the mirror and was naked save for an extremely short miniskirt. 'The great news is that because you're so thin, we've made your skirt shorter than Jason Donovan's or Philip Schofield's,' she added with a smile. I felt very self-conscious as these women stood around admiring their handiwork and giggling at my discomfort. They went through the rest of my outfits: long billowing white trousers and a long white coat tied with a rope for the opening scene; body armour for Joseph's triumphant return towards the end, and a white T-shirt and white jeans for the final scene. Despite these other costumes, there was no getting away from it, though – I was going to be standing on stage with virtually no clothes on for nearly all of the show. The most expensive part of my new clothes was the Amazing Technicolor Dreamcoat itself. It cost more than £3,500 to make – a far cry from the version I had worn back in Llandegfan Primary School, which Mam had crafted from that set of old curtains. There were two versions of the coat that I used on stage – one that I wore most of the time and one held together by Velcro strips. This was so that it would easily tear to pieces in the part of the show where Joseph's brothers threw him into a pit.

The production was midway through its run at the Alhambra in Bradford and the plan was for me to take over for the final five weeks, before doing the show for six months in Blackpool. The producers arranged for a hire car so that Wayne and I could drive north. I had food poisoning the day before I was due to leave and was still feeling queasy when Wayne arrived at Uncle Arthur's flat to pick me up.

It seemed to be a long journey up to the Stakis Hotel in Bradford, where the producers had booked me a suite. For the next few weeks, I would spend each day rehearsing with Wayne and each evening sitting on my own in the hotel, so it was quite a lonely experience. I filled the time on my own in my room just as I was trained to do in Bristol, by writing down everything I had learned that day – where Joseph would stand on the stage and why he was behaving in a certain way at any given time.

Rehearsals started in earnest the next day, when Wayne wanted to run through the opening scene. Joseph is required to stand on a small revolving platform in the middle of the stage about six feet up in the air. The platform then gently rotates and lowers to the stage amid swirling dry ice, creating the effect of him arriving through the clouds. That first morning, I stood on the platform six feet above the stage leaning on a white stick, with Wayne standing below on one side and the stage manager on the other. The stick was taken away from me and the platform started to revolve and lower. At the same time, I began to wobble uncontrollably until I came crashing down towards the ground below. Wayne managed to catch me, so I wasn't hurt.

'There's only one way of doing this,' he said. 'And if you can't do it, then you just can't do the show, because this is how the whole thing starts. Basically, it's all about using your diaphragm and breathing properly – just as it is with singing.'

I did as I was told and discovered that the moment I held myself properly and breathed correctly, the platform stopped wobbling. Although I had mastered it, I still found the first scene the scariest part of the show because had I fallen off, it would have ruined the opening – and it could also have hurt. I always used to worry that because I was concentrating so much on not falling off the platform, I would forget the words to the opening song 'Any Dream Will Do', so I used to talk them through out loud on my way on to the stage each night.

Wayne taught me all of the moves on stage and showed me where I would stand for each of my scenes. We spent so much time rehearsing together that we quickly became good mates. I think that he respected my work ethic – I know that I certainly respected his. Through the time we spent together, we forged a lasting friendship, which I still greatly value to this day.

The next stage of getting me ready to play the part for real was to work on the singing and acting, so the producers hired a church hall at Salt's Mill in Bradford. The stage manager marked out the floor with masking tape so that everything was in the same place as on the main stage. Nichola Treherne, the associate director, then worked through each of the moves that Wayne had taught me, while Robert Purvis, the very loveable musical director, helped me with the songs. It was all very intense, day after day for four weeks. Only then was I allowed to see the show and meet the cast for the first time. I quickly became friends with John Higgins, who played Pharaoh, Alan Morley, who was the butler, and Ria Jones, the narrator.

After five weeks with Wayne and Nichola, we all felt that I was ready to get on with actually doing the show, so they arranged for me to have a run-through of the full production with the whole cast and the entire twenty-piece orchestra at eleven o'clock one morning. I sat in my dressing room and half an hour before the show was due to start, my dresser came in with the opening costume. She made sure the clothes looked right and then five minutes later, the wig mistress came in with my wig on a block. She pinned back and netted my real hair and then placed my new false hair on top, securing it with glue. Just as she was finishing, the sound man came in to put the sound pack into my hair. This consisted of a microphone, a battery and a transmitter. It had to be woven into my wig because I wore so few clothes most of the time that there was nowhere else to hide it from the audience. The stage manager followed close behind, to make sure that everything was ready. Over the intercom, I heard the words, 'Mr Jones, this is your beginners call.' These instructions are given out all the way through the show with cast members being called to various different positions ready for their scenes.

I was starting to get nervous, because everything was so much bigger than anything I had experienced in Bristol. I left my dressing room and walked into the wings. I was confused because all the rest of the cast still seemed to be wearing their everyday clothes, rather than their costumes. I quizzed my personal assistant-come-dresser, Max, and she replied, 'Yeah, you're the only one in costume today.' That made me feel even more self-conscious.

The moment that I started to sing on stage, I found that the wig was extremely hot and heavy, stopping me from concentrating totally on my performance. I also discovered that I was unable to move around as freely as I had done when I was wearing trainers because I had big cowboy boots on my feet. By the end of the rehearsal, a long list of different things had gone wrong and the show even had to be stopped completely by the stage manager, when I was nearly bashed on the head by the prison bars that are lowered to the ground from above. I was standing in the wrong place and would have been hit by them had the stage manager not acted quickly.

I got through it in the end and the rest of the cast were politely encouraging, but I knew that I wasn't quite there yet. However, there was no need to panic because I had a rehearsal with Nichola in the afternoon and then three full dress rehearsals still to go. The first proper dress rehearsal went very well and everyone cheered at the end. I was now genuinely part of the cast and we quickly developed a real sense of family.

By the time my first proper performance started, I knew the show back to front. I stood on the platform and the opening bars of music began, the lights came up, the dry ice was swirling and I felt a surge of excitement. I was lowered safely to the ground. The set was designed to look like a picture frame and I began singing 'Any Dream Will Do' as I walked through the frame. A group of kids from local schools ran on and knelt either side of me as I was singing. It was an amazing opening to an amazing show.

The final scene was equally spectacular. I rode up high above the stalls on a cherry picker until I was level with the circle. The entire stage was covered by Joseph's coloured coat. Then, after Joseph was reunited with his father, the whole auditorium exploded into a spectacular sound-and-light show and the whole cast ran on – with the girls in white body stockings and the boys in white jeans and T-shirts. They did a huge dance routine to the 'Joseph Megamix' that went on for about twenty minutes. I, meanwhile, was out the back, taking off my wig, having a cup of tea and getting changed into my final costume of white T-shirt and jeans – plus, of course, the Amazing Technicolor Dreamcoat. The dresser gelled up my real hair and then, just as the dance routine finished and everyone else in the cast was glistening with sweat, Joseph nonchalantly walked on and sang the end of 'Any Dream Will Do' for the third time.

By this stage, the audience were always on their feet. The whole cast would take a bow and then walk right to the back of the stage, before rushing forward and taking a final bow. The rest of the cast, exhausted, struggled up six flights of stairs to their dressing rooms. The actor who played Joseph, on the other hand, was accorded star status and allowed to use the lift, something which I never felt terribly comfortable about because the rest of the cast had to work just as hard, or in many cases harder, than I did.

That first night, I could sense that the musical director, Robert, was really willing me on to do well. In a big production like this, there are monitors all around the stage, so that the singers can see the conductor without having to look directly at him, but when I sang my solo numbers I was always at the front of the stage straight in front of him. He gave me a big encouraging smile and I was very touched to see a friendly face right at that moment.

Even though the cast and crew were brilliant, not everything went quite as smoothly as it should have done every night during the run. I sweated so much that I ruined four microphones in the first three weeks. In the end the technical team built in an opportunity for me to flick the sweat out of the microphone during one of the scenes where I had my back to the audience.

One night, during the scene where Joseph's brothers have to throw him into a pit, the back of my wig caught on something on the way down and I heard a ripping noise. I felt the back of my head and realised that my wig was torn from top to bottom. To stop it flapping, I had to sing the next song with my hand behind my head, before running off stage to get it fixed. Luckily, the wig mistress had a spare for emergencies, so everything was fine by the time I was next required back on stage.

It was at the end of my five-week run at Bradford that I first understood just how big the production really was. When it came to packing up and moving on to Blackpool, it took no fewer than seventeen articulated lorries to transport the show from one theatre to another.

The training I had received in Bristol had instilled in me a rule that you are never to put on airs and graces. You are never to ask for a personal assistant or wig mistress or make-up artist. Instead, you should do everything yourself. So it took a bit of getting used to that here I was on the biggest show in the world with my own personal assistant and dresser and all the trimmings. Max, my assistant, was employed solely to ensure that the actor playing Joseph functions to the best of his ability night after night. She would even have done my shopping and answered my letters had I asked her to. She made it great fun and when she got married during the run, we all went to Scotland for her wedding and had a fantastic time. Max would stand in the wings with my water bottle throughout the show and, as soon as I came off, she would hand it to me while at the same time helping me to change into my next costume. All I had to do was stand there until I was needed for a scene. The backstage area was like Piccadilly Circus, with people running everywhere and sets flying all over the place – it could be very dangerous if you were standing in the wrong spot.

When you work in the entertainment industry, there is a difference in the sort of working relationships that you develop with your colleagues. It is not like working in an office every day for a number of years, because when you are an actor, or a presenter, or a singer, you spend relatively short but very intense periods of time with people and then move on to another project. With *Joseph*, we all worked together six days a week for six months, so the intensity was even greater and very real friendships were made.

I arrived in Blackpool two days before the show was due to open. I had already found myself a little house to rent for the six months. It was beautifully furnished with a tiny private courtyard out the back, where I would sit and relax in the sunshine.

We did four nights of previews before the opening, just to iron out any problems that had developed during the move from Bradford to Blackpool. On the night of the third preview, I caught a stinker of a cold and felt really ill. Wayne took me to a steam room all day to try to clear my blocked-up nose. When I walked on stage for the first night proper, I was feeling a lot better, but was still not a hundred per cent. I did the performance to the best of my ability and the audience seemed to love it. I was particularly relieved to see that the critics in the next day's papers gave me great reviews – my favourite one being 'a star is born again'. My overwhelming feeling was one of relief.

The audiences were brilliant in Blackpool. They were all there for their summer holidays and ready to have a good time, so *Joseph*, with its infectious tunes and spectacular staging, was the perfect show for them to see. There was one scene where Pharaoh, who looks and sounds like Elvis, summons Joseph and asks him about his dreams. Pharaoh goes down into the audience and thrusts and gyrates in front of the women, who all scream with delight. One night, someone shouted, 'Show us your arse, Pharaoh!' John Higgins, who played the role brilliantly, didn't miss a beat and, staying in character, said, 'Uh-huh. I can't – it's a family show. Uh-huh.' We would always be able to see the front two rows behind the conductor on the television monitors and at the start of one performance we realised that the front row was filled with skinheads. As the opening bars of the music began, you could clearly hear their cans of Stella being opened. John was adamant: 'No way am I going into the audience tonight!'

At the time, I was often asked what it was like to do the same thing over and over again for a long period of time. I know that some actors and singers become really bored with it, but I think that it is fun. Every night is slightly different because musicals hinge on how people act and sing. Sometimes a scene can be particularly poignant when it has not been previously, or another actor might sing a song in a particularly beautiful way that inspires you to give an even greater performance. There is nothing better than if you have a cast of 35 people who are all on fire and you all walk off stage saying, 'Wow! That was great!' It makes you want to get back out there and do it again.

Having said that, I would cheerfully throttle the person who invented matinees because they are the most exhausting thing to do, especially if you are a singer. Whenever you do a show, you want to feel that you have done your best, but on days when you have both a matinee and an evening performance, it is a difficult balancing act between performing well in the afternoon and still having some energy in reserve for the second show. To this day, I am very proud that I did not miss a single performance in the entire seven months I was in *Joseph*.

As the run came to its end, I discovered that there was a tradition of casts messing around and playing tricks on each other in the last matinee of a season. Apparently, the very last evening performance was always taken seriously, but at the matinee the view was 'anything goes'. I was a bit cross about this as Mam and Dad were coming to Blackpool from Llandegfan to see this show and I wanted it to be good for them. But despite my protestations and a very stern message over the intercom before the show began, warning the cast not to misbehave, everyone else seemed intent on having their fun. Looking back, I think that I probably came off quite lightly, considering the number of opportunities there were to have a go at Joseph.

There was a scene where Joseph lay on a bed surrounded by girls fawning over him, running their fingers through his hair and stroking him. 'Close Every Door' followed straight afterwards and on the final matinee, I was blissfully ignorant of the fact that the girls had put my wig into pigtails. I must have looked ridiculous standing there singing the song with my hair in bunches. One of Joseph's brothers came on stage with the biggest Afro wig I had ever seen to sing the 'Benjamin Calypso'. I looked across at him and noticed his T-shirt. At the time, Roy 'Chubby' Brown was in the charts with a song called 'Alice, Alice, who the f*** is Alice?' As homage to this, the words on his T-shirt read: 'Aled, Aled, who the f*** is Aled?'

We had a great party that night and I felt really sad that it was all over. I needed a rest, though, because doing 240 shows had left me vocally and physically tired. I shall always be grateful to *Joseph* because it was the first time that I successfully made the transition from child to adult performer. It was very important for me to have achieved that change – I was very lucky to have done it with such a professional and talented bunch of people.

I have one other major reason to be grateful to *Joseph*, because without the show I would never have met my wife, Claire. So I suppose you could say that by the time I left Blackpool, I had discovered that I did have a new voice, that I could have a new career and that I definitely had the love of my life.

16. LOVE AND MARRIAGE

I was tired but happy the morning after the opening night of *Joseph* in Blackpool. My alarm went off and I scrambled out of bed and into the shower. The performance had been a success but, unusually for me, I only popped my head into the cast party. I was determined to rid myself of my cold, which was starting to get on my nerves. I had wanted as much sleep as possible and left myself very little time to get to my first engagement of the day, a photo call for the press along with the stars of all of the other summer-season shows in the seaside town. There was always a big production that ran for the whole summer in the Opera House, where *Joseph* had its home, as well as a series of variety shows at many of the other venues in the town.

My cab arrived late and we rushed to the North Pier for the photo shoot. I was starving so, mindful of the need to keep up my energy for the show that evening, I bought a large beef and onion sandwich, which I munched while we waited for the photographers to sort themselves out. I stood chatting to Les Denys, Su Pollard, Roy Walker and Joe Pasquale, all of whom were appearing locally.

A photographer from the local paper, the *Gazette*, called across to me. 'Aled, can you come up on this carousel for your shots?' I did as I was asked and he said, 'Now, pick yourself a pretty girl to have your photo taken with.' He gestured across to a group of very attractive young ladies from the Blackpool Tower Circus who were dressed alluringly in high heels, fishnets and elaborate bikinis crowned with tall feathered headdresses.

'I don't really do those sort of photos,' I said shyly. He ignored me completely, pointed at one of the girls and shouted, 'Hey, you! You'll do.'

She walked over and sat next to me on the carousel. 'I've got to apologise because my breath must smell terrible. I've just eaten a beef and onion sandwich,' I said.

We chatted happily, while the photographers snapped away. It turned out that the girl was called Claire Fossett. She was in the circus as a dancer and also did a rope act. Her father, who had been in the circus all his life, had taught her the routine, so she decided to join the circus herself for a year before going away to university. Claire's family had been based at Chessington World of Adventures, Alton Towers and in France for about ten years prior to coming to Blackpool, which meant that she had led a very different life to most people of her age and that she only had a vague idea of what I had done as a boy. It was one of the few occasions that I have met someone when *The Snowman* did not come up in conversation and I found it very refreshing. She asked me which show I was in and what role I played, but didn't seem as impressed as I had hoped she would be when I told her that I was Joseph in *Joseph*.

'Do you want to come to see the show?' I asked hopefully.

'We don't get a day off,' she replied.

'What? Not one night off at all?' I persisted.

'Well, actually, we do get Friday nights off.'

'Come and see the show, then.'

'Thank you, but I'm busy this Friday. But maybe I'll come to see it another time.'

I still hadn't given up hope. 'Well, if you do decide that you want to come along, give me a call and I'll get you some tickets.'

I was delighted a couple of days later when the phone rang and Claire told me that she had decided to come along after all, and could she bring some of her friends too? I could not believe it when she turned up on the night with her mother. She told me that one of the other girls had a stomach bug, but I thought that I was getting the brushoff. I told John Higgins, who was playing Pharaoh, that she could not possibly be interested in me if she had brought her mum with her. At the end of the show, I went up in the air as usual on the cherry picker, which meant I was on the same level as Claire, her mother and her friend. When I saw Claire sitting there, I pointed towards her and waved at her during the song. She instantly looked away and all I saw was her mum surreptitiously nudging her to wave back. But Claire was resolutely not playing the game. Despite things not looking hopeful to me right then, we did meet for a drink at the end of the show and got on very well. During the next six months, we saw more and more of each other and gradually became an item.

When we started going out, Claire gave me an incredibly hard time. We often arranged to meet outside Woolworth's, which was just to the right of the Tower Circus, along the street from the Opera House, where I was performing. If I had been doing a matinee, then we would arrange to get together at four o'clock. Now, even with a baseball hat pulled down tightly on my head, it seemed that everyone in Blackpool knew *Joseph* because it was such a popular musical, so a long stream of people would come and chat to me. After a while, I would look at my watch and realise that I had been waiting for more than an hour, with no sign of Claire at all. On these occasions, when I phoned her to remonstrate, she would say, 'I was there until four minutes past four and you weren't there, so I went back to the Tower.' She really was not prepared to take any messing from me. I found it quite attractive that she played so hard to get, although I have never quite forgiven her for those horrendous waits outside Woolies.

After Claire had been to see me in *Joseph*, I thought that I should return the favour and go to see her at the Blackpool Tower Circus. The first time I went with a group of guys from the cast and the second time I sat next to Claire's mother, Elaine, who is always the life and soul of the party and a very gregarious woman. By then, I knew that Claire was mentally a very strong person, but I was also amazed by her physical strength. I could not believe how she managed to climb up a rope without using her legs. She was clearly also a perfectionist, who took enormous pride in her work. Since knowing her, I have learned a lot about the circus and many of our closest friends now are involved in it. They are all incredibly kind people and, without a doubt, they are the hardest working group of performers anywhere in show business. Most circus people have to travel extensively, although they do go back to the same places each year, so they become almost like home. In Blackpool, it is slightly different, because the circus is always at the Tower and it is somewhere that Claire and I always make a point of going back to each year, although these days I don't have to pay to get in.

Claire's stepfather, Tom Fossett, was a magnificent performer and the circus was the only life he had ever known. By the time I met him, he was a clown called Grimble, who incorporated into his act many of the skills which he had spent a lifetime perfecting. The highlight of his performance saw him balancing on a unicycle while juggling. Claire told me that he had never liked her having boyfriends and always gave them short shrift. I always telephoned Claire at a time when I knew she would be in the house, to minimise the chances of having to speak to her dad, but one day when I called, he picked up the phone. I was in the West Coast Diner, one of the noisiest bars in Blackpool, where all the casts would go to let off steam with a burger and a pint after their shows. When Tom answered, I thought, 'I've got to bite the bullet here or I'll sound like a complete wimp.'

'Hello, it's Aled. Please could I speak to Claire?' I asked meekly.

'Yes, you've been seeing rather a lot of my daughter, haven't you?'

'Yes, I'm really enjoying getting to know her. I'd really like to take you out to dinner sometime and get to know you, too.' I think that this shocked him because none of her previous boyfriends had ever asked to see him before. We met up and had a great evening with a group of his colleagues, becoming firm friends. Tragically, I did not get to know Tom as well as I would have liked because he developed a brain tumour shortly after our first meeting. He died a few months later. Even though I did not spend long with him, I learned that he was a very proud and strong man with a great sense of humour. He was always hugely optimistic and one of the last things he said to me came just after I had been told that I had not been given an acting role for which I had auditioned.

'Don't worry,' he said wisely. 'What's meant for you won't pass you by.' I have often thought since how right he was.

One evening, Claire and I had been out to dinner and she was feeling a little sad about her dad's illness. I suddenly said, 'You should ring him.'

'I don't want to disturb him. He sounded really tired yesterday,' replied Claire.

'No, you should definitely ring him.' She called and one of the nurses wheeled the telephone over to his bed. The next day, Claire's mum called to say that he had died. It was so important for Claire to have said goodbye to Tom and I thank the Lord that she made that call. It was a devastating time for Claire, her mum and her brother, Marcus. I spent a lot of time with them and we went away on several holidays after Tom's death – it was our way of getting through it. Elaine told me that just before Tom died he said that he was glad that Claire and I were together and he knew that he did not have to worry about her any more.

Over the years that Claire and I have been together, she has become my best friend. She is also an incredibly strong person, which I think may have been influenced by her circus background. She is fun to be with, devastatingly beautiful, and has enormous style and panache. But what her love gives me more than anything else is stability – something that I believe is very precious. I realised very quickly that I had found my soul mate, the person with whom I wanted to spend the rest of my life; for me, it was only a matter of time before we would get married.

The setting when I finally asked for her hand could not have been less romantic. It was pouring with rain outside her mum's house in the town of St Anne's in Lancashire. I went down on one knee in Claire's bedroom and proposed. Thankfully, she said yes.

It was never supposed to have happened like that. I had arranged to take Claire away for a romantic weekend to a beautiful country-house hotel just outside Preston called Northcote Manor. The ring was being transported from London to Lancashire and I was due to pick it up from the Leonard Dews jewellery shop in Blackpool on the Friday afternoon. The plan was that I would ask her to marry me on the Saturday. She would hopefully say 'yes' and then we would have a big engagement party with all of our close friends on the Sunday. Unfortunately, the ring was on a train which was involved in a serious crash at Watford, so when I went to the jewellers, it had not been delivered.

The following night, I had nothing to put on her finger, so I kept drawing pictures of different cuts of diamond rings on a napkin, but Claire thought that I was just teasing her. I didn't feel that I could properly ask her without the ring, although she got the gist of what was going to happen and we had the engagement party anyway. Two days later, Michael Hyman, the owner of the jewellers, phoned me to say that he had driven all the way to Liverpool especially for us and had found a ring that was almost identical to the original. That sort of generosity is typical of people in Lancashire, who will do anything for anyone. Although Anglesey is where I come from and I now live in London, there is a little bit of my heart that will always belong in Lancashire. When the ring arrived, I did the honourable thing and popped the question in Claire's bedroom.

We were in no rush to get married and, in fact, we were engaged for five years before we finally walked down the aisle. Claire decided that she was going to study French at the University of Westminster, because it was round the corner from my London home at Uncle Arthur's. We went down to London and took one look at the halls of residence, which were horrible. The awful accommodation seemed to highlight this sad time and we decided it was too soon for Claire to leave her mum. We spent the night at a hotel and travelled back up north the next day.

It was quiet for me on the work front after *Joseph* came to an end, so I made St Anne's my base and got to know Claire's family much better, including her brother Marcus. He and I would watch the Euro '96 football tournament together and we gradually became great friends. I had no choice but to get on with him really because he was always around – whenever Claire and I went for a romantic meal in the local restaurant, Jack's, Marcus would invariably turn up uninvited halfway through and join us for dinner.

Looking back now, I realise that although it was a very happy time personally, these were my lean years, when I had not quite carved a clear niche for myself anywhere in the entertainment world. I had hoped that the work would come flooding in, but it didn't. Just before I did *Joseph*, I had met two guys called George Stiles and Anthony Drewe, who had been on *New Faces* and were then working on a series of new musicals. Anthony fancied himself as a squash player, although he never managed to beat me in the three years that we played regularly together. They were both very witty, talented writers and I used to record all of their demos for them. We even worked together on a song, which we entered for the Eurovision Song Contest under pseudonyms, although we never heard anything back.

Eventually, they decided to put on *Warts and All*, a revue of their music and songs at the Watermill Theatre in Newbury and offered me a part. I said that I would do it and appeared alongside George, Anthony, Jenna Russell, who has starred in the BBC television drama *Born and Bred*, and another actress with a brilliant singing voice called Ali Jiear. The show was directed by the legendary choreographer and director Wendy Toye, who was in her eighties.

We quickly became a very close-knit team, spending most of our days walking in the Berkshire countryside or hanging around the beautiful Watermill Theatre as a group. If you ever have the opportunity to visit this wonderful area, do take it.

One of my favourite parts of the show was a song George and Anthony wrote for me about my voice breaking called 'What's a Choirboy to Do?' I sang the first verse as a boy soprano and used my adult voice for the second verse:

What's a choirboy to do
When his singing days are through?
Once I used to sing higher
In the front row of the choir,
I was walking in the air
Like a cherub with fair hair,
Butter wouldn't have melted
And my songs were never belted.

Who could have known
Something called testosterone just lay in wait?
Then wham! Certain bits and pieces dropped
And my income stopped,
That's when things came to a crunch,
I acquired my own packed lunch,
And my manager pouted
When I told him things had sprouted.

If I'd known testosterone could do all this on its own
I'd have debated getting myself castrated,
I saw the signs tucked inside my Calvin Kleins,
Alas too late,
My voice dropped another notch,
Then bade farewell to concert halls,
Even snowmen have snow balls.

Once I used to sing solo,
Now I have to sing so low,
What's a choirboy to do
When his singing days are truly through?
No longer some precocious pup,

I was forced into early retirement,
My surplice is now surplus to requirement,
Boy, hormones really screw you up!

The Watermill was a wonderful little theatre with around four hundred seats. The run lasted for a month and was well received, although I found it hard being away from Claire for that length of time, especially just after she had lost her father.

George and Anthony became really close friends and helped me through a time when I was not working as much as I would have liked. They had an unerring knack of always managing to fill my life with music and laughter. I recorded the demo version of their musical *Honk*, which was premiered at the National Theatre and is now being performed around the world. I very much hope that sometime in the future I will be able to perform properly in one of their musicals, because they are such a talented duo.

After the revue, I did some radio plays and I presented a one-off Christmas morning programme on BBC Radio Wales, but times were still tough professionally. I was auditioning for stuff and not getting it – something that I hate. Recently, I interviewed Gaby Roslin on my BBC Radio Wales programme and she said that she loved auditions. I am afraid that I have to disagree completely because they always send me into a state of high panic. Claire always says that the jobs I get at auditions are the ones that I don't really want. If I go there wanting a job, it is almost certain that I won't get it.

One job that I did get was with the Good Company from Brighton playing the role of Tom Gradgrind in a touring production of the Charles Dickens classic *Hard Times*. It should probably have been renamed 'Gruelling Times' because it was a tough job. I was playing alongside Philip Madoc, Janet Brown and Ken Farrington, who was the original bad boy, Billy Walker, in *Coronation Street*. Ken and I became great friends and the only thing that kept me going through the tour was our regular tennis matches. I joined the cast a week late because I thought that I had glandular fever, although that turned out to be a false alarm. My character was not the lead, which was quite a levelling experience after playing the best role in *Joseph*. It was also a straight play, rather than a musical, and I realised as soon as I started the rehearsals that the fourteen-week run was going to be a long slog.

The opening night was at the Alhambra Theatre in Bradford, where I had been with *Joseph* before it transferred to Blackpool. Back then, the buzz surrounding the theatre was intoxicating. I was in number one dressing room with a dresser and wig mistress and crowds that I knew were going to get up on their feet every night. Now, with *Hard Times*, I was sharing dressing room number five with three other people. Whereas *Joseph* had an amazing set, our set was one corrugated-iron piece. The hardest performance of all came when we played the Sunderland Empire, which seats 2,000, and there were just 27 people in for the matinee.

I knew that I had to get on with it. I was grateful for the work and my fellow cast members were all fantastic, but my heart just was not in it. I know that it sounds arrogant and stupid – and I hope that it's more of the latter than the former – but I knew that I would perform and do something good again of which I was proud. *Joseph* was a great start to my adult performing career, but things seemed to have stalled a little afterwards. Having said that, a fourteen-week repertory tour is good experience in anyone's book and I am glad that I did it, if only to help me to understand that repertory theatre was not where I wanted to make my future. One huge bonus of having so much time on my hands was that I was able to spend long periods with Claire.

I also took the opportunity of this relatively quiet period to sort out something in my life that had been bothering me for some time – my teeth. In nearly all of the photographs of me as a boy, other than those where I was actually singing, I had my mouth closed. This was because my teeth had always been slightly crooked, the result of sucking my thumb for too many years as a baby. I had not been able to wear a brace at the time when other children usually do because it would have altered the sound of my singing. As well as losing some of the clarity of my diction, the sound of the brace clicking in my mouth would have been quite audible on my recordings. So my dentist filed down my original teeth, which is quite a terrifying experience when you look in the mirror afterwards, before capping the six front teeth at the front of my mouth with shiny new porcelain veneers. I am now very happy to have my picture taken with my Hollywood smile, and I only wish I had taken the plunge and had my original teeth fixed much earlier.

After Claire decided against going to university, she knew that she needed a career of her own and chose to become a flight attendant. She applied to Virgin Atlantic and was chosen from hundreds of applicants to go through to the intensive training course. Having seen what a Virgin flight attendant has to learn, I can assure you that they are far from being trolley dollies; they are all highly trained. The courses that they go on are incredibly detailed, covering health and safety and first aid. They also have to know how to use every single bit of equipment in the cabins, from defibrillators to crash axes. I would test her constantly during her training, and by the end of it, we both knew where each item was kept in each different type of aircraft flown by Virgin Atlantic.

Claire passed the course and I went with her to see her being presented her wings by Richard Branson. When he caught sight of me he wandered over and asked, 'What the hell are you doing here?'

'I'm going out with one of your flight attendants,' I replied.

It was interesting to see that Richard was there throughout the ceremony, making an effort to be seen by his staff. I think that visibility is part of being a great leader and I was impressed that he was taking just the same interest in them as he had done in me when he signed me to 10 Records all those years ago.

On my first night in *Hard Times* in Bradford, Claire was making her first flight. She rang me just before the curtain call to say that they had taken off and were in the air and the pilots had radioed back to the cabin crew requesting help because there was smoke in the cockpit. Claire did not lose her cool and assisted the more experienced crew members to place smoke hoods over the pilots. They managed to bring the plane safely back down to the ground.

'Leave your job – I don't want you to fly any more,' I told her. But she ignored me completely and jumped back on to another plane and flew off to New York.

We had a great time while Claire worked for Virgin Atlantic. All staff members were given free flights and I used all of hers, so that we could then spend time together in her destinations on her days off. I became an expert in working out how to get upgraded to Upper Class and we had some fantastic mini-holidays together. I managed to go to Hong Kong with her five times in two months. My favourite memory of our visits was on China Day, the year after the handover of Hong Kong. We stood together at the top of the Peninsular Hotel and down below, as far as our eyes could see, was a sea of people, looking like little ants. The fireworks were spectacular, with fountains floating in the air. Every explosion was synchronised with music that was played simultaneously in every single public place in Hong Kong. It was unbelievably spectacular and you could probably only have achieved such a feat of organisation in a totalitarian state.

I would only get a seat on the plane if there was space, and flying as a standby passenger is a nerve-racking experience. I would check in and wait. Occasionally, when they knew that a plane was particularly empty, I would be ushered straight on board. On most occasions, I was held back until about ten minutes before the plane took off. Everyone else hoping for standby flights would be standing around me with a look of panic on their faces. If we got on the flight we would be told to run straight to the plane, which always seemed to be the furthest possible gate. There was an enormous sense of relief all round when we finally got on board.

Virgin Atlantic has beauticians working in Upper Class to give passengers massages during the flights. On one flight, I was sitting in Economy when I was tapped on the shoulder by a husband-and-wife couple behind me. They turned out to be from Wales and the parents of a girl who was working as a beautician on the flight. Shortly after takeoff, half a bottle of champagne arrived with their compliments. I returned the favour and sent back a bottle of champagne to them. The wife came up to me and held my hand. Looking earnestly into my eyes, she said, 'I'm so glad that you're on the flight. I was so nervous but when I saw you walking down the aisle I thought, "I know we won't crash now".'

The only time that I didn't enjoy flying Virgin Atlantic was around Christmas, because 'Walking in the Air' was one of the pieces included in the pre-flight music and everyone would look at me. That was a small price to pay for what was a very exciting period of our lives and we were both so lucky to be able to visit cities all over the world. I always liked us to eat out at fashionable new restaurants and would spend some time researching where to go before we left the UK. On one occasion, in Los Angeles, I was wearing what I considered to be a particularly trendy pair of glasses – at least, they were trendy in London. The waitress in the restaurant sauntered up to our table, took one look at me and drawled, 'What is it? Have you got some sort of Austin Powers thing going on?' I thought that Claire was going to pass out because she was laughing so much.

Claire's brother Marcus has always loved his food and absolutely adores great restaurants, one of the highlights being Heathcotes in Longridge near Preston, run by Paul Heathcote, who is one of the best chefs in the north of England. From when I first met Marcus, he always had books by the likes of Marco Pierre White and Gordon Ramsay – they were like bibles to him and when we were in St Annes, we regularly went out to fantastic restaurants.

Eventually, Claire and I moved down to London. On 13 February 1997, I belatedly realised that we were less than 24 hours away from Valentine's night and I had not booked anywhere for the two of us to go out for a meal. So I went through the *Good Food Guide* and telephoned the restaurants where I had become a regular. Every single one of them responded with, 'We're full, I'm afraid,' laced heavily with a tone that implied that I must be barking mad to have expected them to have had a free table at such a late stage. I flicked through the book and the page opened at Les Saveurs, which was owned by Marco Pierre White. The head chef there was a guy called Gary Hollihead, whose name I recognised from another restaurant where I had previously had a fabulous meal. I realised that it was a long shot, but I decided to give Les Saveurs a call anyway. A very well-spoken English voice answered the phone.

'You could probably save my life,' I said with an air of desperation in my voice. 'I haven't booked anywhere for tomorrow night.'

'How many for, sir?' replied the well-spoken voice.

'Two, please.'

'Name?'

At this point, I usually just say 'Jones', but for some reason on this one occasion, I said, 'Aled Jones.'

'How was your birthday meal at Quo Vadis?' said the voice. Six weeks earlier, I had indeed been there.

'It was absolutely brilliant,' I replied.

'And what about the meal before Christmas in the Criterion?'

'Your computer must be awesome,' I said admiringly.

'No, there is no computer.'

'Then, how do you know where I've had dinner over the past two months?'

There was a pause and the voice replied, theatrically: 'Because I *am* Marco Pierre White.'

'If my fiancée's brother knew that I was speaking on the phone with you, he'd die of excitement.'

'Why?'

'He absolutely loves you.'

'What does he do at the moment?'

'Well, he works in Oddbins because he loves wine.'

'Tell him to come in next week and I'll have a chat with him and will probably be able to give him a job.'

Claire and I had a wonderful Valentine's meal at Les Saveurs. Marco gave us a bottle of champagne and came and talked to us. A week later, he took Marcus, Claire and me out to dinner at Quo Vadis. By the end of the meal, he had told Marcus not to bother with Oddbins and that he would train him up as a sommelier instead, starting from the following Monday.

Marco and I got to know each other very well over the next few months. My favourite restaurant of his was the Oak Room. The food there was simply amazing. He was a whirlwind of a man and would walk into the restaurant smelling of some sort of animal that he had shot in the afternoon on a hunting trip. He would sit at our table and order a few dishes for us all to try, which he would then proceed to demolish in front of our eyes. Then he would go into the kitchen and would cook for us. We would never quite know what was coming because he always insisted on choosing on our behalf to ensure that we had the best of everything. I met Marco during the time when I was not working again and he treated me with such great respect. He was always interested in what I was doing and in my voice. He was – and still is – for me, the ultimate chef. I have eaten all of the best meals that I have ever had in Marco's restaurants.

Claire and I had decided to set a date for our wedding – Epiphany (6 January) 2001 – and we had also found a venue, the actors' church, St Paul's in Covent Garden. The only problem we had was in finding somewhere close by for the reception. I had asked Marco's assistant if he would allow us to hold the reception in one of his restaurants and he promised to relay the request. One afternoon, the phone rang at home.

'Aled, it's Marco. Come to the Mirabelle now,' said the by-then familiar voice on the other end of the line. So Claire and I went to the Mirabelle and he told us that he would let us use the Criterion to hold our reception. He was in a great mood and every time Claire drank a glass of champagne, he knocked a thousand pounds off the cost of the restaurant. The poor girl could not even look at a glass of champagne for months afterwards.

I knew the vicar of St Paul's, Mark Oakley, very well because he has always been involved in a charity event of which I am vice president, called 'The Story of Christmas'. He was also the Deputy Chaplain to the Queen. Mark has a wonderful sense of humour and a great way with religion. He makes it new and fresh, while acknowledging the fact that we are not all perfect. I have never portrayed myself as an angel in any shape or form. Just because I sang the sort of music that I did as a child and the fact that I sing religious music now doesn't mean that it is easy living a perfect life – far from it.

The night before the wedding, Claire's brother Marcus, who was my best man, took me for dinner at the Ivy. I was so nervous that I could hardly eat the delicious food in front of me and he ended up polishing off my meal along with his own. When I got back to the hotel, I sent Claire a text message saying, 'I can't sleep. I'm so excited.' Moments later my phone beeped with the reply: 'Me too'.

When the big day finally arrived, I was petrified to receive a call from Mark Oakley saying that a group of paparazzi had gathered outside the church. We had told nobody in the press about the wedding. Marcus decided that a good fry-up would calm my nerves, but the sight and smell of it was too much for me and I had to rush off to the lavatory to be sick. It was the thought of the photographers gathering outside rather than the wedding itself that made me nervous. At that stage, I really had not been in the public eye for a long time.

I arrived at the church and it was beautifully decked out. All of our family and friends were there. In the half-hour after I had gone inside, about thirty photographers had gathered outside and I knew the moment that Claire had arrived because the inside of the church was lit up by flashes as they took pictures of her walking through the doors.

A company called Mirror Mirror, who had also made wedding dresses for Zoë Ball, Amanda Holden and Kym Marsh, created Claire's dress. When I turned around and saw Claire standing at the door of the church, she looked simply stunning. Her dress was very elegant and drew looks of admiration from everybody in the congregation. She was followed down the aisle by her half-sister Louisa, who was her bridesmaid.

Throughout the service, I was a blubbering wreck because the boys choir Libera sang one of my favourite songs called 'I Will Sing for You'. We all sang 'Dear Lord and Father of Mankind', which was very special for me because I have always associated it with the wedding of Bob Geldof and Paula Yates. It was a Eucharist service so everyone received the bread and wine. Bishop Ivor Rees from Bangor Cathedral was officiating and when he lifted the cup to Claire's lips, he started to shake and I saw this red wine going towards her white dress, so in a split second I put my hand out and took most of it down my sleeve. I managed to prevent Claire having to walk around with a large red stain down her front, although both our outfits had red-wine splashes on them for the rest of the day. We have since found out that this is a sign of luck.

The reception was fantastic and Marco had done us proud. The menu was magnificent, starting with a Fois Gras and Gewürztraminer terrine, followed by mussels and saffron soup, ribeye of beef with Yorkshire puddings and a chocolate *cadeau* box with raspberries. They also made us a *croc en bouche* wedding cake, which is basically a huge mountain of profiteroles. Tim Payne, who is one of Marco's head chefs, had persuaded all of the other head chefs who worked for Marco to join him in the kitchen. I went in to see them to say thank you just after the starter and they were all happily sitting there drinking champagne. Because they were all at the top of their profession and everything that they did was about preparation, the entire meal was ready and they just had a great time chatting.

More than 130 of our closest friends and relatives came to the wedding and it was a day that I will always cherish. It went by so quickly and we had so much fun that I struggle to remember it all. I was relieved to get my speech out of the way, although I was particularly proud of the last line: 'Me and Mrs Jones, we've got a thing going on', which I had pinched from the Billy Paul song. I was even more proud that, on this occasion, I had written the speech all by myself and didn't have to call on Brian Kay's expertise, as I had done all those years before at the Royal Academy of Music. After the speeches, we partied the night away to the brilliant band Mal Pope and the Jacks. We ended the night with a very loud rendition of the Welsh national anthem.

Claire and I spent our first married night in an amazing round room at One Aldwych, which is, in my opinion, simply the best hotel in London. We honeymooned at the Datai Hotel in Langkawi in Malaysia, which was a lovely break full of nothing but total relaxation. Before that, I had always been on holidays where you were expected to 'do' something, so it was great to just unwind for ten days. We stayed in a suite that had previously been occupied by Phil Collins. I could not work out why people were nudging each other and pointing at me so much whenever I walked around the hotel. I wondered if they had re-released all my albums in Malaysia. The mystery was cleared up the day before we were due to leave, when a waiter asked me, 'Are you a famous singer?' I was amazed that somebody would recognise me so long after I had been singing professionally. The waiter soon put things straight by saying, 'Are you H from Steps?' This band was at the height of its popularity at the time and it turned out that somebody in the hotel had said I was H. This rumour had spread like wildfire around the area. I was gobsmacked, because I don't think I even look remotely like him.

On the way home, we stopped off at Singapore for two nights in the infamous Raffles Hotel, which was a fantastic end to a wonderful holiday. On the flight home from Singapore, I felt very happy and content with my lot in life. I had a beautiful wife with whom I would spend the rest of my life. As a bonus, it looked as though my career was going to take an exciting new direction towards more work in television and radio. Little did I know that within a year, my life would change completely as two became three.

17. A NEW LIFE AND A NEW ROLE

Once the Millennium had been and gone, I started to do more television presenting back home – for both BBC Wales and S4C. Around the same time, Julie Barton, the controller of BBC Radio Wales, asked me if I fancied presenting a programme for them. I came up with a concept where a guest chooses five pieces of music that they think I might like and I do the same for them. We throw our musical choices up in the air and see where they land. I might like their choices and they might like mine, or then again, we might both strongly dislike what we hear.

I have presented one series of the programme each year and, so far, I have interviewed more than a hundred different celebrities ranging from Dame Judi Dench to Ian Hislop to Ann Widdecombe. The powers that be at BBC Radio Wales must like it because it has gradually moved up the schedule to its current peak-time slot on a Sunday morning from ten o'clock to eleven o'clock. It is always a real thrill to be able to talk to these people and both my delightful producer Lynne Rosser and I feel that the music brings out the best in all the interviewees. The guests really seem to enjoy the programme because they are not just talking about themselves, but are sharing very personal reasons for liking a particular piece of music. Working for BBC Radio Wales feels like coming home because we used to listen back in Llandegfan when I was a boy and the station also played such an important role in the early part of my career.

Previously, I had done some television presentation for BBC Wales in Welsh from the Eisteddfod. My role was to be the roving reporter out and about in the field interviewing people. I had never done anything like it before and I could not believe my luck – I was being paid simply to stand and talk to interesting people. My career as a presenter of television programmes in Welsh really started to take off after this. I was asked to present a programme on S4C called *Heno*, which means 'Tonight'. I was very familiar with the programme, which had been going for years and was particularly popular in North Wales. The show was on air every evening from six until seven, with an extra live three-hour programme on S4C Digital from three until six in the afternoon. It was made at an old supermarket that had been converted into a television studio in Llanelli. The topics covered by the show were enormously wide ranging: cookery, fashion, celebrity interviews and music were all on the agenda, so it meant that the presenters had to be very versatile. Many, such as Angharad Mair, were regarded as being among Wales's finest. She was one of the team of presenters when I was there and is still fronting a version of the programme now.

I was asked to be one of the main presenters of the programme for two days a week for a year. By that time, I was living in London so it was a big commitment. I was incredibly nervous on my first day. When I said 'yes' to the job, I don't think I really had any idea what I was letting myself in for. I suppose it only really dawned on me when I was making the journey to Llanelli for the first time. I started to work myself up into more and more of a state, so that by the time I arrived I was a bag of nerves. I called Claire from the car and said, 'I've never done live TV in Welsh before. If I'm interviewing someone, I've got to be able to converse with them.'

As usual, talking to her calmed me down. It was silly really, considering that Welsh is my first language and I spoke very little else for the early part of my childhood. My fears turned out to be unfounded and I learned so much about live broadcasting by doing the programme, although by the end of my year in the presenter's seat, I was ready for a break because I was absolutely exhausted. Each week, I would hire a car in London on the Thursday morning and would arrive in Llanelli at around lunchtime. As the weeks went by, I came to know the M4 very well indeed. On average, it was a three-hour journey door-to-door from my home to the studio.

Llanelli is a tiny little town with a great rugby team that has made the place famous across the world. My first job at the studio would be to write the script for that day's programme. After we had done the show, I would then jump in the car for the hour-long drive to Cardiff, where I stayed in the Hilton Hotel every Thursday night for a year. On the Friday morning, I would drive back to Llanelli, prepare that day's show, present it and then get back in the car and drive home to London some time after ten o'clock in the evening.

Things do tend to go wrong an awful lot in live television, so I became adept at dealing with unexpected technical difficulties. The trick is not to look like a rabbit caught in the headlights and instead to relax and tell the viewers what is going on. I have a theory that viewers actually enjoy seeing mishaps take place on their screens, so long as it does not happen with too much regularity. On *Heno*, each programme would always contain a couple of SNG satellite link-ups to reporters or guests in locations around Wales. Although most of them worked perfectly, they did provide the biggest possible opportunity for things to go wrong. So I became used to saying something like, 'Now, we're off to Swansea. Rhodri's there in Wine Street. Sounds like you're going to be having a good time, Rhodri? . . . Rhodri?' There would be nothing but a crackle at the other end and the line would go dead. As it was a live programme, we would still have to fill the time which that item would have taken up, so there would be a frantic reshuffling of the rest of the items on the running order to ensure that we had enough material to keep us on air until seven o'clock. I loved the buzz of having to think on my feet and the time I spent on the programme has stood me in excellent stead for all of the other television and radio presenting that I have done since.

Occasionally Claire used to come with me to Wales when I was working on *Heno*. I would drop her off in Cardiff, where she would spend the day shopping or swimming before we met up later that evening at the Hilton. One particular Thursday, Claire was there, so when I arrived back at the hotel, I stopped off in the bar and ordered two huge glasses of Chablis. I took them up to our room, where Claire was waiting for me.

She stood up when I walked into the room and said, 'Sit down.'

'Righto,' I replied nonchalantly, before telling her about my day. As I was talking, I looked over to the bin and noticed that it was brimming with cellophane and cardboard.

'Listen,' she said. 'Have a huge gulp of wine.' I did as I was told. 'I'm pregnant.'

My immediate response was plaintively to ask, 'How?'

'Well, you know how,' she smiled.

'But you've got polycystic ovaries,' I countered. Just the week before, Claire had undergone some hospital tests and we had both been devastated to learn that she might have difficulty becoming pregnant because of these cysts. We were both upset by the news, but as it turned out, the results were wrong.

'Listen,' she said again. 'I've taken about five tests today and all of them say that I'm pregnant.'

It turned out that she had felt strange earlier in the day and had suddenly developed a massive urge to eat pickled-onion crisps all the time. So she went to the shops and bought a multipack of crisps and a pregnancy test kit. When she got back to the hotel room, she took the test and forgot about it while she watched *Neighbours* on the television. Afterwards, she went back into the bathroom and was shocked to see that there was a blue line on the test kit. She rushed from the Hilton to the nearest branch of Boots, where she proceeded to buy one of every single brand of pregnancy testing kit that they had in stock. All of the results came up the same as the first kit.

I was in a daze. I ordered some food on room service and quickly downed both glasses of Chablis – after all, Claire was not allowed to drink now, so I was going to have to do it for the both of us. We ate our meal giggling and crying at the same time. I had never felt emotions like it. I was incredibly happy, but yet at the same time I felt so worried about the little person who was growing inside Claire. I felt a sudden sense of responsibility, of my place in the world now being to look after Claire and the new baby and to protect them from all the bad things that could happen. That night, I was scared of cuddling Claire too tightly in case I hurt the baby.

During the pregnancy, all went well for the first seven months. Claire had all of the scans and the doctors told us that everything looked normal. We set about learning more about what was going to happen, by reading a couple of books about pregnancy and at an excellent session with a midwife at the Portland Hospital in London, where we had decided the baby would be born. It turned out that the best thing that the midwife taught us was that there is a particular place to put your hands on the mum-to-be's lower back when she is having contractions that halves the pain.

At the time, we were living in a little cottage in southwest London and just two days after we had first visited the Portland, I was on my way to Homebase to buy some bits and pieces for the spare room that we had nearly finished converting into a nursery. Claire phoned me on the mobile and said that she really didn't feel well. I screeched to a halt, turned the car around and raced back home.

I drove her to the Portland where she was thoroughly examined. The doctors said that there was nothing abnormal showing up, so we returned home. It gave us a bit of a fright and the first thing that we did as soon as we arrived at the house was to pack an overnight bag, so that it would be ready if we needed to make a quick exit. That evening, we were sitting together on the sofa watching *Inspector Morse* on the television. Claire suddenly turned to me and said, 'I think my waters are breaking.'

I telephoned the hospital in a high state of panic and the wonderful midwife on the other end of the line said, 'Darling, just bring her in.'

By the time we got there, it was after ten o'clock at night. Claire was examined by a doctor, who was amazingly good with us, and straight away we saw a second doctor. In all honesty, I was expecting to be told that everything was fine and that we should go home and not come back again for another six weeks. But the doctor had other ideas.

'You're not going home,' he said. 'The baby's going to come. Probably not tonight. But you're not going to leave here without a baby.'

The hospital was very busy and they only had a small room available. 'Well, I'm not leaving Claire,' I told the nurses. So they managed to rustle up a z-bed. That night, I pulled it into the room, put my blanket over it and slept there beside Claire. I would do the same thing for the next seven nights. As I lay there that first night, I felt terrified about what the next few days would hold for my wife and I was equally terrified that my baby could have all kinds of damage because she would be born six weeks early. I was in a hell of a state, really, and I needed someone there for support. I phoned Claire's mum and she came straight down from Lancashire in a taxi.

The next morning, the doctors scanned Claire again and tried to reassure us by saying that they thought the baby would be all right because she was a good size. Our baby would be delivered by a terrific woman called Maggie Blott. She was one of those people in whom you had total confidence as soon as you set eyes on them. She was, in fact, not due to be our doctor, but because we were in hospital far earlier than everyone had anticipated, the obstetrician who had been looking after Claire through the early stages of her pregnancy was away on holiday, so Maggie stepped in to take care of us.

When we woke up the following morning, Claire and I sat together watching Saturday morning children's television. She started to have contractions at around midday that went on until nine o'clock that evening. She was in agony throughout that time. I remembered the lesson I had been taught by the midwife at our antenatal session and stood for hours with my hands on Claire's back. Every time I took them away, she would moan in agony. As soon as I put them back, the pain became just about bearable.

Then the birth started for real. I still cannot believe that I went right through it alongside Claire, because even now when I see something like that on television, I feel like I am going to faint. I don't like blood at all, but with the birth of my daughter actually happening right in front of me, I did not have a problem. Maggie Blott arrived in our room covered in water because she had just delivered another baby. Our midwife, Maria, was another wonderful woman who stayed on way longer than her allotted hours to look after Claire. I was there with cold towels, hoping to help the best I could and trying not to get in the way.

Claire pushed and pushed and eventually they used forceps. The first time I saw the crown of the baby's head coming through, I noticed that she had jet-black hair and I said, 'That's not mine!' Everyone laughed and it broke the tension. Despite the pain that Claire was going through, it was a very happy time. We were doing it together, as a team. Apparently I was calling her 'pal' all of the time and the doctor said afterwards that it was the nicest birth she had been to for ages, although I am sure she says that to everyone.

Suddenly the pushing stopped and Emilia, our daughter, had arrived. She weighed six pounds – considering that she was six weeks early, she would have been enormous had the pregnancy run its full term. After I had made sure that Claire was all right, I went to see Emilia properly for the first time in the special-care baby unit. The room was quite dark, with peaceful music on Classic FM playing gently in the background. There were babies everywhere with two nurses looking after them. One of them turned around as I walked into the room and said, 'Hey, it's the snowman!' I smiled, but inside I was so worried about Emilia. Despite the fact that some of the babies in the room were very poorly, the nurses always remained calm and relaxed. I think that it takes a very special kind of person to be a doctor or a nurse and I don't think that we value them as highly as we should do in our society today.

I was instantly struck by how tiny all of the babies looked – one of them was no bigger than my hand. They lay there on their fronts in incubators with tubes coming out of their little bodies. Just one baby was lying on her back on a plastic bed outside of an incubator. She opened her eyes and took a long hard look at me. Then she spat out her dummy and started to cry. I turned to the nurse and said, 'This looks like mine.'

Emilia was on a drip and had marks on her head from the forceps, but to me she was simply the most beautiful thing I had ever seen. Later, I pushed Claire up to see her in a wheelchair. We sat beside the little plastic bed for ages watching Emilia and felt an incredible wave of happiness surrounding us. The next morning when we visited, the nurses in the special-care unit said that she was fine and was coming off the drip. She was wheeled down to our room and we sat together for the first time as a family.

After a while, I popped out to get some coffee from the Starbucks near to the hospital. When I arrived back with my cappuccino, Claire burst into tears. Just after I had left, Emilia had turned blue and looked poorly. She was rushed to the hospital's emergency area. One of the paediatricians, Mr Massoud, scanned her and checked her over thoroughly and, to our enormous relief, she turned out to be fine, having had what they called a 'dusky moment'. He was another of those doctors who instantly inspired confidence.

I am full of admiration for the doctors and nurses at the Portland Hospital. They are dedicated beyond belief. Emilia had not developed her sucking reflex because she was premature. It was only the patience and persistence of the nurses helping Claire that meant that Emilia was able eventually to breastfeed. Everything in the hospital is geared towards supporting the mother through any difficulties that she may encounter.

I was due to be presenting a TV show in Preston the day after the surprise birth. The whole team were brilliant and instantly the decision was taken to rearrange all of the filming to a new date a couple of weeks later. This meant that I was able to stay at the hospital alongside Claire for a whole week, only nipping home a couple of times for a change of clothes. After a week, the doctors told us that Emilia had put on sufficient weight to go home. The journey back to our house took about three times as long as normal – I was so frightened of damaging the baby that I don't think we went over about ten miles per hour for the whole trip. I was just as petrified during that first evening that she was at home, because I had not realised how much babies sleep at that age. I spent the whole time staring at her to make sure that she was still breathing.

Being a dad is the most amazing thing in the world. My greatest sadness about the first few weeks of her life is that I still had television commitments to fulfil away from home. I had cleared my diary around the time that she was due to be born, but because she came into the world six weeks earlier than we had anticipated, I still had programmes to make. It is very difficult to spend time away from a new baby because they tend to bond with whoever is there. I am so lucky to have Claire looking after Emilia all of the time. We followed the advice about 'controlled crying' in the book *The Contented Little Baby* by Gina Ford and within a few days, Emilia was sleeping through the night, as she has done ever since. For eight months, Emilia slept in our bed on a big pillow between the two of us. For someone so small, she took up an enormous amount of room. Claire and I were on opposing edges of the bed while she spread out like a starfish. Eventually, we thought 'enough is enough' and she moved into her own room.

Because my work means that I have to travel for long periods of time, I have been the guy who comes in, spoils Emilia, and then goes again. That has been quite hard sometimes, especially as she grows older. When I went away to Australia to perform for the first time, she kept asking, 'Where's Daddy?'

As for Claire, she is the most naturally talented mother that I have ever seen. She has read every available book about babies and has brought up Emilia immaculately. Claire has a very elegant, classic style and even though she eats a massive amount of food, she still wears dresses that are size eight. Within a week of giving birth to Emilia, she was back to wearing her normal clothes. All the other mums hated her for it, but as soon as the baby had come out, she went back to being more or less her normal size right in front of my eyes.

We are now very much a family. Emilia is a very strong fighter – you can tell that from her earliest days. She is also very witty and Claire and I do wonder if she will become an actress because she is a natural mimic, as well as being musical. She regularly wakes us up early in the morning by singing at the top of her voice. I really wanted to have a little girl first – I think it is probably because little girls always have a special relationship with their fathers. I hope that she has a happy life and I want her to know that I will always look out for her. I know that I spoil her like mad, which sometimes makes Claire a little bit cross. Emilia is so precious to me, even more so now that she is growing up and every day something new and interesting happens in her life. I just want to be there to experience it with her. She is a real character and I want to savour every day with her. I thank God that those original tests suggesting that Claire had polycystic ovaries were wrong.

Through having Emilia, I have changed my outlook on life completely, with many of the things I used to place great importance upon not seeming to matter nearly as much these days. I remember being so scared standing in St David's Hall in Cardiff for a concert to launch my new adult voice. My dad walked around the corner with Emilia in a papoose. She saw me and beamed and I thought to myself, 'What are you worried about? As long as Claire and Emilia and the rest of my family and friends are healthy, it doesn't matter.'

I came off stage after that concert thinking, 'I'm not a little boy any more.' That is something that I have had an even greater sense of over the past couple of years. I suppose that until Emilia came along, I never really had to grow up and I do hope that I always have a fun side to me. When I was working as a boy, I was extremely mature for my age and then I regressed like mad when I was at the Royal Academy of Music. In my twenties, I continued to live life to the full and now that I am in my thirties, I have found out that that sort of thing is not really important to me any more. Instead, it is far more vital for me to have a constant. Claire and Emilia are definitely that. All the rest can come or go.

18. *SONGS OF PRAISE*

I first presented *Songs of Praise* when I was fourteen years old. I did two programmes – one from Aberystwyth and one from Pwllheli. Thinking back to it now, I suspect that at that time I was the worst presenter the programme had ever had. What struck me back then was that all of the interviewees had to answer the questions posed to them in one go with no editing. Many of the people featured on the programme were unused to being interviewed, so it was pretty tough. After my two editions were finished, I thought to myself, 'I don't want to do that show again.'

When I was eighteen and just off to music college, the BBC offered me the chance of becoming one of the regular presenters on the programme, but I turned it down. They wanted me to do a screen test, but I told my agent that I was not interested, because it was not the sort of show that I wanted to do at the time. More than a decade later when the call came once again from the BBC, I felt much more ready to become a presenter for *Songs of Praise*, especially because the particular programme that they wanted me to introduce was far closer to home. I would be working with the programme's executive producer, Medwyn Hughes, whom I had known from my childhood career when he had been based at BBC Bangor working in the sports department. I instantly hit it off with Medwyn and with the programme assistant, Heulwen Lewis, who was also from Wales. Both have become great friends and I owe a lot to Medwyn, who played a big part in guiding my career at this stage.

The nature of *Songs of Praise* is that once every so often they go back to where they have been years previously. When they had been to Bangor Cathedral before, I was interviewed as a former chorister whose voice had just broken. I talked about how the cathedral was a very significant part of my life. In 2000, my agent received a call from the BBC asking me if I would be interviewed once again for the new edition of the programme. Just a day later, they received a call from a BBC researcher called Rowan Morton-Gledhill, who told my agent that the BBC producers had changed their mind and did not want to interview me any more. Instead, they wanted me to present the whole programme.

Rowan has since become a great mate of mine. She hails from Huddersfield and is frightfully intelligent and extremely extrovert. She had seen footage of me presenting programmes for S4C from the Eisteddfod and had persuaded the *Songs of Praise* editor, Hugh Faupel, to allow me to present this one-off from Bangor. I have always been grateful for her absolute belief in my ability to pull it off.

I was really pleased with how the programme went. When I walked back through the doors of Bangor Cathedral, it all seemed very familiar and yet at the same time I felt very strange, as if I did not really belong there. So much of what goes on there had not really changed since I was a boy, but there I was twenty years later and a completely different person. I was given such a friendly welcome by everyone there and was truly humbled by the warmth shown towards me.

As soon as I walked through the door of the choir room for the first time since I had been a chorister, that old familiar smell hit me straight away. I had a great chat with the choirmaster, Andrew Goodwin, about old times. In fact, I probably spoke to him for longer on that occasion than I ever had done when I was a choirboy.

It was lovely going back, but I was very aware that I was presenting a network television programme for BBC1 and it was serious stuff. The director, Mary Colhane, did everything possible to put me at ease and, despite my apprehension, I actually started to enjoy myself. It was a really action-packed programme – we even went up in an RAF Sea King helicopter. I sang the Michael Jackson song 'Heal the World' on the end of Bangor Pier. We recorded it in the freezing cold at about eleven o'clock at night and it looked great. It was the first time that I had worked with the *Songs of Praise* music supervisor, Robert Prizeman, who has since become the producer of all of my albums. In all, it took five days to record the programme and I was full of admiration for the attention the crew paid to every last detail. However, while I was making the programme it never crossed my mind that it was anything more than a one-off opportunity, so I enjoyed it while I could.

The programme went out and then suddenly my agent had another call from the *Songs of Praise* office.

'They want you to go to Coventry,' said my agent.

'But I've got no link with Coventry,' I replied, remembering that my connection to Bangor was the only reason I had been asked to front that particular edition.

'No, they just want you to present it like anyone else,' he said. In all, I was given nine programmes in the year that followed. Now, I present nineteen editions of *Songs of Praise* each year – and I love making every single one of them. It is a genuine honour to be associated with the programme because everything about *Songs of Praise* is done properly. A producer spends two months preparing each edition and the presenter spends five days working alongside the crew to make those preparations a reality. Every piece-to-camera (where the presenter talks to the camera on screen) is done to perfection, the production values are incredibly high and there are never any sound interruptions or strange lighting. It is a joy to be involved in the process.

The music on the programme is particularly uplifting. Many hundreds of thousands of viewers have actually been involved in making the programme over the years, but those who have yet to take part might be surprised that putting it together is much more than just a half-hour sing-along. We actually record the outside broadcast from the location over two nights and during that time the congregation may well have to sing a particular hymn around fifteen times. We always get to the stage where we think that the conductor and the congregation have got it spot on, but then the little white telephone which is always just out of shot next to the conductor will suddenly give a shrill ring. The conductor will pick it up with trepidation and Robert Prizeman will be on the other end saying something like: 'Third verse . . . the sopranos were a little bit out.' And everybody will have to sing it all over again. It is a huge commitment from everybody involved and you can hear the groans of mock exasperation when the phone rings for the umpteenth time.

At the start of the recording session for each programme, I always do a little speech to the congregation where I explain how everything works. 'However crestfallen you feel when the phone goes for the fifth time and you are asked to sing a hymn for the twenty-fifth time,' I always say to them, 'just keep the thought in your mind that the producer of my albums is on the other end of the line and imagine how hard he is on me when we are recording them.'

I first started going to Sunday school and church when I was a little kid. For a while, as a teenager and a student, I stopped attending, but through working on *Songs of Praise* my faith has changed completely – and for the better. I suppose that when I was a child, the music was a far bigger pull for me than anything else. Even today, I still consider sacred choral music and especially hymns as being the best music ever to have been written. You simply cannot better them in any other musical genre – the devil definitely does not have all the best tunes. For me, a really rousing rendition of 'Dear Lord and Father of Mankind' is equally exhilarating as a performance of Wolfgang Amadeus Mozart or one of the other truly great composers. I have enjoyed becoming far more familiar with modern hymns through working on *Songs of Praise*, but my personal all-time favourite has to be 'How Great Thou Art'. This wonderful work is passionate and stirring. It is great fun to sing and I always find myself humming it for days after I have performed it.

One of the most important roles played by the *Songs of Praise* presenter is to talk to people on camera. When I first started the job, I used to turn up having prepared carefully but thinking to myself, 'This is a job and I'm interviewing someone.' Over time, as I have become more involved in the programme, that has changed. Nowadays, if I speak to a father or mother who has maybe lost a son or daughter, I genuinely feel for them. As an interviewer, you have to be real and respect them.

Invariably, we arrive at their house to find them dressed in their best outfits and it always amazes me that they want to talk about something that is so personal and so important to them. I admire them so much and I have come to realise that the only reason they are able to get through it is because of their faith. I always feel a slightly better person afterwards, as if their faith has rubbed off on me. I do my best to put people at ease before the interview and we never have a director standing in front of them shouting 'Action!' Instead, we just start recording our conversation. Usually we talk on tape for around 45 minutes, of which only two and a half minutes will actually make it into the programme. On many occasions, the quality of the interviewee is so strong that the producer has a real struggle to choose which segment to include in the final edit of the programme.

My job allows me to meet so many inspirational people who have had such horrendous things happen to them and I come away thinking how extraordinary these people are. They are part of God's creation and I would much rather talk to them than interview another politician or celebrity. Of course, nearly all of them simply have no idea how inspiring to others they actually are. Instead, they are just getting on with life and I suppose that is what I always try to do. Yes, I swear sometimes. Yes, I enjoy the odd glass or two of wine. But neither of these things makes me any less of a Christian.

I feel that my life is so much more enriched because I have *Songs of Praise* and I can honestly say when I stand on stage that I am singing 'How Great Thou Art' to God. It is my way of saying 'thank you' to Him for giving me what I have got and even to thank Him for giving me the gift of being able to sing at all. Some of my mates who are not religious say, 'Get out of it,' when they hear me talking like that, but that is truly how I feel and I am sure that the time I have spent on *Songs of Praise* has only strengthened that feeling.

Without doubt, I do have a faith. I am not sure that I would be able to exist without it, which I realise may sound odd to some people. I have never delved too deeply into it because I am not intelligent enough to do so, but when I look back, I realise that it has always been there even if I was unaware of it at the time. For example, I always believed that I would see people again in heaven. My faith is not quite as simplistic now and I do question a lot, which can only be healthy. The best example I can give of what having a faith is like is to equate it to when I started to regularly have singing lessons again as an adult. My teacher told me that I should breathe differently and that it would give me support. The difference between whether or not you have a faith is just like that breathing technique. With it, you know that you have support – there is somebody there looking after you.

I suspect that if you sat down and wrote a list on a piece of paper of all the character traits that a really good Christian is supposed to possess, then I would turn out to be a really bad Christian. But I always try to do my best and, more than anything else, I always try to treat everyone with respect, to love my fellow man and to lead a good life – but saying it is much easier than doing it.

The minute I walk into a cathedral, I instantly become calm because they are such special places. I feel a sense of space, of the oxygen swirling around me, of lifeblood. Outside, I can have the biggest worries in the world on my shoulders, but as soon as I go through those doors the stillness overwhelms me and everything seems all right. There might be an organ playing or there might be absolutely nobody else in the building. As I look around, I can almost see the people who have worshipped there over the centuries in the fabric of the building. Cathedrals have a warmth and serenity that for me is like nowhere else in the world.

I am usually someone who charges around the place at full speed, but I am always overcome with the desire to just sit down in a pew and relax. Often, I will sit and think quietly in the breaks while we are recording *Songs of Praise*. At those times, I feel completely open to God. I do pray, but I worry about putting too much pressure on God. If everyone is praying all of the time, He must have a pretty hard job to do. I am also somebody who just gets on with life, although there have been times when I have prayed harder than others.

When people meet me for the first time, they often know that I present religious television and radio programmes and they have an idea in their minds of what sort of person I must be. I am not sure that I match their stereotype once they have got to know me. It's a really tricky one, because there is nothing wrong with being God-fearing; however, I would much rather be God-embracing. There is no need to be awestruck and cowering, because it seems much more natural to me for religion to be open-armed and welcoming. Yes, *Songs of Praise* is a religious programme, but it is also a piece of television that uplifts and spiritually enhances its viewers, and whether or not they are Christian, they should feel comfortable watching the programme.

There is no doubt in my mind that religion has a relevance to 21st-century life. People often say that churches are empty, but it was fascinating to see the growth in attendance for services after the terrorist attack on the Twin Towers on 11 September 2001. In the following weeks, the number of people visiting churches rose sharply because they needed some spirituality in their lives at that moment. I am sad that Sunday is no longer the special day of the week that it once was, having been relegated to being the equivalent of Saturday with all of the shops open these days. I do believe that if the big stores stayed closed, more people would have time to go to church, but as it is, they opt to do something else.

Having said that, I am afraid that some churches are stuck in a rut. There is nothing worse than going to a service and feeling that everyone else around you is simply going through the motions. Religion is real, it's now, it's happening and it's exciting. It's certainly not sedate or simply part of history. Take, for example, when Jesus toppled over all the market stalls in the synagogue. They were not the actions of a calm person, were they? He was not the sort of person who wouldn't say 'Boo' to a goose. This is a person with passion, a person with love, with blood running through his veins, and that's what religion is all about for me.

If the vicar understands this, then it may well be that the best way of relating to his congregation is to hold a short service in a B&Q car park on a Sunday morning. My vicar at St Paul's in Covent Garden, Mark Oakley, is what I would call 'the future of religion' because of the way he shows that the Gospel is as relevant to our lives today as it was to the lives of the people for whom it was first written. He has an amazing ability to catch his congregation's attention during his sermons.

I have had the privilege of interviewing Dr Rowan Williams, the Archbishop of Canterbury, three times – twice for *Songs of Praise* and once for my BBC Radio Wales programme. Without question, he is an amazing man. He is unbelievably intelligent and can speak many different languages but, as somebody said to me before I had first met him, he is a holy man. As soon as I saw him, I knew instantly that this was true. When he walks into a room, you feel that he has a kind of very special glow around him. It is really hard to define holiness, to put that glow into words, but I would say that Archbishop Rowan is enlightened by God's passion and is alive with God's spirit. At the same time, he is an incredibly nice bloke.

We had a great time spending an hour together making the BBC Radio Wales programme at Lambeth Palace. I chose him pieces by musicians such as the Incredible String Band, the Beatles and Will Young – the last one because his daughter is a big fan. When I went through the front door at Lambeth Palace, I saw a bike with stabilisers and a football sitting in the hallway. It was a sign that the archbishop is a real person, with kids and a family life, not somebody sitting in an ivory tower preaching from on high. He gave me a wonderful interview, talking about his childhood and why he decided to become a theologian. He also told me that his favourite television programme is *The Simpsons*. Now how many vicars up and down the land would have felt comfortable admitting that?

Celebrity guests on *Songs of Praise* tend to fall into two categories: those who find it easy to speak about their religion and their relationship with God – and those who find it difficult to do so. My favourite interviewees include the late Fred Dibnah, who became famous for making television programmes about climbing up tall buildings and was one of life's great eccentrics; Portsmouth defender Linvoy Primus; singer Chris De Burgh; the author Susan Howatch; the former Prime Minister, Sir Edward Heath; Graham Kendrick, who is one of our greatest living hymn-writers (he penned the classic 'Shine, Jesus, Shine'); and Lord Montagu of Beaulieu, whom I interviewed in a wonderful vintage Rolls-Royce from his collection of magnificent cars.

I always enjoy talking to Sir Cliff Richard, but everyone knows about his faith, so when I interview him I like to try to get some fun out of him because it's nice to see the real man underneath. As a singer, I admire Sir Cliff enormously – he is the consummate professional and is every bit as great today as he was in the 1950s when he first started making hit records. I also have a really good relationship with the record producer turned *Pop Idol* judge, Pete Waterman, who was another great interviewee. People are sometimes scared of him because he can be quite a tough cookie, but he has been great on the occasions that he has presented *Songs of Praise* because he used to be a chorister himself and has a very genuine love of choral music. People often forget that to be a successful record producer you need to be very musical – I would love him to produce something for me one day.

The first really big programme I did for *Songs of Praise* was the fortieth anniversary edition, which came from a special concert at the Royal Albert Hall. It is easy to forget how big the programme is internationally – at the last count, it had twenty million viewers around the globe. We were making two programmes out of the concert, with Pam Rhodes presenting one and me fronting the other. We each had about thirty pieces-to-camera to do without an

Autocue, so we had to learn all of our lines. Everything had to be finished very quickly because we had to record our bits in real time while the acts were performing on stage. The magnificent Gloria Gaynor, best known for her hit 'I Will Survive', was one of the headline acts and it was my job to interview her backstage in her dressing room after her performance. I could tell that she was a big star because they had two cameras to record our conversation, instead of the usual one. For someone who has been so famous for so long, she proved to be a wonderful interviewee who talked very lucidly and openly about her life.

I worked with Pam Rhodes again on the live edition of *Songs of Praise* to celebrate the Queen's Golden Jubilee. Pam is a lovely person and a brilliant presenter with a memory like nobody else on earth. She is a true professional and one of the most technically proficient broadcasters I have ever worked with. I really respect her and have learned so much from her, so there was nobody I would have rather been standing next to in front of five thousand people in Centenary Square in Birmingham.

It is very rare for the programme to be completely live, so when we all gathered together in a hotel in Birmingham the night before the big day, we all took things very seriously. With a live programme, nobody has a second chance. The director, Medwyn Hughes, talked us through everyone's role and then the floor manager took Pam and me through what we would have to do. On the day, we rehearsed the whole programme all day. There was a real buzz and dozens more people involved behind the scenes than on a normal pre-recorded programme. Just before we were due to go on air, Pam and I were given our earpieces and we stood in front of the 5,000-strong crowd who were eagerly anticipating the programme.

David Dimbleby was anchoring all of the coverage from a studio in London just outside Buckingham Palace. Through our earpieces, we could hear him wrapping up the commentary about the parade along the Mall. Suddenly his words were drowned out by an announcement on the loudspeaker in Birmingham saying, 'Ladies and gentlemen, we will be going live on air in just under a minute. Please standby to cheer.' Pam and I were taking deep breaths and feeling rather anxious. There was no Autocue to fall back on and all we could hear in our ears was David Dimbleby talking. We were jolted by the master control room in London cutting in over the top of him and a disembodied voice saying, 'Birmingham ... Birmin-

gham . . . this is London. We'll be coming to you in thirty seconds
. . . twenty seconds . . . ten seconds . . .'

And then we could hear David saying, 'And now over to
Birmingham, where Aled Jones and Pam Rhodes are waiting for us.'
And we were on. The adrenaline rush that we had as we realised
we were part of this massive outside broadcast was just fantastic.
The programme went swimmingly, apart from one tiny hiccup
caused by a small person not unrelated to myself.

Mam, Claire and little Emilia had come along to sit in the
audience for the programme and they were given seats in the front
row. Emilia was completely silent during the countdown, but just
as Pam opened her mouth to say, 'Yes, we're here in Birmingham
having a wonderful time, aren't we, Aled?' Emilia began to scream
piercingly behind me. I knew instantly that it was her. Consequently, in the background as we are talking, the viewers could quite
clearly see Claire trying desperately to quieten Emilia down,
because she realised that I was doing my live piece-to-camera in
front of I don't know how many millions of people around the
world. In the next shot of the crowd, during the first hymn, Claire
was still struggling to quieten Emilia down. By the time the second
hymn has come around, Claire has taken Emilia away and Mam is
there on her own, and one hymn later, none of them was there at
all. Despite that, it didn't put a dampener on what must rank as one
of my proudest ever presenting engagements.

Early in 2002, I heard on the grapevine that the *Songs of Praise*
team were planning to make a programme in the Falklands and I
was very keen to present it. I was delighted when I heard that I had
got the job, but I did not fully understand how gruelling the trip
would be. The team arrived at RAF Brize Norton in Oxfordshire:
Susan Kirby, the production assistant whom I had known since my
first programme in Bangor; Mike Jackson, the cameraman; Adrian
Tomlin, the sound man who is known as 'Wombat' to his friends;
and the very young but very talented director, Richard Caruthers.

We checked in and immediately I realised that flying with the
RAF was a little bit different to the great service, good films and
fine food that I had been used to when I flew Virgin Upper Class –
a mode of transport for which I had developed quite a taste while
Claire was working for Richard Branson. In fact the hot, cramped
and uncomfortable DC10 we flew on could not have been more of
a contrast.

After we had checked in, we walked through an area for the squaddies where about three hundred soldiers sat patiently watching television while they waited for the flight. Susan turned to me and said, 'I think we're allowed into the Officers' Mess.' We managed to get past the man on the door and sat down.

'Hey, Aled! How are yer, lad?' came a shout from across the mess. I turned around and saw it was the pilot of the RAF Sea King helicopter who had flown me around Bangor on my very first *Songs of Praise*. His second officer was also from RAF Valley in North Wales, along with a group of others going out to the Falklands for their training. We became so engrossed chatting in the bar that they had to make three announcements for the *Songs of Praise* crew to get on the flight, which made us laugh all the way out there.

We were lulled into a false sense of security eight and a half hours into the flight, because we stopped to refuel in the Ascension Islands, where the weather was baking hot. The plane landed in between two mountains and the helicopter pilots all jumped out into the barbed-wire enclosure surrounding the runway and ran straight into the shop to buy six-packs of lager for the rest of the flight. Two hours later we got back on to the plane, which by now was swelteringly hot. The next time we touched down, though, we were in for a rude awakening – the temperature at our final destination had plunged to minus 15°C.

We shivered in the freezing cold as we left the DC10 and got into a Land Rover, where Richard the director was waiting for us. He had flown out three days ahead of the rest of us and seemed to be delighted that he finally had some company. We spent dozens of hours in the vehicle over the next week. Susan, Adrian and Richard squashed into the back and Mike the cameraman sat in the front. I had to squeeze into the middle between him and the driver, trying to avoid being skewered on the gear stick.

We drove to the Malvinas Hotel in Port Stanley. There are only two hotels in the Falkland Islands' capital, the other being the Upland Goose, where Margaret Thatcher stayed when she visited after the islands had been liberated. As I checked in, the receptionist gave me a knowing wink and said, 'Don't worry, Aled, we've sorted you out. You've got Jim Davidson's room.' It turned out that the only people who had stayed in this room prior to me were Jim Davidson when he was entertaining the troops and Alan Titchmarsh when he recorded his *Ground Force* programme there. The room was lovely and the hotel was warm but when I ventured outside, I had never experienced a temperature anywhere near as low as it was there. I was also struck by how desolate the islands are – there is nothing there, literally nothing there. On the first morning, I did a live interview back to London with Don McLean on BBC Radio Two.

'How are you enjoying it?' he asked.

'Well, Don, to be honest with you, I got off the plane last night after having one of the least comfortable flights of my life and went straight to the lovely hotel. I'm loving it so far,' I replied.

'Well, if they ask me, I'd never go back,' he said. 'I'll tell you that for nothing. I hated it. You can survive it the once – but never again.' After having spent a week there, I have to admit that it was a struggle, but I do think that the place has a real magic to it.

The Falkland Islanders are amazing and are inordinately proud to be British, with pictures of Margaret Thatcher everywhere. In the Upland Goose Hotel, it seemed as if every frame was filled with a photograph either of her or of Sir Denis Thatcher. There was a very serious side to our trip and I felt very privileged to be presenting the Remembrance Sunday edition of *Songs of Praise*, so despite the cold and discomfort, I knew that making a programme that was worthy of commemorating the lives of the men who had fallen in the battle to liberate the islands was a very important job that we had to do.

One of the most special tasks I was given was to carry over to the Falklands the ashes of a soldier who had died on a ship there. He had been cremated in the UK and his wife had asked that his final resting place be on the islands. I handed the ashes over to a priest in Stanley Cathedral. He took the ashes out in a boat and scattered them on the sea, close to where the ship went down. So I knew when I left the Falklands that he was being looked after.

While we were there, the weather gradually worsened. A few days into our stay, we planned to fly to the second island, but the wind and rain was so bad that the helicopter would not have been able to land. The weather there is changeable at the best of times and anybody flying over to the other island is instructed to take a sleeping bag and emergency food with them in case they become stranded. I was quite relieved that we were unable to go because I had heard horror stories of people being forced to stay there for days because the weather had changed completely within a few minutes of them landing. By this stage, I was keen to go home on our scheduled DC10 flight, because it was the longest I had been away from Claire since Emilia had been born.

It is hard to convey just how cold the Falklands are to somebody who is not used to the weather there. For the first time, I really understood the meaning of the term 'biting cold'. It was so chilly that it felt as if any exposed part of your body was being slowly chewed off. Never again will I complain about the cold winds and driving rain that can blow across Anglesey. That simply pales into insignificance when compared to what the islanders have to put up with down there. Even in good weather, it is still freezing. As part of the programme, I was singing a song and reading a poem. These were filmed with me standing on a beach. All over the Falklands, you see signs saying: 'Danger! Mines!' next to a cordoned-off area, of which you are wise to steer clear. There are other signs which warn that there might be mines present and walkers go into the area at their own risk.

Now the director, Richard Caruthers, is a bit of an action man – he had already had me surfing on an edition of *Songs of Praise* from Cornwall. He led us down the pathway on to one of these deserted beaches. I was terrified that I was going to be blown up any minute. I stood there singing a song with the waves lapping around me, looking suspiciously out of the corner of my eye at any object that was floating past in case it was a mine. Richard asked me to take my coat off to read the poem and very quickly my eyes started to stream and my lips started to quiver. There were dewdrops forming on the end of my nose. Afterwards, so many people said to me that it was the highlight of the whole programme for them, because I was crying my eyes out as I recited the poem. In truth, although reading the poem was a very emotional experience, which did bring tears to my eyes, they were already streaming because of the intensity of the cold, which made me feel as if my body was out of control.

At the same time, we knew we were making a programme that meant such a lot to us and to our viewers. We visited both the British and the Argentine cemeteries and I was struck by the enormity of the human loss during the war. The age of everyone who died, particularly in the Argentine cemetery, seemed to be seventeen, eighteen, nineteen years old. The loss of life of such young men, no matter whose side they were on, seemed to me to be such a waste. We went to the place where the Royal Navy ship *Sir Galahad* was blown up and I was shocked to see shells from guns of war still lying on the beach, almost like a permanent memorial to the men whom they killed and maimed.

The soldiers who are on the Falklands today are a long way from their loved ones, but the army does its best to ensure that they do have some home comforts. I was very much aware that I would be going back to my house to see my wife and daughter very shortly, whereas many of them still had months away from their families ahead of them. They work hard on their training exercises in the inhospitable terrain, but their bases contain gyms and swimming pools. I would not have missed making the programme for the world and felt especially honoured to be the presenter of my first Remembrance Day *Songs of Praise*. It was very special to make a programme from a place so difficult to get to, that most people will never have the opportunity to visit. Having said that, when we got back on to the DC10 for the long flight home, I was very thankful to be leaving – not least because I had totally lost my voice. By the time we arrived back at RAF Brize Norton, I could only speak in a croaky whisper. It was the one and only time in my life that I have been completely unable to speak.

I owe a lot to Hugh Faupel, the editor of *Songs of Praise*, who has always backed me to the hilt. He was with me when I was named Religious Broadcaster of the Year in 2004 at the Churches' Media Council Andrew Cross Awards. Believe it or not, no *Songs of Praise* presenter had ever won anything like it before. It was the last award of the evening and many of the top religious broadcasters in Britain had been nominated. Winning frightened me in a way, as I told the audience during my acceptance speech. I said on the night that I felt it was the sort of award that somebody should win when they are about sixty years old. I am still learning to be a broadcaster and I am privileged to work with people whose skills are far greater than mine. I have set myself the target of winning it again. To pick it up once was brilliant, but if I can do it twice, it will mean that I am really making my mark in religious broadcasting.

I also hold the rather less auspicious honour of being the first *Songs of Praise* presenter to appear on Terry Wogan's programme *Auntie's Bloomers*. My own particular gaffe came when we were recording the programme I presented from Bangor Cathedral. The camera was focused on a small group of us in the congregation as we sang the last few bars of a hymn. I did not realise that the hymn also had an 'Amen' at the end. So I sang the final line with a flourish and then tried desperately to hide my embarrassment when everyone around me carried on singing. I could not stop myself from collapsing with laughter.

My television work has continued to grow and in the summer of 2004, I was asked to be the main presenter of *On Show* on BBC1 Wales. Previously, I had been a roving reporter, but it was great to get my feet under the table as the programme's host. It was always hard work because we recorded two editions of the programme in one evening, but it enabled me to meet and have long conversations with all sorts of fascinating people, including the Welsh composer Alan Hoddinott and the actor Matthew Rhys. I ended up comparing notes with him on screen about the trials and tribulations of wearing a jockstrap as an actor. It was also an opportunity for me to meet up with old friends such as the composer Karl Jenkins and the conductor Owain Arwel Hughes. I have been lucky to continue to cover the Eisteddfod and the Brecon Jazz Festival for BBC Wales.

I also presented *Songs of Praise* from my all-time favourite location – Highbury Stadium, the home of Arsenal football club. It enabled me to fulfil my life-long fantasy of being a professional footballer for just one day. The programme started with a shot of me heading and kicking the ball. On the day we recorded the show, the new pitch had just been laid ahead of the 2004–05 season and it looked simply stunning. Even I have now come to terms with the fact that I will never lead the Gunners out on to the pitch as their captain in a game against their arch rivals Manchester United, but as I said earlier, I do still harbour a hope that one day I will be invited to sing there on the pitch before a match.

I receive many letters from *Songs of Praise* viewers, most of which are very complimentary. However, there is a common thread running through a number of them: the fact that I don't often wear a tie with a suit. One of the more bizarre occurrences of this is a letter that turned up in the *Songs of Praise* office in Manchester after my appearance at Highbury. Even though I wore very little but the Arsenal strip throughout the programme, I was still chastised for not wearing a tie. I am not convinced that collars and ties will ever become standard kit for footballers on the pitch.

19. THE BIRTH OF A BARITONE

M y first attempt to relaunch myself as an adult soloist was not a success. It came about before I started working properly on *Songs of Praise*. The BBC asked me to sing the theme tune for a television series called *Get Well Soon*, which starred Anita Dobson. The song was written by the genial Irish singer/songwriter Christie Hennessy. When Christie and I began to work together we hit it off very well, so we continued collaborating after we had finished recording the television theme tune.

Christie has written hundreds of songs and is very well known in Ireland. I started to record some of them and we also wrote some new material together, as well as laying down some old favourites in the studio. I had worked with Telstar when I was a boy and so I went to see the bosses there, Sean O'Brien and Neil Palmer. They were both very enthusiastic and said, 'Make an album with Christie.'

So we went to Battery Studios in North London, where Robbie Williams has recorded his albums. We were there for a month and made an album largely of ballads, which ended up being called *From the Heart*. It was a really exciting process. Christie made me sing in a very different way from what I had been used to. Instead of singing out, he asked me to use only about an eighth of my voice, so I would almost be whispering the songs. It worked brilliantly for some, but others really did need my full voice. I know now that my classical adult singing voice was not ready at that stage. It needed a few more years of development before being unleashed on the listening public. Nevertheless, it was a very beneficial experience for me, because so many great musicians took part in the project and I was allowed to become involved for the first time in all aspects of making a record, as opposed simply to just turning up and singing.

After recording the album, I did a photo shoot for the cover and made a couple of videos. Suddenly, Telstar decided they were going to release it a year later than planned. I was completely crestfallen. It meant that I had to wait in limbo for another twelve months. I had made no secret of the fact that I hoped that *From the Heart* would relaunch me as an adult singer.

Eventually, the album did come out and nothing really happened. I did a few television and radio interviews to promote the record, but it failed to capture the public's imagination. Shortly afterwards I received a very nice letter from Neil Palmer at Telstar saying, 'I have got to let you go, but I am sure that the pendulum will swing one day and you will start to sing again.'

And he was right. The pendulum did swing back very firmly in my favour with the release of what I consider to be my first proper adult album, simply called *Aled*, in the autumn of 2002. It all came about through *Songs of Praise*, really. In the second programme that I presented, I was asked to sing a song called 'Vespera' and so I began to work closely with Robert Prizeman, the programme's music supervisor. From the start, it was a real pleasure to record with him. After that, they asked me to sing with Mal Pope, who is a Welsh songwriter, singer and presenter, whose band was to sing at my wedding. I went down to his studios in Swansea and a producer called David Tavener asked me to sing 'For Once In My Life', the song made famous by Stevie Wonder, but he made me slow it right down so that it was much more a ballad. I was very nervous about recording a song that was so closely associated with Stevie, because he is one of my favourite singers and I wanted to make sure that I did the song justice.

The *Songs of Praise* viewers liked it so much that many of them wrote in to *Points of View* to ask to hear the song again. Mark Wilkinson, who is in charge of classical music at the massive record label Universal Classics & Jazz, was one of the people watching *Points of View* that afternoon. He liked what he saw – and more importantly, heard – and asked me to go to see him. By now, I was being managed by Peter Price, who had looked after my career at

10 Records all those years before. Mark was very encouraging and was keen to sign me on the back of the one piece he had seen me perform on the television. I met with the label's big boss, the very cuddly Bill Holland, and the marketing director Dickon Stainer, and they asked me to do a few more recordings with Robert Prizeman. This was the easiest thing in the world because by then I had already recorded four or five pieces with him for *Songs of Praise*. They signed me for a five-album deal as the first artist on the brand-new UCJ label, which has since signed people like Katherine Jenkins, John Rutter and Myleene Klass. I was delighted – I just hoped that I could repay Bill, Dickon and Mark's faith in me by delivering them a successful album.

At around the same time, Peter Price and I were invited for lunch at the Conran restaurant, Sartoria, in London's Savile Row. Our host was Roger Lewis, the managing director and programme controller of Classic FM. I had not met him before, but was delighted to find that he too was Welsh, which instantly endeared him to me. By the end of the meal I liked him a whole lot more. He was very jovial and bouncy and we had a lovely lunch. I had been told beforehand that there was a chance that I would present a one-off Christmas special for Classic FM, which I was delighted about. Ever since the station first began broadcasting in 1992, I had always wondered whether I could fit in as a presenter. At the end of the meal, Pete asked, 'When would you like Aled to do the programme?'

'Oh, we'd like him to do a lot more than that,' replied Roger with a smile. 'We were thinking that maybe he could become the permanent presenter on Classic FM on Sunday mornings between seven o'clock and nine o'clock. We'd be happy to commit to Aled for a year.'

'Wow!' was all I could manage to stammer in reply. I left the restaurant on cloud nine. Pete and I went to a pub around the corner and shared a bottle of Chablis as a celebration. I was over the moon, I really was. It was not just because I love classical music and I have been involved in it all of my life, but because Classic FM is a radio station that is listened to by so many people across the UK. I still get a buzz about that every time I go on air or when I hear one of my songs being played on the station now.

In the summer of 2004, I met the Queen for the first time as an adult after a performance at Westminster Abbey. She told me how pleased she was that I was back singing again. Then she told me that her husband listened to my Classic FM programme each week. Prince Philip turned to me and said, 'Oh no. I only listen to that Jones fellow.'

'That's me,' I said.

'Oh yes, Sunday mornings,' he replied with a smile. Now, while I am presenting the show, I think about the Duke of Edinburgh sitting in his study listening each week.

Making records these days is slightly different from how I used to do it when I was a boy. All of my recordings are made at Robert Prizeman's house overlooking the beautiful Surrey countryside. He is the consummate musician and I respect his musical expertise more than anyone else with whom I work. When I arrive at his house, a microphone has always been set up in his living room, which has a magnificent view through the French windows. The wire runs all the way through the house, through the kitchen and into a room that was once the garage but has now been turned into a recording studio. Robert works alongside Ian Tilley, who is the co-producer and sound engineer. It is just the most relaxed environment possible in which to make an album. Robert sits there listening and making suggestions. Occasionally, he plays the piano to accompany me and he then mixes in the other instruments afterwards.

Now that I have a taste for making records this way, I always want to work like this in the future. Robert and Ian know just how to get the best out of me and they are very strict about not letting me dwell on anything I feel has gone slightly wrong. This is good news because I am such a perfectionist that I could happily spend a week recording a single line in a song if they indulged me more. Instead, we always aim to share a genuine performance with the people who buy the albums so we record each piece all the way through.

I probably do about three or four full performances of each song, but I never know how they will turn out because Robert absolutely refuses to allow me to hear them played back on the day of recording. Instead, a week or two later, a CD lands on my doormat and Claire and I sit on the sofa at home and listen through it together. The first time this happened, I was pleasantly surprised at how I sounded, because I had never before heard myself properly singing as an adult. On my first album, I am still particularly proud of 'Pie Jesu' by John Rutter. The last phrase of the song seems to go on for ever and I recorded it all in one breath, moving into the falsetto at the end. It was such a voyage of discovery for me to understand what I could achieve with my voice, and my principal emotion each time I heard a finished song for the first time was a sense of relief.

I would describe the repertoire that I sing now as being a mixture of church and easy-listening classical music. It is what I have always done and it is the area of music in which I definitely feel the happiest. I was very relieved that Universal did not ask me to go down the musical-theatre route, which I would not have wanted to do at the time. It was very brave of them to allow me to revisit my heritage. I know when I have sung well: I feel physically drained afterwards because I have put so much emotion into the song. The best way for me to describe in words what I feel about the music that I sing is that it makes my heart soar. I hope that through my records, people are rediscovering some of the great religious pieces that have been written over the years. Funnily enough, since the release of *Aled*, I think that other people have been copying our formula like mad.

Singing and recording songs are only the first things that you have to worry about when you set out to make an album. There is all sorts of other stuff involved and I try my hardest to keep control as much as possible of everything else that is going on around the edges. I am very lucky that Mark at Universal allows me to become involved. I value his opinion on my singing because he has a great musical ear, which is something that can be rare among record company executives.

I like to work with the fantastic stylist Peter Hawker when I am having my photograph taken for an album cover. Peter has been working in show business for years and has styled the likes of Bros, Atomic Kitten and Kylie Minogue, although he is best known for his work with Tom Jones. He has a unique style as well as being outrageously funny. The cover shot for an album is one of the most important things to get right after the music, not least because it lives with you and follows you everywhere for an entire year.

Just as when I was a boy soprano, the most important thing for me is to have a team around me whom I trust and like. We all exist really closely together for a long period of time and, so far, I have been really lucky about everyone who has worked with me on my albums.

I thought I was going into this business to become a singer, but it is amazing how many hours I have spent over the years having my photograph taken. It is something that I had to get used to when I was a boy so it does not really bother me now. Although, I have to admit to always being a little bit disappointed with the end results of virtually all the photo shoots I have ever done. The pictures never quite come out how I imagine them beforehand. Of course, my ugly mug might have something to do with it.

For *Aled*, my first adult album, the record company decided to whisk me off to Dungeness to have my pictures taken on the desolate beach in the shadow of the nuclear power stations. It was pretty cold, although at this stage I had yet to go to the Falkland Islands, so I had no comprehension of the true meaning of the word 'freezing'. We wanted the first album to have quite a 'real' look to it, with a sense of the elements – wind, rain, sunshine – and that is what came through in the photographs with pebbles, old sheds and peeling paintwork in the background of each of the shots.

The boys choir Libera have appeared on all of my albums and they are truly brilliant. They are all ordinary lads with extraordinary voices, who sing in a church in Surrey on Sundays and who appear in concerts and make records as well. Robert Prizeman is their music director and he treats them like adults rather than kids and they respond accordingly. They have all got nicknames and are great fun, but at the same time they are incredibly professional about their singing. The sound that they make is simply divine with the whole group singing together as one, just as all the best choirs do. I am pleased how much their style has fitted in with what I have tried to do on each of the albums.

Once a singer has finally made their record and it is on sale in the Virgin Megastore, HMV or W.H. Smith, it is time to get out and promote it. Now, I love this part of my job and I cannot for the life of me understand singers who record an album of which they are really proud, but who then don't seem to want anyone to buy it. Now, to do it properly is definitely hard work, but it can also be fun. I have always had great support from Des O'Connor and Melanie Sykes on their programme *Des 'n' Mel*, which goes out every weekday on ITV1. It has become one of the most influential television shows in the UK for classical-music artists – appearing on *Des 'n' Mel* can be the difference between having a number-one bestselling album and being just an also-ran. They are both great fun and work incredibly hard at producing so many hours of quality live television each week. I was lucky that they had a good response from their viewers to my first performance, and I ended up singing on the programme three times during 2002.

One of the more gruelling things that I did was to be interviewed by BBC local radio stations up and down the land – not because the interviewers were ever anything less than intelligent and charming, but because I had to do all of them in one go, one after another. I went to BBC Broadcasting House in central London and walked up to the first floor, where I was directed to a very small cubicle containing a microphone and little else. Each of the local stations had a twenty-minute slot to interview me. So first off, it might have been BBC Radio Cambridgeshire with a live programme and next it might have been BBC Radio Kent with a pre-recorded show. Because each of them were talking to me about exactly the same subject, the questions tended to be remarkably similar. It is absolutely exhausting, but I always try to remember that the people at the other end will only ever hear one of the interviews, so I try my hardest to answer in a different way and to keep my responses as fresh as possible. By the end of the day, I could accurately predict how each of the presenters would introduce me on air: 'You remember that cute-faced little boy who sang "Walking in the Air"? Well, he's got a new album coming out. So, what have you been doing since then, Aled?' I usually try to make a joke by saying that I hibernated in a cave in North Wales and only ventured out when it got warm enough.

Some people say that I must have a screw loose because I enjoy doing regional press, television and radio interviews and perform-ances, but I just ignore them. True, charging around the country cramming as many appearances as possible into the shortest period of time is physically draining, but I love meeting new people and going to new places. I always try to find the fun in each and every situation as it occurs.

I launched my new baritone voice as an adult in St David's Hall in Cardiff at a special live concert edition of *Songs of Praise*. Libera were there, as were the all-female quartet Bond and an orchestra of about thirty musicians. I was especially pleased when the great cellist Julian Lloyd Webber agreed to perform. Julian has been a great friend ever since we first appeared together in concert when I was a boy soprano. In essence, our friendship revolves around me teasing him about how badly his beloved Leyton Orient football team are doing. I have been lucky to perform with him many times in concerts and on records. He is a very generous, warm and exciting performer and underneath his studious-looking exterior he has a wonderfully cheeky personality, which shone through when we competed together on *Ready Steady Cook!* Modesty prevents me from gloating about the fact that I beat him hands down.

The Cardiff concert happened about a month after I had flown back from the Falklands. I was having real trouble with my voice after catching a cold over there. It got so bad that I could not speak, let alone sing. I was unable to rehearse for my big night and was becoming increasingly stressed. I knew how important for my future it was to get that one performance right. In truth, my voice was not at its best on the night, through no fault of my own, but I got away with it. In fact, I more than got away with it and the evening was hailed as a big success. I went on stage and gave it everything I had. I actually began to enjoy myself. When I walked back on at the end of the concert to take a bow, the audience cheered loudly and I felt like a proper singer again for the very first time since I was sixteen.

The promotion for the album then got under way in earnest and I toured the country, singing on television shows in Leeds, Manchester, Glasgow, Cardiff, Dublin and Belfast over the next month. On each occasion, I would meet my fabulous regional press and publicity manager, Joe O'Neill, at Heathrow Airport, usually very early in the morning. We would always stare sleepily at each other before grunting a greeting. The conversation only ever started to flow once we had imbibed a couple of strong coffees in the British Midland lounge. Once the television show had been broadcast, we would head back to London on the plane, only for the whole performance to be played out again the following day, this time with a different destination.

Joe is huge – well over six feet tall – and he always teased me for pre-booking my seat on the aisle, as one of a pair, rather than near the window or in the part of the plane where the seats run three across. I love flying, but I am very particular about where I sit because I believe in making it as pleasurable an experience as possible. Joe always tended to leave his seat booking to chance, but after the first week of regional promotion for the album, where on a couple of occasions he was sandwiched between two people on a row of three, he finally saw the light. I have a sneaking suspicion –

and more than a little pride – that he has now turned into as much of a plane spotter as me. Joe never ceases to amaze me when he flies, because the moment the plane leaves the jetty and starts to taxi down the runway, he falls soundly asleep. His snoring only stops when there is any hint of the food being served, at which point he sits bolt upright and wide awake.

One of my favourite regular television interviews is in Belfast, where I have been a guest on the Gerry Kelly show every year since I started singing again as an adult. He is on Ulster Television week in week out, right through the year. The other guests I have met have all been particularly interesting: pop stars Gabrielle and Westlife, the boxer Frank Bruno, the designer Linda Barker and the explorer Sir Ranulph Fiennes. He had to leave to fly back to London before I was due to sing on the programme, but he asked the researcher to pass on a message to me that he loved my singing. I was very touched and it never ceases to bowl me over when people say things like that. Ever since, I have wondered if he has taken any of my CDs with him on his adventures.

Aled was finally released on Monday 14 October 2002. The first day was horrible because I had no idea how it was selling. The record company only starts to get an inkling of how a new album is doing on the Tuesday after its release, when they can analyse the first day's sales figures. The only thing I knew in advance was how many copies the record shops had pre-ordered. Universal seemed encouraged, but it did not stop me from worrying about whether anybody would actually go out and buy one. By the Friday evening, they were confidently predicting that *Aled* would be number one in the classical chart and among the Top 30 bestselling pop albums as well. Still I worried, because there was still one day's sales to go on the Saturday afternoon. What if somebody else had a sudden surge of fans going out to buy their album? Would I be knocked off the top spot?

Record companies and broadcasters receive the new chart on a Sunday afternoon. Mark Wilkinson phoned me with the news that we were definitely number one in the classical charts and number 25 in the pop charts. I was unbelievably relieved. After trying for so long to relaunch myself as an adult performer, it looked like our plan was coming together. From then onwards, my feet did not touch the ground until after I had finished presenting the Classic FM breakfast show on Christmas Day.

Being a singer is different to being any other kind of musician because your instrument is inside you. So if you go out and overindulge the night before a concert, the following day it will be hard work on stage; whereas if you have an early night and get enough rest, it can be the most enjoyable thing in the world, because you are communicating with people. After the success of *Aled*, I became more confident about my new voice and I started to enjoy singing far more. Now, I really have fun when I am up on stage – I cannot get enough of it. I still have regular singing lessons, which help me to improve my voice and I am feeling more powerful and strident as a singer. My teacher, Penny Harvey Piper, says this is because I have started singing from the very centre of my body. I even feel that it has had an effect on my speaking voice, which is more resonant than before. These days, you just can't stop me.

My fans have always been very important to me. After all, there is no enjoyment in making music unless you have somebody else to share it with. The letters I receive about my singing from listeners to Classic FM or viewers of *Songs of Praise* are very special to me. Many of the writers say that my music has actually touched them. No performer could ask for anything more and whenever I read these letters, I find it a completely humbling experience.

I have now stopped listening to myself singing on stage, which is a real breakthrough because I used to listen so much that it would prevent me from giving my best possible performance. Now, all I want to do is communicate and the less a singer listens to themselves, the more their audience will hear. Basically, I suppose that I give more of myself on stage now than I used to. I am always aware of the responsibility I have to my fans to give them records and concerts that they will enjoy. I have brilliant fans who have been with me from the beginning. They have really hung around and they didn't have to and I will always appreciate the way in which they have stuck by me over the years.

Before Christmas 2002, *Aled* achieved gold-disc status, meaning that it had sold more than 100,000 copies in the UK. For me at the time, this was the most important gold disc I had ever been awarded. I put it up in my office at home and felt that I could then put all the discs I was given as a boy soprano up on the wall beside it.

One of the highlights of that period was appearing on the front cover of *Classic FM Magazine* with the headline 'Aled's back!' That time, I had to share the cover with the clarinettist Julian Bliss, the violinist Chloe Hanslip and the mighty Bryn Terfel. However, two years later I was very proud to finally grace the cover of the magazine on my own to promote my Christmas album. It was worth the wait.

In May 2003, my manager Pete flew with me to Australia where *Aled* was being released. I did a series of television and radio interviews and I was delighted to see that it zoomed into the number-ten position in the pop charts. Australia is an amazing country and I loved getting off the plane and seeing Sydney Opera House and Sydney Harbour Bridge. The first week I was there, I was number two in the classical charts, with my old friend Sarah Brightman preventing me from taking the top position. The second week I was there, I was disappointed to see that she was still at number one, despite all the hard work I was doing to promote the album.

One of the most influential breakfast radio shows in Australia is presented by Alan Jones (no relation) on 2GB Radio in Sydney. Alan was a larger-than-life character who actually cried when he played 'O Holy Night' on his show one morning while I was there. He implored his listeners to go out and buy the record as a Mother's Day present. Just after takeoff on the way home, I telephoned Alan in the studio to say thank you to him for all of the support he had given me while I was in Australia. He was live on air and he put me straight through. 'You're number one!' he bellowed. It was the perfect end to the trip – just as I was flying out of Australian airspace, I discovered that I had cracked it there after all. It was a job well done in a country that is a long way from home.

The other radio show that I particularly enjoy appearing on every time I am in Australia is presented by Ernie Sigley on 3AW in Melbourne. We have a strong repartee, based on his own experiences as a choirboy.

The main difference between doing television programmes in Australia and in Britain is that you have to sing live in Oz – miming is never an option. This means that an intensive publicity tour is always going to be very tiring, as I found out on my first visit. One of the country's biggest television shows is *Good Morning Australia*, presented by the legendary Bert Newton. It runs throughout every weekday morning and my first appearance on the programme was due to go out at an incredibly early hour – even so, I was made to sing live. Nowadays, whenever I am going to guest on Bert's show, I always make sure that I go to bed early the night before. My musical director Ian Tilley, on the other hand, does not always follow this sensible course of action. On one occasion, I came downstairs for a very early breakfast at our hotel and found him still in the bar, drinking brandy with Robbie Williams's father, who was staying with Robbie in our hotel.

I am very keen now to go back to Japan as an adult performer. My fans there used to be teenage girls, but now they are more likely to have children of their own. The toughest country for any performer to crack is the USA, but I would love to give it a go. There is a strong tradition of Christian music there and I hope that my style of singing would find an audience.

If I thought I had put myself under pressure by releasing *Aled*, then I had no idea how much of a challenge I would face in getting ready to release my second adult album, which was called *Higher*. By anybody's standards, the first one had been a success. In fact, it has remained in the classical charts for more than two years after its release – something I find unbelievable considering how many classical albums are released each week. I needed to prove to myself that the first album had not just been a flash in the pan and that I was more than just a 'one hit wonder'.

My voice, which was baritone for the first album, had actually moved slightly higher in pitch, towards that of a tenor, which is why we eventually settled on the title *Higher* for album number two. I gave Mark Wilkinson a list of more than a hundred songs from which to choose. I knew that I was singing better than I had been the year before and I was keen to make sure that the new developments in my voice were reflected on the record.

We went through the whole process of choosing the tracks before I went off again to Robert Prizeman's house to lay them down on tape. When it came to the front-cover photograph, Universal decided to stick me right up on top of the London International Press Centre building. The view was magnificent, with St Paul's Cathedral on one side and the building known as 'the gherkin' on the other. This would also be the backdrop for the promotional video for the album. Once again, my stylist Peter Hawker gave me a fantastic 'look' for the cover shot and video. In fact, I liked that picture so much that we have used it again for the cover of this book.

Off I went again around the television and radio studios to tell everyone what I had been up to over the previous twelve months. Robert Prizeman had been hugely encouraging throughout the production process, saying that he believed my voice was better than it had ever been as an adult. *Higher* was finally released and I was more than a little relieved to see it enter the classical charts at number one and the pop charts at number nineteen – considerably higher than *Aled* the year before. I was particularly pleased that an album called *Higher* had not charted *lower* than its predecessor.

I did not feel anywhere near the same amount of pressure with the release of my third record at the end of 2004, *The Christmas Album*. Believe it or not, it was exactly nineteen years before that I first brought out an LP of that name. This was something that I had really wanted to do, because although a lot of people associate me with the festive season due to the success of 'Walking in the Air', I had only ever made the one specific Christmas disc as a boy – all my other childhood albums were released at other times of the year.

The *Songs of Praise* executive producer, Medwyn Hughes, had come up with the idea for a Christmas edition of the programme that I should duet with the young Aled singing 'O Holy Night', so Robert Prizeman took the original and cut it up. I sang along with it in the studio. When the two versions were mixed together, it was uncanny – all of the musical phrasing was exactly the same. The only difference, of course, was that I sang in a deeper voice. That duet appeared on *Aled* and it started me thinking about the possibilities for doing more Christmas repertoire. Medwyn had the idea in the first place of me working with Robert Prizeman and Libera. That is why he's credited as 'Mr 10%' in the acknowledgements on my first album, 'Mr 15%' on the second and 'Mr 20%' on the third. Although, as we always joke, it is only a percentage of my love rather than any hard cash.

I do love carols and every Christmas I have presented quite a few special programmes for Classic FM, including the breakfast programme on Christmas morning. The music just makes me feel great and I set out to make the definitive Christmas album that I had always wanted to do, packed full of everyone's favourites, but with one or two surprises thrown in as well. For example, the version of 'In the Bleak Midwinter' had a very atmospheric, almost eerie quality to it. My favourite track on the album was 'The Coventry Carol' that featured no musical accompaniment at all. Instead I sang a cappella accompanied by a group of male singers. The album contained the big loud hits such as 'Hark the Herald', but also there were quite a few more intimate tracks as well. I have always loved the traditional carols, but during the course of researching the tracks for this album, I have come across some modern carols such as one from Germany called 'Still Still Still' and John Rutter's stunning 'Candlelight Carol'. These are now also among my personal favourites.

Challenging myself vocally does not always mean belting out a song, it can also mean doing something like 'My Life Flows On' on the first album, where I played around a little with the tune. When I do that, it makes it more difficult for me to sing, but at the same time somehow gives the song more emotion. Once again, when recording my Christmas album, I noticed some real development of my voice compared with *Higher*. It is much stronger than in previous years and I can now comfortably hit the top B at the end of 'Hark the Herald'. The work I have done with my singing teacher Penny has given me a lot more confidence here.

I was really pleased with the sleeve for my third album – the photograph was taken by Stuart Weston, who often takes pictures for Vogue. It was studio based this time, rather than being shot outside. In all, the album contained sixteen songs, including a duet of 'Silent Night' between Hayley Westenra and me, which we also performed together on a *Songs of Praise* Christmas special from the Royal Albert Hall. The reaction that evening in the hall was fantastic. Having Hayley on my album comes full circle for us, as I introduced her to British audiences before her first CD came out, when we sang together at the Classical Brit Awards in 2003, also in the Royal Albert Hall.

I particularly enjoyed coming up with the track listing for *The Christmas Album*. I always sit down with a completely blank sheet of paper and then build up a list. At the same time, Robert Prizeman and Mark Wilkinson put together lists of tracks that they think might be suitable. We usually end up with around 65 possibilities, which then get knocked down to around 30 probabilities. Mark, Pete my manager and I then get together in a restaurant and whittle the list down to a final twenty. Robert and I then start recording in the knowledge that some of that twenty will fall by the wayside and others will spring on to the list at a late stage. For instance, with *The Christmas Album*, we were not going to do 'The Angel Gabriel' at first, but in the end it found its way on to the album. And then, I was sitting on the sofa at home talking to Claire about the album and she said, 'Are you going to do "Whence is that Goodly Fragrance Flowing"?'

'I can't believe that nobody has thought of that before,' I replied. So on to the final list it went. I am glad that I took her advice.

Some of the tracks on *The Christmas Album* were suggested by listeners to Classic FM and viewers of *Songs of Praise* through my website. New technology has meant that it is much easier for me to keep in touch with fans around the world. I regularly join them on the discussion forum, posting answers to their questions.

One day, I plan to reveal my countertenor voice with a hidden track on the end of an album. It is something that I have always had a bit of a thing about, because I do have a strong singing voice at this very high pitch, but I have never previously revealed it in public. Maybe one day, I might even make a whole album as a counter-tenor. Who knows?

20. ON THE ROAD

In 2003, I went on my first-ever proper tour, with eighteen dates around the country. As the first concert started to loom large, the rest of the team began to panic about what exactly we were going to do for two hours a night to entertain each of these audiences. So, one Sunday morning after I had finished my Classic FM programme, I pulled a piece of paper from the computer printer in the office just outside the studio and I sat down and said, 'Right, this is what we'll do.' I mapped out the whole evening on the spot and then we stuck to that plan right through the tour.

The first of the two acts who supported me on stage was Duel, the excellent violin duo Greg Scott and Craig Owen. They were great to work with and were massively keen, always turning up at each of the venues with hours to spare. It also seemed logical for me to work once again with Hayley Westenra, who back then was still to become the massive recording artist in the UK that she is today. She alternated with Katherine Jenkins, who was on the same record label as me and who the guys from Universal Classics and Jazz were determined would break through as a big star.

We had three full-scale rehearsals before actually going on the road. At first, my band was made up of Greg and Craig from Duel, a harpist and a pianist – now we have added a viola player and a cellist to the team. Ian Tilley, who works with Robert Prizeman on all of my albums, was the musical director. I knew that it really was going to happen on the day before we were due to set off on the road, when security passes with 'Aled Jones Tour – ACCESS ALL AREAS' emblazoned across them arrived through the post. I must admit that I was quite scared about how the tour would go. What frightened me most was that there was no ensemble for me to fall back on if I was having an off day. Even though I had played the lead role night after night in *Joseph*, this was a different kind of pressure. It was only my name above the door and all of these shows would succeed or fail on my performance. After the first couple of nights, I realised that my fears were misplaced. The tour was shaping up to be great fun.

On the morning of the first concert in Croydon, our extremely professional tour driver picked me up from home. We also had a tour manager in charge of getting everything and everyone from venue to venue in one piece. Again, he had learned his craft over the years with some of the great names in rock'n'roll.

We spent a lot of time together over the next few weeks zigzagging up and down the country from places as far apart as Glasgow and Eastbourne. Very quickly we felt like a family, with great camaraderie developing. Pete and Ian travelled everywhere with me in a massive Mercedes people carrier. We felt like film stars as we languished behind blacked-out windows in the back, sipping iced drinks from the built-in fridge. Our driver would always be waiting for me with gallons of water whenever I came off stage. Performing in a concert is hot work and I need to keep my voice well lubricated, so I can easily drink six or seven bottles of mineral water. As well as the personnel, there was also a huge amount of gear that had to be hauled to and from each of the concert halls. The set, the lighting rig and the sound equipment were all driven around in two huge articulated lorries. As soon as one concert had finished, we would jump back into the Mercedes, the tour manager and technicians would load up the vans, and we would disappear into the night as we headed for the next venue. I never failed to experience a surge of excitement when we arrived at a venue and saw 'Sold Out' written across the promotional poster by the front door.

The audience was incredibly generous and supportive in every single venue. Everyone certainly appeared to have a good time and it was a real thrill at the end of the tour when I realised that we had been given standing ovations at every single performance. It was something that I had never experienced to that degree before. By the fourth or fifth night, we started to know what to expect because the audiences were surprisingly similar in each of the towns and cities we visited. Undoubtedly the best crowd was when I was on home turf in Llandudno. The audience in Northampton was also particularly good and I suppose I do consider the town to be part of my home 'patch' as well, even though it is a long way from North Wales. It felt a little strange to be on stage at the Derngate, when I had been acting for Michael Napier-Brown next door at the Royal Theatre all those years before.

One of my greatest regrets with having all of a tour's dates crammed together into a relatively short period is how little time I have to spend in each of the places I visit. Often, there can only be a couple of hours to spare before each concert once we have done all of the sound checks, and I always try to use this time to conserve my energy before going on stage. I also like to give my voice a rest and so don't do too much talking. Funnily enough, keeping quiet can often prove to be quite a challenge for me.

As well as the support acts and my performances, I always like to include a question-and-answer session in each of my concerts. So we put a card into each of the programmes with 'Ask Aled a Question' printed at the top. I then tell members of the audience to write on it the one thing that they have always wanted to find out from me. At the end of the interval, the cards are handed to me backstage and I then randomly select a question or two to answer between each of my songs in the second half. It is a nice way to involve the audience more closely in the evening and I never quite know what to expect. The questions can be about absolutely anything at all, from the sensible: 'What is your most favourite piece of music that you have ever recorded?' through to the ridiculous: 'Is it true that you have nice legs because I heard Jane Jones talking about them on Classic FM?'

I make it a policy of never reading the questions beforehand, which is fairly unusual. It works for me because it keeps me on my toes on stage and makes every night different. My favourite question of all came from a twelve-year-old called Sam, who wrote: 'Dear Aled, Is it true that you are a fine concert pianist and that you studied at the Royal Academy of Music?' The band started to laugh at this suggestion and the audience very quickly followed suit. So I walked to the back of the stage and gave Nick the pianist a fierce look. 'Up!' I barked at him. Taking his place on the stool behind the beautiful Roland piano which came everywhere with us, I broke into a fine performance of the opening lines of 'Walking in the Air' in a falsetto voice, while accompanying myself on the piano. The audience erupted with laughter, but I think that the band thought that my piano-playing was even more hilarious.

It was the first time the guys from Duel had ever been on a concert tour and I was really chuffed to read on their website afterwards that they had enjoyed it so much. In fact, they described it as being 'laugh-a-minute', saying that it had been the time of their lives. In the end, that is what it is all about for me. There are no hissy fits or prima-donna tantrums. Instead, we all know that we have a job to do and we simply get on and do it, making the most of the opportunities and having a laugh along the way. I try to make sure that all of the musicians are as involved as possible in what happens on stage throughout the evening.

There was one particular technological innovation that I tried for the first time at the beginning of the tour and which made a huge difference to the way I perform in a live concert setting. I started to work with 'in-ear monitors'. Basically, these are moulds of your ears containing an ear piece, which are often used by pop singers. It is very important for singers to be able to hear themselves and I always hated the alternative: a line of speakers at the front of the stage, known to everyone as 'wedges'. Using the 'in-ears', I was at first very conscious of my own voice, so that when I sang I would listen to every nuance. As I have said before, when you do that, you fail to give a good performance because you are using up too much energy on self-analysis. I only wear one of the monitors in my right ear so that in my left ear, I can hear clearly what is going on in the hall. This works perfectly for me because now it does not matter where I am, whether the concert is in a cathedral or a field, the sound is the same for me.

As I have more singing lessons as an adult, I am pleased that I am becoming less self-conscious about my voice. I believe that going on tour and singing regularly to a concert standard has helped me to continue to develop. I know that my adult sound has not yet achieved one hundred per cent of its potential, but I am delighted that it is changing for the better all of the time. I reckon that right now I am probably about 65 per cent of the way there.

Our final night of the 2003 tour was in Southend. During the afternoon, I did an interview with my old friend Henry Kelly on his afternoon programme on LBC Radio. When we left the LBC studios in West London, we thought that there was plenty of time to spare, but the traffic was horrendous between London and Essex. I sat in the back of the Mercedes and became increasingly agitated as the clock on the dashboard raced towards the concert's start time of half-past seven. We finally arrived at the Cliffs Pavilion with literally one minute to spare. I had already changed into my stage suit in the back of the car. We screeched to a halt outside the stage door and I ran into the theatre. I rushed to the toilet, which is always a must before a performance. There is nothing worse than being caught short standing on stage in front of a couple of thousand people. Then I stood in the wings and heard Pete making the pre-performance announcements. I think he may well be a frustrated performer, because he gradually built up this role during the eighteen nights we were on the road. It never failed to make me smile to hear him saying something along the lines of: 'And this evening, the role of the soprano will be played by Katherine Jenkins.'

That night in Southend, I breathed a sigh of relief that each of the eighteen nights had gone so well, even if we were all absolutely exhausted by the end of the tour. I took my shoes off my aching and sweaty feet and ceremonially threw them straight in the bin in my dressing room. We had enjoyed eighteen exhilarating nights of laughter and fun and I was itching to get back on the road around the UK once again. So just over a year later, at the end of 2004, we went on a countrywide tour for the second time. We set out to build on the success of the previous year, but also decided to do everything much bigger, with more lights and effects. As it was just before Christmas, all of the concerts had a very festive flavour, with the audience joining in with some of the carols. Another of my favourite parts of the tour was the moment when I sang a duet with a recording of my younger self on stage.

The tour began in Lancashire and then took in dates in Scotland, England, Northern Ireland and Wales before three magical nights at the Cardiff International Arena, the London Palladium and the Guildhall in Preston in the week just before Christmas. By the time of the party on the last night I was exhilarated and exhausted in equal measure. I certainly spent a lot of time snoozing after Claire served up the turkey on Christmas Day that year.

As soon as the 2003 tour finished, I went straight to Australia for five concert performances in Brisbane, Melbourne and Sydney. The highlight for me had to be singing on stage at the Sydney Opera House, which has always been a dream of mine. While I was there, I found out that my old friend Nigel Kennedy would be using my dressing room shortly afterwards, so I left behind a cheeky message for him. It read: 'Aston Villa are rubbish. Arsenal Rule. PS I am a better footballer than you.' I bumped into Nigel at the Classical Brit Awards about six months later and he told me how surprised he was to receive my note.

I love Australia and I always enjoy the relaxation of the long flight over there as well. I was once asked in an Australian radio interview if I would ever consider living there full time and I thought long and hard about the question before answering that I probably would not emigrate. The truth is that, much as I really adore the place, I have to confess to being scared of their poisonous snakes. We simply don't have those sort of creatures on Anglesey. Having said that, the idea of visiting Australia and New Zealand every year for the rest of my life would be bliss.

Later on in 2005, I am going back down under for a far bigger tour, which will be incredibly exciting. I also hope to spend some time discovering some new parts of that wonderful country with Claire and Emilia, who are coming with me this time.

In the summer of 2004, I went back to the Llangollen International Eisteddfod for my first performance as an adult. I sang alongside the Opera Babes, who have become great friends. Walking out on stage took me back down memory lane and I don't think that I have ever had such a warm reception from an audience. It was a real buzz from start to finish. Ironically, it was one of the unhappiest times I have ever spent on stage because I had a chest infection and a sore throat. The arena was packed with thousands of people and there was not a seat to be had anywhere. To sing the sort of songs in my repertoire properly, you need to have some tenderness in your voice, but when your throat is playing up you are unable to perform in that way. As a result, I had to project powerfully through all of the songs, performing each one at full pelt. I concentrated incredibly hard and thought that any minute my voice would crack, but thankfully I made it through the concert.

The Llangollen International is probably my favourite of all of the Eisteddfodau because it is all about performing, rather than just being inward looking. I think it is fantastic that the winner of the 'Soprano Under Eighteen' category in 2004 came from Singapore.

Initially, I wondered what on earth someone from that far away was doing in Llangollen and then I remembered how widely respected the competition is around the world. It is a great showcase that underlines the vitality of live performance in Wales. It is so important that people want to come to our country to perform and after all, Llangollen was the place that launched the great Luciano Pavarotti. As I walked around and saw competitors in the national dress of countries from the four corners of the world, I felt immensely proud of everything that has been achieved in Llangollen over the years. I was even more proud that such a magnificent event happens so close to the place I will always call home.

21. *STRICTLY COME DANCING*

I was invited to take part in the first series of *Strictly Come Dancing* on BBC1, but had to turn the producers down because I was in Australia on tour when the programme was on air. I am not sure that I would have been brave enough to have done it anyway. I must be on a hit list for reality TV programmes somewhere because during 2003 and 2004 I was asked about taking part in *Celebrity Boxing*, in aid of Comic Relief, *The Games*, a reality athletics event on Channel 4, and *I'm a Celebrity Get Me Out of Here*.

When the offer came through for the second series of *Strictly Come Dancing*, I really fancied having a go because it would help me to get fit and also because I knew that it would be a big challenge to try to master something that I couldn't do. Even though I had been to all those dance classes at the Bristol Old Vic, I was still seriously inept on the dance floor; I even hid in the bar at my own wedding reception because I was scared about having to show up my inadequacies in this department when the time came for Claire and me to have our first dance.

My family and friends all thought that I was mad to agree to take part in the programme and that I was setting myself up for a huge fall. However, I remembered my days playing Joseph in Blackpool. Often, on Thursday evenings, the cast would go down to the Tower Ballroom and we would see these people who had walked in off the street and who were able to just get up and ballroom dance with unbelievable proficiency. It was a real art that I fancied mastering.

The BBC made me wait for about six weeks before announcing that I was definitely going to be one of the contestants on the show. From the moment the news became public knowledge, I never looked back and *Strictly Come Dancing* became one of the most rewarding things I have ever done.

My dance partner was Lilia Kopylova, who, together with her husband and regular dance partner, Darren Bennet, was the South American Showdance Champion and World Professional Rising Star Champion of 2003. Darren was also taking part in the programme, dancing alongside the *EastEnders* star Jill Halfpenny.

My first meeting with Lilia was captured by the *Strictly Come Dancing* cameras. None of the celebrity contestants had been told anything about their partners. Each of us was filmed talking about what we expected, before our partners were revealed to us. My rather embarrassing initial reaction to being introduced to Lilia was to say, 'Oh, I'm so pleased you're not a man.' She was rather miffed about this comment, but I had this nagging fear at the back of my mind that the producers would set me up to dance with a bloke.

Lilia and I hit it off instantly and we joked about putting glass in the other dancers' shoes to knobble them ahead of the first week's programme. As soon as our meeting had been filmed, we were driven straight to BBC Television Centre for our first wardrobe fitting. As we arrived I was struck by the huge buzz surrounding the programme. Even though I had been presenting *Songs of Praise* for BBC1 for five years, I had never experienced anything quite like it. This was a big budget, mainstream Saturday night entertainment programme with a team of around 150 people working behind the scenes to make it happen.

I was taken to wardrobe and make-up ahead of our first photo session. Lilia wore a striking green dress which was slashed right across the front and back, while they put me in a sparkly wraparound shirt with black trousers and high-heeled shoes. 'What have I done?' I thought to myself. I was absolutely petrified, although just a few weeks later I would become completely comfortable with the garish costumes.

The next day, they filmed the advert for the programme, which would run on BBC1 ahead of the first show. The guy who was making it was a little naughty because he said that all the other celebrities were doing a lot of dancing in their ads. He suggested that I dance down the aisle of a church wearing my glittery outfit.

Being a complete fool I said, 'Ok, fine.' There was no choreographer there and I just made up what I presumed to be something approaching dance moves as I jiggled between the pews. Just as I moved close to the camera, I looked into the lens and blew a kiss. When I watched it being played back, I realised that it was probably the campest thing I have ever done on television. I was certainly ribbed about it more than anything else while I was on the programme.

The pace started to hot up very quickly after this with my first training session with Lilia taking place just a day later. It was horrendous because the cameras were there the whole time. Lilia and I got on very well. She was similar to me in attitude, but her teaching methods were very frightening. I think that she realised pretty soon into our first training session that I respond best to being pushed hard. Despite the workload, we always had a lot of laughs during training and our mishaps would often appear on *It Takes Two*, the daily BBC2 show which ran alongside the main Saturday night programme.

In the first week we did 16 hours of rehearsals and in each of the weeks that followed we put in about 25 hours of work, only having Sundays off. Our main training base was in Ballet Rambert's studios in West London. I found it hilarious because there were posters of people with beautiful bodies all over the wall. I was pretty fat on the first day that I went in there. Lilia pointed to a picture of one particularly muscle-bound dancer and said, 'I will get you like that one day.' Despite my scepticism, it became closer to being a reality the longer we stayed in the competition.

I had one added complication during the eight-week run of *Strictly Come Dancing* – a real lack of time. I was in the middle of a thirty-date concert tour and was also recording a series of Christmas specials for *Songs of Praise*, as well as presenting my weekly Classic FM Sunday morning programme. Lilia joined me in Ely for a rehearsal after I had sung for *Songs of Praise* at the Cathedral. She hit me with the news that our first dance in front of the nation would be to the Ricky Martin hit 'She Bangs'. I nearly died of laughter because I thought she was joking. Of course, it turned out that she was deadly serious and, in the end, the song proved to be an inspired choice.

We rehearsed for three weeks before the first show. I have to admit that I was shocked at the amount of sheer hard work that was necessary. It reached the stage where I was putting every available hour into dancing, whatever time of the day I could squeeze it in to my schedule. Often, this meant getting up incredibly early in the morning and creeping out of the house while trying not to wake Claire or Emilia.

I met my fellow contestants on the Friday night before the first show. They came from a variety of backgrounds: the actresses Jill Halfpenny and Sarah Manners; the television presenters Diarmuid Gavin, Quentin Willson, Carol Vorderman and Esther Rantzen; the athletes Roger Black and Denise Lewis; and the comedian Julian Clary.

The programme went out live from Studio One in Television Centre on Saturday nights and that Friday before week one was the first time that any of us had been given the opportunity actually to practise dancing in the studio. It threw me completely and I went in totally the wrong direction a couple of times, dancing backwards when I should have been dancing forwards. There were so many differences from rehearsing in a dance studio, not least the flashing lights and a cameraman running around filming close-ups.

I didn't sleep well on the Friday night and awoke early on the Saturday morning. I arrived at Television Centre at around ten o'clock, by which time Lilia had been in make-up with all of the other female dancers for about two hours. I was so pale that they spent quite a lot of time on me, and in subsequent weeks I was treated to a regular all over body tan, which was another new experience for me. At eleven o'clock, we had our first rehearsal for that evening's show. Then, at half past two, there was a rehearsal with the band. This was the first time that each of us had heard the exact music we would be dancing to that night as, up until then, we had all been working from CDs. The music was played through twice – the first time so that the contestants could hear it and the second time so that they could have a practice dance. One of the big thrills for me in taking part in the programme was being able to dance with the live musicians playing right next to me – it always seemed to spur me on.

At 3.45 p.m., we all took part in a dress rehearsal of the full show, which went reasonably well. It was a real thrill to work with Bruce Forsyth, who was amazing. He is a proper entertainer who worked brilliantly with his two co-presenters, Natasha Kaplinsky and Tess Daley. Bruce was particularly generous to all of the contestants. Once we had finished rehearsing, there was a gap of about half an hour before the actual programme. Lilia was unhappy with my costume because I had lost weight since the first fitting and so it was too loose. She insisted that the wardrobe department sew my shirt and my trousers together, which meant that I had to wait another four-and-a-half hours before I was able to go to the toilet again. That proved to be testing!

The worst moment of performing each week occurred just before we went on as we heard the voiceover man, Alan Dedicoat, saying: 'Will Aled Jones and his partner, Lilia Kopylova, please take to the floor.' It was horrendous because I knew that I had the hardest ninety seconds of live television I would ever do in front of me.

On the first programme, my levels of apprehension and excitement were at breaking point as we walked past the band and down the steps onto the dance floor. I had prepared for it so much and I was aware that I had to deliver. This may sound overly dramatic, but I do believe it was something of a turning point in my life. I became a man properly because I didn't chicken out or shirk at all. I really faced up to the pressure – this was much more the Aled of Bristol Old Vic days rather than the Aled of the Royal Academy of Music days.

We threw everything into our cha-cha-cha and it seemed to go down a storm with the crowd in the studio – no doubt helped by the choice of 'She Bangs' as our song. The judges, led by the legendary Len Goodman, were all positive with their comments and it felt really good as I walked back to the green room with Lilia to talk to Natasha Kaplinsky while we awaited our scores. I was thrilled when we were propelled into second place. The atmosphere back stage was always very supportive. During the programme itself, there was always a mixture of contestants standing around – those who had danced already and those who had yet to prove themselves. Much was said in the press at the time that none of us got on, which was complete and utter rubbish. There was no bitchiness or back-stabbing whatsoever.

Once the main programme had finished, we had a rehearsal of the results programme, which was broadcast live about forty minutes later. The trouble was that nobody had told Lilia and me that it was just a dry run. I was sweating like mad and felt so relieved when Bruce announced that I would be staying in. We trooped backstage afterwards and Denise Lewis whispered to me, 'You know that was a rehearsal, don't you?' I could not believe that we had to go through that tension all over again.

My big aim had been to stay in the competition beyond the first week, so a huge wave of relief swept over me when I heard that the result of the public telephone vote and the judges' scores added together would keep us dancing for another seven days.

Very quickly, my every waking hour became defined by training for the programme. Things were no easier in the second week, when we danced the quickstep to 'Life is a Cabaret'. I had convinced myself that our success the previous week was a flash in the pan and that I would come undone doing ballroom, rather than Latin, dancing. I felt great dancing in tails, but I must admit that I was more than a little surprised when Lilia turned to me, looking pale, and said, 'I can't believe I'm doing this – I haven't danced ballroom for fifteen years!' I found myself reassuring her, rather than the other way around.

When the viewers' votes and the judges' scores were added together, we were in second place again. I was on a high as I went to the bar for a drink afterwards. I walked into the lift to find the football pundit Alan Hansen there, on his way to the *Match of the Day* studio.

'Hello. Are you still in?' he asked.

'Yes', I replied.

'Oh, fantastic! Well done mate!' he said.

I was amazed at how quickly the programme had gripped the public's imagination. It seemed as if the whole of Britain was talking about it. I was truly astounded by the level of interest at home in Wales. Every Monday and Friday, while I was in the competition, I gave interviews to Radio Cymru, BBC Wales, Swansea Sound, Red Dragon FM and the *Western Mail*. The support they gave me was fantastic.

In the third week we danced the jive to the Queen song 'Crazy Little Thing Called Love'. By this stage, I had been rehearsing so much that I had lost three inches around my waist, much to the annoyance of the man who made my costumes. Once again, our performance went down well with both the judges and the audience at home, even though I actually forgot a couple of moves in the middle of the performance. My hastily made-up replacements seemed to pass unnoticed.

By now, my concert tour was well underway and this meant that Lilia and I had to train in venues ranging from a church in Cambridge to the Wiggles Dance Club in Southend-on-Sea, taking in Liverpool, Manchester, Bolton, Cambridge and Glasgow along the way.

In the fourth week, we danced the foxtrot to 'It Ain't What You Do, It's the Way that You Do It'. It was the first dance where I was totally confused by the whole concept. I really struggled to remember to lead with the heel rather than the ball of my foot as I moved forwards across the dance floor. I didn't enjoy it nearly as much as I had the other dances because I felt that it was very restrictive. To help me master the dance, Lilia made me draw our routine on a piece of paper, which really did help. Despite that, I was still suffering from blanks because we would learn a certain section before moving on to mastering another section, but I would not always manage to join them together in my mind. I suppose that learning a dance did have similarities to learning a song, but I found the former much harder. Everything had to be black and white. I needed to know exactly what I was doing with my feet before I could move on and be expressive with my arms or my head.

Things didn't go well with the judges in week four. They said that I looked nervous and as though I hadn't be enjoying it. I have to admit that my primary concern was getting through the dance without forgetting any of it. I was concentrating like mad and so I guess I didn't perform. I was just too focussed and I think that is what caused the problem with the judges. It was the week that my love affair with ballroom ended and I decided that Latin American dancing was much more my cup of tea.

The fifth week of the competition saw us going to the Tower Ballroom in Blackpool, which was an amazing place to dance. It has a very large sprung floor, massive floodlights, a hugely ornate ceiling – and the tiniest glitter ball you have ever seen. It looks as if they ran out of money when they were building it. That week, we were dancing to the Tom Jones hit 'It's Not Unusual' and I was especially proud that I even managed to choreograph a couple of moves for myself. The biggest buzz of the whole competition came when our names were announced and we walked down the stairs onto the dance floor. The crowd gave us an enormous cheer.

We had a lot of fun dancing the samba. The judges and the audience enjoyed it and, for me, it was the musical highlight of the whole series. The programme's musical director, the great Laurie Holloway, created a fantastic arrangement. I was especially excited to find out that some members of the band actually played on the original Tom Jones recording.

The following week, we were back in Television Centre and, for the first time, had to dance twice in one programme – first the waltz and then the rumba. It made rehearsals especially tough because we had to do twice as much work as we had done in previous weeks.

We made it through to the semi-final where our two dances were the passodoble and the tango, both of which are aggressive dances. I tried to inject into my performances the passion that the judges said had been missing in the previous week. I had a sneaking suspicion that this was to be our turn to be voted out of the competition. As soon as I woke up on the Saturday morning, I said to Claire that I just didn't see how I would get through to the final because Jill Halfpenny and Denise Lewis were both technically very proficient and Julian Clary had done extremely well in the public votes in previous weeks. My premonition turned out to be correct and Jill, Denise and Julian went through to the final. I did however have one dancing swansong, in the Christmas special a couple of weeks later when Lilia and I danced to . . . you've guessed it . . . 'Walking in the Air'.

I was extremely disappointed not to get through to the final, as was Lilia. Bruce came up to me and gave me a big hug and a kiss and all of the other contestants crowded around after we had been told who was going through. However, my *Strictly Come Dancing* journey was nothing short of brilliant from start to finish. I have no doubt in my mind that it ranks as the most enjoyable thing I have done during my adult career. At the end of the series, I had lost two stone in weight, I felt stronger mentally and physically, and I felt as though I had become a better performer. It boosted my confidence enormously and was the first television programme that I have done where I have been able to relax completely.

I don't think that I will dance again. I was very lucky to have the opportunity to dance with a champion like Lilia, who was so full of energy and fire. She made the whole experience huge fun and we had a lot of laughs along the way. However, I think that my dancing shoes will remain hanging in the wardrobe at home unused, although I would never say 'never again'. I am certain that Lilia and Darren will go on to truly great heights in the dance world though.

Making the programme meant that I was incredibly busy for nearly three months and I missed being able to spend time with Claire and Emilia. I know that not having me around much was hard for them, but I did enjoy the pressure and the buzz of the programme, which was nothing short of being a life-changing experience.

22. *THIS IS YOUR LIFE*

I never imagined for a moment that I would ever become a victim of Michael Aspel and his big red book. Looking back on it now, the signs that something was going on were there in the days and weeks leading up to my being surprised by him live on stage at the Royal Albert Hall in 2003, but at the time they just passed me by completely.

Claire seemed a little strange in the days beforehand and I did not speak to Mam or Dad for a whole week, which is certainly not usual. I was to be a performer and one of the two presenters at the *Songs of Praise Big Sing 2003* at the Royal Albert Hall, which is one of the biggest programmes of the year for us, with a huge number of people both in the audience and on stage, making it a bit of a logistical nightmare for everyone in the production team. To add to the pressure, I was just getting over a nasty bout of flu, which is probably what comes of having a small child. They do seem to catch every cough and cold within a ten-mile radius of wherever they happen to be, before lovingly sharing them with their parents.

I met the *Songs of Praise* director, Medwyn Hughes, the day before the programme was due to be recorded to check if I could read the Autocue in the hall, because it was a long way from the stage. These special programmes are always really high-pressured. Pam Rhodes is amazing in the way that she learns all of her lines word-perfect. I much prefer to work from a mixture of learned lines and Autocue – it is a great safety net. As we were together, he seized the opportunity to take me through the running order. The first 56 items were very tightly scheduled, but when it came to item 57, it rather starkly said, 'Aled and Pam talk about the evening . . . how special it's been . . . will script individually.'

'Why do you want us to do that?' I asked.

'I'm moving a camera and need to fill the time,' he replied nonchalantly.

'Well, surely I could just go off stage for that bit. It doesn't really matter does it?' I said, because I did not really see the point of standing there waffling on stage.

'Listen, just do it!' barked Medwyn, with a force that surprised me.

I arrived backstage in plenty of time for the script meeting on the morning of the concert, where the director goes through what each of the presenters has to say and where they need to be on stage when they say it. By this point in the production of the programme, everything is usually set in stone. We finally arrived at item 57 and Medwyn started laughing. I was feeling quite sorry for myself because I was not well, and I thought, 'Right, what's going on here? They're finding something about me really funny. It must be because they think I can't fill when he's moving his camera.' I felt even glummer when I went on stage to rehearse with the BBC Concert Orchestra. I started to sing 'I Believe', which was one of the songs on my first adult album *Aled*. After struggling through two verses, I said, 'Listen guys, this isn't working, I'm afraid. I'm fighting a losing battle against my flu. I just can't get any notes out.'

'That's no problem, we can play a backing track and you can mime the song,' replied Medwyn calmly.

I trudged off stage feeling dejected and noticed that Pete, my manager, seemed to be hanging around for no particular reason. Then I wandered into my dressing room only to find that Mark Wilkinson from my record label had turned up.

'What on earth are you doing here?' I asked grumpily.

'Oh, I just came to see how it's all going,' he said with a big smile.

Rowan, who had been responsible for getting me on to *Songs of Praise* in the first place, then came and joined Pete and Mark in my dressing room. I started to become slightly annoyed because they were all just standing there chatting and getting in the way. My stress levels rose. Didn't they realise that I wasn't feeling my best and I needed to concentrate on performing on stage in front of five thousand people in the hall, let alone all of the millions watching at home?

Eventually, I persuaded them all to leave and had a bit of a rest in my dressing room – a quiet period before the storm. Pam and I went on stage to a fantastic reception from the audience. Everything went very smoothly and I started to enjoy myself. The rush of adrenaline from being in front of such a big crowd seemed to have kept my flu symptoms in check. Then it came to item 57 on the running order, the part where we had to fill time while Medwyn moved his camera. Before we did that, Medwyn asked Pam to retake a link because something had gone slightly wrong in the background when they had recorded it the first time. She walked to her position and I started to walk off into the wings. As soon as I started to head for the edge of the stage, Medwyn literally screamed at me through my earpiece, 'Stand where you are!' I was shocked because he was actually yelling and I had never heard him talk like that before. 'Don't you move a muscle. You're spoiling my shot.' I felt like a small schoolboy who has been given a severe telling off by the headmaster. Had I not been standing in front of five thousand people who were unaware of what was going on in my ear, I might well have started to sob.

Then Pam walked over to me and said, 'Well Aled, these sort of evenings are just magnificent.'

'Yes, this is what it's all about,' I replied. 'Five thousand people are here raising their voices to God in celebration.' As I finished speaking, I heard a gasp from the audience and sensed that something was happening behind me. I looked over my left shoulder and there was Michael Aspel with his famous big red book. The first thing that ran through my head was that it was Pam who was his intended victim. Whenever I think of what occurred over the next minute of my life, it always seems to happen in slow motion. Michael walked slowly towards me, put his hand on my shoulder and smiled.

Now I have never been shot, and I very much hope that I don't find out what it feels like for real in the future. But the way I felt at that moment would be exactly how I would imagine being hit by a bullet to feel. It was as if all the energy had drained out of my body. My mouth instantly went dry and I could not move my lips. People often talk about their legs turning to jelly, but mine seemed to go rigid. A dull ache streaked right through my body. My heart seemed to be missing beats. All that I could hear was wild applause from the audience in front of me. Behind me, the BBC Concert Orchestra were laughing like mad people and clapping enthusiastically.

When I watched the broadcast of the programme, I could see that the shock had made me do some very weird things on stage. I bent down. I stood up. I had a look of bewilderment in my eyes. I was so surprised that I had lost control of my faculties.

'Did you know?' I asked Pam.

'Yes, I did,' she replied, grinning broadly.

And she was not the only one. It turned out that everybody was in on the act: from my wife and parents, to my manager and record company, to the entire production team of *Songs of Praise*. I found out afterwards that there was a totally different camera script for *Songs of Praise* in existence from the one that I had seen. Not only were Medwyn and his crew filming *Songs of Praise* that day, but they were also filming me being set up by *This is Your Life*. They had even rehearsed it with a stand-in, before I had arrived. It almost went wrong when I decided to walk off stage because Michael Aspel was waiting in the wings to come on. Had I walked much further, I would have seen him and rumbled what was going on; hence the ferocity of Medwyn's commands to stand still which crackled through my earpiece.

Michael Aspel waited for the applause to die down. 'Aled Jones,' he said slowly and deliberately. 'This is your life.' I rabbit-punched him and playfully pushed him. Much later, I interviewed him for my BBC Radio Wales programme and I felt that I had to apologise for the force of my reaction, citing intense surprise as my excuse. 'Yes, it was rather hard,' he told me with his trademarked understatement.

My only response to hearing the words 'This is your life' on stage at the Royal Albert Hall that night was to stammer plaintively, 'But I am only thirty-two.'

From then onwards, it was a whirlwind. I was subjected to a military-style operation. It was quite late at night by this stage, probably about half-past ten in the evening.

'Do we go to film the programme tomorrow?' I asked innocently.

'No, we're doing it right now, tonight,' came the reply.

A woman producer from *This is Your Life* walked into my dressing room with me. Miraculously, a suit for me to wear had appeared from somewhere and was already hanging up in the corner. Rowan and Sian from the *Songs of Praise* team came in and burst out laughing. I gave them both a hug, before saying a few choice words to them when I found out that they had known exactly what was going on for some time. 'Please, please, please,' I begged. 'I need a drink to help calm my nerves.' Despite their best efforts, all they could come up with was a Diet Coke, because there was no bar open backstage.

The *This is Your Life* producer then took control. 'You don't need to pick up anything, just leave everything here in the dressing room. People will come in and sort out all of your stuff.' Pete was the only person with whom I was allowed any contact and he was standing in the corner smiling broadly at me. I suppose he was fulfilling the role of 'Prisoner's friend' while I was transported to the *This is Your Life* studio at Teddington. Right at that moment, I didn't know whether to hug him or run away from him.

We left the Royal Albert Hall through the stage door before the *Songs of Praise* audience started to depart. They still had one hymn left to sing when I had been whisked off stage. I was led to the newest, shiniest, most blacked-out Mercedes I had ever seen in my life. Pete sat in the front next to the driver, and the producer and I were in the back. Even though it was some time after the 'hit' by Michael Aspel on stage, I was still shaking. In a way, it was horrible because I was not allowed to see anyone other than Pete. I turned to the producer and said, 'I feel really, really uneasy. I don't like surprises. I like to be in control of what's going on.' She smiled and reassured me.

'Are my Mam and Dad down then?' I asked.

'Sorry, I can't tell you who's going to be there,' she said. 'Although your Dad's stayed at home on Anglesey.' This is what I had expected – appearing on television really is not his thing and he prefers to remain in the background proudly watching at home. The producer started to make an increasing number of calls on her mobile phone and as we drove up towards Teddington Studios, she gave a running commentary of our exact whereabouts.

I was very familiar with the studios, which are the home of *Des 'n' Mel*. I was used to parking in front of the building, getting out of the car and walking to the studio through the main entrance, but we seemed to be taking a completely different route right round the back of the studios, to an area which is usually out of bounds. It was eerily quiet because there was absolutely nobody else around.

As we were approaching Teddington, the producer said urgently into her phone, 'We're twenty seconds away from the studio now.'

Somebody had been knocked off their bike and I remember the flashing blue lights of an ambulance, but looking back now it seemed to be happening as if it was in slow motion. When you read a detective novel by somebody like Patricia Cornwell, she describes places in a way that makes them almost 'otherworldly' and I was feeling that sensation right at that moment. The lights on the ambulance still seemed to be rotating really slowly. 'I haven't got a clue what's going to happen to me now,' I thought to myself. As I climbed out of the Mercedes, I looked around but could see absolutely nobody at all in the darkness apart from a couple of security guards with walkie-talkies. They hurried me into the building, which appeared to be devoid of all human life.

What I did not know until afterwards was that as soon as the producer had told the rest of the production team that we were just twenty seconds away from arriving, all of the other guests on the programme were quickly moved out of the way behind closed doors. I arrived in my dressing room with Pete and the producer. The door was shut firmly behind us. There was a huge plate of sandwiches on the table alongside two bottles of Chablis on ice.

'Can I see Claire?' I asked.

'No,' came the answer.

'Is she here?'

'I don't know.' They are that brutal with their victims because they want to capture every last ounce of surprise on stage in front of the television cameras. I gently sipped a glass of wine. My mind was buzzing with questions.

'So what will happen now?'

'Well, we'll take you down to the studio in a minute when everyone's in their place.'

I had my make-up applied there and then in my dressing room, which is unusual because normally everyone is made up in a dedicated area. The very jovial make-up lady asked me how I was feeling and whether I was excited. By way of answer, I turned to Pete and said, 'I'm really not enjoying this.' The thing that was scaring me more than anything else was that here was something to do with my professional life over which I had absolutely no control. I choose the tracks on my records. I choose which television programmes I appear on. And now I was sitting in Teddington

Studios in the middle of the night, without a clue about what was going to happen to me. At that stage, it felt really uncomfortable. Little did I know that the biggest surprises of the night were still to come.

The production team had edited the recording of Michael Aspel pouncing on me earlier in the evening. It was played out so the *This is Your Life* studio audience could see what had happened. I was amazed to find out afterwards that a couple of hundred of these hardy souls had turned up in Teddington at half-past eleven at night without knowing who the programme's victim was going to be. I stood next to Michael behind the sliding doors watching the 'hit' on a small monitor.

'That's one of the best "Gotcha's" we've ever done,' he whispered to me as we watched the Royal Albert Hall audience erupting on the tape. Suddenly, we were surrounded by the sound of the familiar strains of the *This is Your Life* theme tune. I kept on having flashbacks of sitting at home in Llandegfan as a youngster with Mam. I was so small that Mam and I could sit comfortably together on the same armchair watching as Michael Aspel's predecessor Eamonn Andrews surprised another poor unfortunate.

The two doors in front of Michael and me slid open and we stepped out on to the stage to applause from the studio audience. I looked around and my past was sitting there in front of me. I noticed a bizarre assortment of people whom I would never have expected to see grouped together: Ken Bowen, my singing teacher from the Royal Academy of Music, Henry Kelly, actors Ken Farrington, Philip Madoc and Janet Brown along with members of my family including Mam, who was waving. Then I looked again and saw my Auntie Pat and Uncle Colin, Richard Fleming and Guy Lankester from Bristol Old Vic and George Muranyi from the Royal Academy of Music. I was told to go and sit down. The seat next to me was empty, which was a real jolt. No Claire. My mind raced with possible reasons for her not being there. I knew that she would not have wanted to speak on television, so maybe she had been too nervous to appear? Or perhaps Emilia was ill and she had needed to stay with her?

Then the first person to come through the door was, of course, Claire with an enormous smile on her face. 'Are you all right?' she asked as we hugged.

'I love you . . .' I mumbled, looking completely shell-shocked. She, on the other hand, looked absolutely stunning.

All sorts of people had come from all over the country to take part in this programme, which was being recorded just before midnight on a Sunday night on the outskirts of London. The two guests who stick in my mind above everyone else and whose presence on the programme I found incredibly moving were Terry Wogan and Bob Geldof. Terry was unbelievably generous, saying that he was so proud of me for coming back and having a new career and that he had always been proud of me for singing on *Wogan* so many times. He said that he felt as if I was his protégé. By now, I was struggling with my emotions.

But nothing prepared me for the big, big surprise of when Bob Geldof appeared on the screen in front of me. He talked very movingly about his wedding to Paula, saying that I had made their day by singing during the service. I was almost crying, but in true Bob style, he finished his speech by saying that he had not seen me for years and that I was probably a hairy-arsed geezer now. The audience roared with laughter. I turned to Michael Aspel and said, 'Michael, what's a hairy-arsed geezer?'

As quick as a flash he said, 'Ask the Bishop!' and pointed to Bishop Ivor Rees, who was sitting in the front row, laughing hysterically. Bishop Ivor had come all the way from St David's Cathedral and he said some lovely things about me. Just like his boss Rowan Williams, he is one of the truly holy people that I have been privileged to meet in my life.

Just before the end of the programme, the doors opened and Libera came out on stage. They performed 'I Will Sing for You', as they had done at my wedding a couple of years before. On that day, it had made me cry, but this time, on television, I thankfully managed to keep my emotions in check and did not dissolve into tears once again.

Right at the end of the programme, just before Michael handed me the book, the doors opened for a final time and there was Emilia with our friend Penny Poppins, who sometimes looks after her. Emilia had just started to walk and toddled on to the set in a pretty white dress. Feelings of intense love and pride welled up inside me. I walked to the front of the stage with Claire next to me, Emilia tucked under my one arm and the big red book tucked under the other. All of the feelings of bewilderment and shock which had been swirling around my head earlier in the evening were by now long gone. Instead, they were replaced by a sense of intense happiness as

I looked around me and saw so many people that I loved very dearly.

There was a huge party afterwards for all of the guests in the studio that went on until about two o'clock in the morning. Then we went to a hotel in Teddington where all of the people who had come down from North Wales were staying. The *This is Your Life* producers very generously loaded us up with a case of white wine and a case of red wine to help the party go with a swing, saying that they knew that I would want to catch up with all of my old friends. I finally got home to bed at a quarter to five in the morning. By then, I had forgiven everyone for their duplicity during the previous few weeks because it had all been in such a good cause. Even now, though, I still cannot quite believe how involved in the meticulous planning people like Medwyn had been. One of the things that made it even more significant was that the BBC decided to end the series with my programme. Not long afterwards, Michael Aspel announced his retirement from the show, meaning that it was the last new edition of *This is Your Life* ever broadcast.

For me, the programme brought my life into sharp focus. My time as a boy soprano seems a whole world away from the person I am now, although everything I learned back then and all the people I have met along the way have come together to influence my personal and professional life today.

Whether it was singing my first solo in Bangor Cathedral, performing 'Walking in the Air' on *Top of the Pops*, my role as Huw in *How Green is My Valley*, playing the lead in *Joseph*, presenting television and radio programmes, learning to ballroom dance for *Strictly Come Dancing* or singing on stage and on disc today as a baritone, I have always tried to give my best performance and to enjoy the moment.

I don't know where my career will take me in the future. All I can hope is that, God willing, the life that I have still to come will be as rewarding and action packed as the life that I have led so far. The words that I said to Michael Aspel when he first appeared with the big red book on stage at the Royal Albert Hall still echo in my mind: 'But I'm only thirty-two.' Two years later, I still look backwards and forwards with an equal sense of awe.

DISCOGRAPHY

BOY SOPRANO ALBUMS:

Diolch Â Chân (Sain Records, 1983):
Panis Angelicus
Diolch Â Chân
Llansteffan
Y Fwyalchen Ddu Bigfelen
Sara
Caro Mio Ben
Ddwyfol Iesu (Pie Jesu)
Where E'er You Walk
How Beautiful are the Feet
Rhosyn Coch
Lilil Ddwr
The Little Road to Bethlehem
Ave Maria

Ave Maria (Sain Records, 1984):
Ave Maria
Tosturi Duw
Ombra Mai Fu
O Holy Night
Breuddwyd Glyndwr
Amarilli Mia Bella
Defaid a Gânt Bori'n Dawel (Sheep May Safely Graze)
O Köntt Ich Fliegen (O for the Wings of a Dove)
Hwn Yw Y Sanctaidd Ddydd (Plaisir d'Amour)

Nunc Dimittis
To Sylvia
Agnus Dei
Bugeilio'r Gwenith Gwyn
Bethlehem
Ar Adain Yr Alawon (Upon the Wings of Song)
Nant Y Mynydd
Yr Ehedydd
Lausanne
Mae Hiraeth Yn Y Môr
Y Gylfinir
Tylluanod

Voices from the Holy Land (BBC Records, 1985):
Let Us Break Bread Together
Ave Maria (Schubert)
My Lord, What a Mornin'
Deep River
The Holy City
There is a Green Hill Far Away
How Beautiful are the Feet
Ave Verum Corpus
Easter Hymn
Jesu, Joy of Man's Desiring
The Little Road to Bethlehem
The Shepherds' Farewell
Ave Maria (Bach/Gounod)
O for a Closer Walk with God
O for the Wings of a Dove
Tue Bethlehem Dref
O Holy Night
De Virgin Mary Had a Baby Boy

All Through the Night (BBC Records, 1985):
Bridge Over Troubled Water
Yesterday
Intermezzo (Cavallera Rusticana)
All in the April Evening
Where E'er You Walk
Ombra Mai Fu

Hallelujah
All Through the Night
Bless This House
Lift Thine Eyes
Solemn Melody
Star of Bethlehem
Silent Night
O Holy Night
Jerusalem

Christmas Album (BBC Records, 1985):
Away in a Manger
Come Unto Him
Sussex Carol
O Little Town of Bethlehem
St Joseph's Carol
Christmas Star
Ding Dong Merrily on High
Deck the Hall
The Holy Boy
Jesus Christ the Apple Tree
Gabriel's Message
Rocking
Ave Maria
My Heart Ever Faithful
Good King Wenceslas
Hwiangerdd Mair (Mary's Lullaby)
Unto Us is Born a Son

Aled – Music from the TV Series (10 Records, 1986):
O Worship the King
Sheep May Safely Graze
The King of Love
Alleluja (Exultate Jubilate)
O My Saviour Lifted
Thy Hand O God Has Lifted
How Lovely are Thy Dwellings Lord
Love Divine
Bist Du Bei Mir
All Thanks to Thee

Benedictus
Let There Be Peace on Earth

Pie Jesu (Virgin Classics, 1986):
Art Thou Troubled?
If I Can Help Somebody
Zion Hears the Watchmen's Voices
Jesu, Joy of Man's Desiring
Lullaby
I'll Walk Beside You
Pie Jesu
The Crown of Roses
Lausanne
I Know That My Redeemer Liveth
Laudate Dominum
God So Loved the World
At the End of the Day
Pie Jesu

An Album of Hymns (Telstar, 1986):
Morning Has Broken
The Lord's My Shepherd
All People That on Earth Do Dwell
The Day Thou Gavest
Dear Lord and Father of Mankind
O Little Town of Bethlehem
In the Bleak Midwinter
All Hail the Power of Jesus' Name
Amazing Grace
O Come, O Come, Emmanuel
Oh Jesus, I Have Promised
All Glory, Laud and Honour
Angel Voices
There is a Green Hill Far Away
Abide with Me
How Great Thou Art

Handel: Athalia (L'Oiseau-Lyre, 1986):
With Joan Sutherland, Emma Kirkby, James Bowman, Anthony Rolfe Johnson, David Thomas. The Academy of Ancient Music conducted by Christopher Hogwood

Sailing (10 Records, 1987):
Sailing
Scarborough Fair Canticle
Reverend Eli Jenkin's Prayer
Puff the Magic Dragon
Trees
Watching the Wheat
Sea Fever
Bright Eyes
To Music (An Die Musik)
David of the White Rock
The Little Horses
At the River
Simple Gifts
Christopher Robin

Faure: Requiem
Bernstein: Chichester Psalms (RPO Records, 1986):
Royal Philharmonic Orchestra and London Symphony Chorus
conducted by Richard Hickox
Recorded at the Henry Wood Hall, London

The Best of Aled Jones (BBC Records, 1985):
Memory
Yesterday
The Little Road to Bethlehem
O Holy Night
How Beautiful are the Feet
Ave Maria (Bach/Gounod)
Where E'er You Walk
Bridge Over Troubled Water
Ave Maria (Schubert)
Ombra Mai Fu
O for the Wings of a Dove
Star of Bethlehem
Bless This House
All Through the Night
The Holy City

The Best of Aled Jones (10 Records, 1987):
Walking in the Air

Scarborough Fair Canticle
Sailing
All Through the Night
Art Thou Troubled?
Where E'er You Walk
Bright Eyes
Love Divine
Pie Jesu
Panis Angelicus
Jesu, Joy of Man's Desiring
Ave Maria
O My Saviour Lifted
Laudate Dominum
O for the Wings of a Dove

The Very Best of Aled Jones (JVC Victor, 1988):
Pie Jesu (Lloyd Webber)
Alleluja
At the End of the Day
My Heart Ever Faithful
Lullaby
Love Divine
O Worship the King
I'll Walk Beside You
O Little Town of Bethlehem
Ding Dong Merrily on High
Art Thou Troubled?
The Holy Boy
The King of Love
God So Loved the World
If I Can Help Somebody
Come Unto Him
How Lovely are Thy Dwellings
All Thanks to Thee
Unto Us is Born a Son
Pie Jesu (Faure)

Hear My Prayer (Sain Records, 2003):
Hear My Prayer
Laudate Dominum
The Lord's Prayer

Silent Worship
The Children's Home
Panis Angelicus
Diolch Â Chân
Llansteffan
Y Fwyalchen Ddu Bigfelen
Sarah
Caro Mio Ben
Ddwyfol Iesu (Pie Jesu)
Where E'er You Walk
How Beautiful are the Feet
Rhosyn Coch (Heiden Roslein)
Y Lili Ddwr (Schumann – Lotus Flower)
The Little Road to Bethlehem
Ave Maria
Bridge Over Troubled Water
Too Young to Know

BARITONE ALBUMS:

From the Heart (Telstar, 2000):
Tears in Heaven
Father and Son
Tell Me, Boy
Christmas Song
Whenever God Shines His Light
Morning Has Broken
I Found a Dream
Amazing Grace
Garden
Make Me a Channel of Your Peace
Because
Heal the World
Because (four-part harmony)

Aled (UCJ, 2002):
I Believe
Ave Maria
My Life Flows On
Panis Angelicus
All Through the Night

Nunc Dimittis
Suo Gan
Pie Jesu
How Great Thou Art
Do You Hear What I Hear?
Vespera
O Holy Night

Higher (UCJ, 2003):
San Damiano
Deep Peace (Gaelic Blessing)
You Raise Me Up
Where E'er You Walk
Abide with Me
David of the White Rock
Be Still
Silent Night
Aberystwyth
Dear Lord and Father of Mankind

The Christmas Album (UCJ, 2004):
O Come, O Come Emmanuel
Away in a Manger
Silent Night (with Hayley Westenra)
Candlelight Carol
O Come All Ye Faithful
Coventry Carol
The Little Road to Bethlehem
God Rest Ye Merry Gentlemen
In the Bleak Midwinter
Still, Still, Still
O Little Town of Bethlehem
The Angel Gabriel
Whence is the Goodly Fragrance
O Holy Night
Hark the Herald
Do You Hear What I Hear

SINGLES:

Memory (BBC Records, 1985)
Too Young to Know (Sain, 1985)

Walking in the Air (HMV, 1985)
Pictures in the Dark (10 Records, 1985)
Morning Has Broken (RCA, 1986)
A Winter Story (HMV, 1986)
I'm in This Over My Head (Warner, 1998)

VIDEOS:

Carols for Christmas (NVC, 1985)
Voices from the Holy Land (BBC, 1986)
The Road to the Cross (BBC, 1986)
Born in Bethlehem (BBC, 1986)

AUDIOBOOKS/NARRATIONS:

A Christmas Carol by Charles Dickens

Under Milk Wood by Dylan Thomas (EMI, 1988)
Voices by Anthony Hopkins, Jonathan Pryce, Freddie Jones, Windsor Davies, Ruth Madoc, Sir Geraint Evans, Sian Phillips, Nerys Hughes, Alan Bennett, Aled Jones
Music by George Martin, Elton John, Mark Knopfler
Produced and directed by George Martin

Prokofiev: *Peter and the Wolf*
Britten: *The Young Person's Guide to the Orchestra*
Saint-Saens: *Carnival of the Animals*
(JVC Victor Records, 1989)
Royal Philharmonic Orchestra conducted by Robin Stapleton

The Story of Classical Music by Darren Henley (Naxos Audio-books/Classic FM, 2004)

INDEX